CULTURAL STUDIES IN PRACTICE

General Editors: JOHN STOREY AND GRAEME TURNER

Also in this series:

CULTURAL CONSUMPTION AND EVERYDAY LIFE   John Storey

FEMINIST THEORY AND CULTURAL STUDIES

Stories of Unsettled Relations

SUE THORNHAM

Professor of Media and Cultural Studies,
University of Sunderland

A member of the Hodder Headline Group
LONDON
Co-published in the United States of America by
Oxford University Press Inc., New York

First published in Great Britain in 2000 by
Arnold, a member of the Hodder Headline Group,
338 Euston Road, London NW1 3BH

http://www.arnoldpublishers.com

Co-published in the United States of America by
Oxford University Press Inc.,
198 Madison Avenue, New York, NY10016

The advice and information in this book are believed to be true and
accurate at the date of going to press, but neither the author nor the publisher
can accept any legal responsibility for any errors or omissions.

British Library Cataloguing in Publication Data
A catalogue record for this book is available from the British Library

Library of Congress Cataloging-in-Publication Data
A catalog record for this book is available from the Library of Congress

ISBN 0 340 71897 8 (hb)
ISBN 0 340 71898 6 (pb)

1 2 3 4 5 6 7 8 9 10

Production Editor: Anke Ueberberg
Production Controller: Bryan Eccleshall
Cover Design: Terry Griffiths

Typeset in 10 on 12 pt Sabon by Cambrian Typesetters, Frimley, Surrey
Printed and bound in Great Britain by MPG Books Ltd, Bodmin, Cornwall

What do you think about this book? Or any other Arnold title?
Please send your comments to feedback.arnold@hodder.co.uk

For my mother

Contents

General Editors' Preface

Cultural studies is a rapidly developing field of pedagogical practice and theoretical enquiry. Among its distinctive characteristics is the way its influence has spread across disciplines and research areas. While the effect of cultural studies on a wide range of disciplinary or sub-disciplinary fields has been substantial and in some cases profound, most publication in the area is less interested in that influence than in mapping the current hierarchies of positions and knowledges seen to define the field. The work of definition and clarification has preoccupied cultural-studies publishing for most of its history. This series hopes to move forward by mapping the ways in which the approaches and politics of cultural studies have affected both the detail and the overall shape of work within the humanities snd social sciences today. The series will produce textbooks which critically describe and assess the contribution of cultural studies to specific areas of research and debate.

John Storey and Graeme Turner

1

Introduction
Telling Stories: Feminism and Cultural Studies

I want to begin with two narratives:

> In relation to our own work, one of our main intellectual and political difficulties has been making effective interventions into work that was going on in CCCS. . . . We found it extremely difficult to participate in CCCS groups and felt, without being able to articulate it, that it was a case of the masculine domination of both intellectual work and the environment in which it was being carried out. Intellectually, our questions were still about 'absences'. Socially, but inseparable from our intellectual presence, as one woman put it at the time, we could either strive for a sort of 'de-sexualized' intellectual role, or retain 'femininity' either through keeping quiet, or in an uneasy combination with being 'one of the lads'. (Women's Studies Group 1978a: 10–12)

> For cultural studies . . ., the intervention of feminism was specific and decisive. It was ruptural. It reorganized the field in quite concrete ways. (Hall 1992a: 282)

What is most striking about these two narratives is their difference, in both content and tone. The first is tentative, its speaking voice clearly still caught in the contradictory identities – 'woman', 'feminist', 'intellectual' – which it describes, and unsure, as Charlotte Brunsdon has pointed out (1996: 284), to whom it is addressed. Its sentences are full of qualifiers, its tone uncertain (its protagonists 'found it . . . difficult', were not 'able to articulate', might 'strive for', could 'keep quiet'). The second is assured, authoritative, organizing its narrative to quite specific effect. It is an account of strategic, even military action. They are narratives of the same events.

The difference is partly one of date. Stuart Hall's account of feminism's impact on cultural studies at the Birmingham Centre for Contemporary

Cultural Studies (CCCS) was written some 12 years after the account by the CCCS Women's Studies Group. Nevertheless, despite Stuart Hall's scrupulous and self-ironic qualifications and disclaimers, a quite specific narrative is being recounted in his 1992 'autobiographical' history of 'Cultural Studies and its Theoretical Legacies', from which the second extract above is taken. It is a narrative in which, to borrow the terminology of structuralist accounts of narrative, the 'narrating subject' (the one who tells the story) and 'subject of narration' (the one who is the subject of the story) coincide (see Cohan and Shires 1988), although in this 'autobiography' it is 'cultural studies' that is the protagonist. Here then, at more length, is Hall's account of the 'ruptural' intervention of feminism into cultural studies:

> We know it was [accomplished], but it's not generally known how and where feminism first broke in. I use the metaphor deliberately: As the thief in the night, it broke in; interrupted, made an unseemly noise, seized the time, crapped on the table of cultural studies. . . . But I want to tell you something else about it. Because of the growing importance of feminist work and the early beginnings of the feminist movement outside in the very early 1970s, many of us in the Centre – mainly, of course, men – thought it was time there was good feminist work in cultural studies. And we indeed tried to buy it in, to import it, to attract good feminist scholars. As you might expect, many of the women in cultural studies weren't terribly interested in this benign project. We were opening the door to feminist studies, being good, transformed men. And yet, when it broke in through the window, every single unsuspected resistance rose to the surface – fully installed patriarchal power, which believed it had disavowed itself. (Hall 1992a: 282)

Charlotte Brunsdon's 1996 response to Hall's narrative points to his emphasis on 'the materiality and particularity of power'. Hall 'reminds us', she writes, 'that what we might consider theoretically and politically desirable can be very difficult to handle' (1996: 279). His account, she argues, at the same time as it registers 'the sense of betrayal and rejection' felt by Hall and his colleagues, also recalls for his 1990s audience that 'the second-wave women's movement . . . was once potent in its disruptive challenge in the name of "women" ' (1996: 280). But she also reminds us, by quoting from documents of the time, what it felt like to *be* a member of that Women's Studies Group. She wrote then about the problems caused by the 'notion of a women's studies group which is "filling in the gaps" in an already existing analysis, and which has a kind of "what about women" public presence' (1976, quoted in 1996: 283). In 1996 she summarizes these problems:

> it seemed almost impossible to imagine what a feminist cultural studies bibliography would be. Did it have to include all feminist books of the period – there weren't very many, and our reading was voraciously

cross-disciplinary. . . . At what level of theory could one defend a concept like 'women's oppression'? What order of concept was 'patriarchy'? And did we have to do it all ourselves – a double shift of intellectual work – while the boys carried on with the state, the conscious and the public? Were there going to be two spheres of cultural studies – 'ordinary' (as before, uninterrupted) and a feminine/feminist sphere? (Brunsdon 1996: 282)

It is clear from Charlotte Brunsdon's writings elsewhere that for her, the answer to these last questions is yes. In 1997 she writes of 'the quite elaborated existence of what we might call academic parallel universes'. 'I turn out', she writes, 'to have been working in a girlzone, a subordinate field which although it has had to transform its own foundational category, "woman", and has produced quite a substantial literature, still seems to have had remarkably little impact on the wider contours of the discipline' (1997: 169).

These issues will recur throughout the course of this book. But what I want to return to here is the question of the kinds of narratives Hall and Brunsdon are constructing here. Elsewhere, Stuart Hall has written about the key function which narrative plays in the construction of identity. It is in telling stories about ourselves, he writes, that we construct our sense both of who we are and of the 'imaginary communities' in which we position ourselves (1987: 45). Identities, then, are provisional, the product of a specific telling at a specific time; they imply an arbitrary ending and an arbitrary structure to a story. But it is only by constructing them – and their accompanying stories – that we are able to act in the world; and the narratives we construct 'have certain conditions of existence, real histories in the contemporary world, which are not only or exclusively psychical, not simply "journeys of the mind" ' (1987: 45). In the same way, then, the narratives of cultural studies have been important in constructing its identity as a field, and I want to pursue a little further the question of their nature.

There are two obvious points to be made about Stuart Hall's 1992 narrative: one is that 'cultural studies' is unquestionably its protagonist, and the second is that that protagonist is male. That these points are obvious, however, does not mean that they do not have consequences. In both the 1992 narrative and Hall's earlier account of the development of cultural studies, written in 1980, the metaphors chosen are frequently spatial, with the narrative figured as a journey or as a territorial struggle. In 1980 Hall writes of the CCCS beginning 'to desert its "handmaiden" role and chart a more independent, ambitious, properly integrated space of its own', with cultural studies becoming 'no longer a dependent intellectual colony' (1980a: 22, 26). In 1992, he writes of 'the opening of [a] new continent in cultural studies' (1992a: 282) which the 'unsettled relations' with feminism made possible. In these accounts, it is clear not only that feminism is *outside* this space, a hostile, potentially invasive force;[1] it is also the case that what marks the growing maturity of cultural studies as a discipline is an increasing masculin-ization – as it leaves behind its 'handmaiden' role. Finally, we can point to Hall's identification in 1980 of the 'originating texts', the 'founding moment' in cultural studies, which he locates in the work of Richard Hoggart, Raymond Williams and E.P. Thompson in the late 1950s and early 1960s (Hall 1980a: 16). The story being told thus takes shape as one in which the protagonist strikes out from his 'fathers' and, achieving a growing maturity, stakes a claim to his own intellectual, political and institutional territory.

The point I am making here is that the marginalization of women and feminist theory is implicit in the very construction of these narratives. Told from this position and in this way, feminism cannot *but* be seen as enter-ing/interrupting cultural studies' story at a point some way into the narra-tive, thus forcing certain renegotiations or remappings of the field. It is not surprising, then, that even feminists like Elizabeth Long telling the story of 'Feminism and Cultural Studies', have tended to describe the ways in which 'feminists have contributed to cultural studies "in general" ', arguing that their contribution lay in having '*extended* not only the Centre's substantive interests but also their methodological program' (Long 1989: 427, 429, my emphasis).

The reason is partly, of course, strategic. Ellen Rooney has described 'feminism's triple practice as women's studies, feminist theory, and the women's liberation movement' (1990: 17), but for the feminist scholar, such a structure offers only a very insecure space in which to work. Whilst women's studies has provided feminism with an institutional base in British universities since the 1980s, this has become both increasingly marginalized and increasingly precarious, with some women's studies programmes becoming the more 'mainstream'-sounding 'gender studies' and others disappearing altogether. Cultural studies, with its frequent institutional linking to media studies, has offered a more secure institutional base for the feminist scholar, and opportunities to work within a field which, inflected as 'feminist cultural studies', is very close in its broad outlines to that of *feminist* studies as Teresa de Lauretis defines it in 1986. The field of femi-nist studies, writes de Lauretis, encompasses 'feminist work in the fields of history, science, literary writing, criticism and theory, with the relation of feminist politics to critical studies . . . as its general and overarching concern' (1986: 1). As Terry Lovell writes, then,

> it is clear that cultural studies offered a peculiarly appropriate institu-tion 'to harbour and focus a scholarship of its own' to a feminism which had always found itself crossing disciplinary boundaries. . . . Cultural studies, in locating a wide variety of types of text and of meaning as integral to contemporary society and culture, opened up a space where feminists could study women's lives as well as women's texts as part of the broad socio-cultural construction of gender in capitalist society. (1990: 276)

Thus, as Charlotte Brunsdon points out, if feminism itself 'has gone out of fashion without ever becoming mainstream' within the academy, the feminist scholar can still find spaces to teach, research and publish within the fields of cultural and media studies. In occupying such ground, however, she finds herself constantly within 'a space of difference . . . cultivated alongside, in opposition to and sometimes in dialogue with, the mainstream', writing the 'special chapter' on gender, working in a 'subaltern field . . . the very existence of which indicates the continuance of patterns of discrimination articulated through gender' (1997: 169, 170).

Other Stories

> [T]heir history, their stories, constitute the locus of our displacement. It's not that we have a territory of our own; but their fatherland, family, home, discourse, imprison us in enclosed spaces where we cannot keep on moving, living, as ourselves. Their properties are our exile. (Irigaray 1985: 212)

There are, however, other narratives that can be told, as Stuart Hall himself reminds us (1992a: 277). '[W]e think back through our mothers if we are women', writes Virginia Woolf in *A Room of One's Own* (1993: 69). If we do this, then we may find a rather different narrative of feminist cultural studies emerging, one in which it is feminism, rather than cultural studies, which is the protagonist. Despite recent attempts to 'reclaim' the work of Raymond Williams for feminism (see Probyn 1993), this may prove for feminists a more productive way of tracing the story than following the Oedipal narrative I have outlined above, even when that narrative includes daughters as well as sons. The very concept of culture, as Celia Lury has written (1993), is profoundly gendered, so that early feminist theory emerged as a 'theory of gender oppression in culture' (de Lauretis 1990: 267). By tracing the contours of both that theory and the feminist theory which was the product of the 'new consciousness among women' (Rowbotham 1973: ix) in the early 1970s, we can perhaps produce an alternative story which, if it does not succeed in altering the 'displacement' described by Luce Irigaray in the quotation above, will at least offer a rather different vantage point from which to view the 'unsettled relations' of feminism and cultural studies.

This book, then, sets out to trace such a story. Chapter 2 begins by attempting, in Virginia Woolf's words, to 'think back through' the work of four of the 'mothers' of feminist cultural theory in order to trace this narrative and to explore the difficulties, compromises, inconsistencies and dislocations which mark its progress. I begin with Mary Wollstonecraft, whose *A Vindication of the Rights of Woman* (1792) addresses many of the questions that have concerned later feminist cultural theorists: questions about women's relation to (the dominant) culture, to power, to discourse, to identity, to lived experience, to cultural production and to representation. It also manifests all the difficulties of speaking position inherent in such a project: how to write *as a woman*, within a public discourse of rationality from which Wollstonecraft was excluded by virtue of her sex. In the process of seeking to answer these questions, I argue, the discursive boundaries by which gender difference and the privileged position of masculinity were marked out in the 1790s, are constantly subverted.

Charlotte Perkins Gilman's *Women and Economics* was published in 1898. Like Mary Wollstonecraft a century earlier, Gilman appropriates the dominant public discourse of her day – in her case the emerging field of the social sciences – for the analysis of women's position in terms which, by definition, exclude her. Like Wollstonecraft, her purpose is subversion and change, and like Wollstonecraft, too, her work is marked by an uncertainty – or play – of speaking voice. In arguing that the key structures determining women's position are socio-economic, or to use Gilman's term, *sexuo-economic*, she anticipates later feminist cultural analysis, arguing that femininity is a culturally and ideologically constructed state of oppression. Like Wollstonecraft, she writes as a cultural outsider, inside and outside both femininity and the masculine discourse that for her is both constraint and weapon.

Virginia Woolf's *A Room of One's Own* (1929) and *Three Guineas* (1938) are concerned not only with the restricted access of women to the means of literary production, but also with issues of representation and the social context of reception, with the texture of writing itself, with psychological aspects of the creative process and with issues of consciousness and identity. Like that of Wollstonecraft and Gilman, Woolf's writing also embodies the contradictions inherent in her enterprise – that of writing theoretically as a woman – though now in a far more self-conscious way. Women, Woolf argues, are both inside and outside all the symbolic structures which construct identity: outside nation, outside class and outside history. What this exclusion produces, argues Woolf, is a difference in what she calls the 'angle of vision'. Women 'see' differently as cultural producers and as readers, and the representations of the world that they produce are also different. This is a matter of both cultural construction and embodied difference. Woolf comes close here to later theorists like Luce Irigaray (1985), who argues that, in Western patriarchal society, representation is the product of the 'male imaginary', so that its structures and rhythms are always implicitly male. Like Irigaray, Woolf speculates on what a *female* 'imaginary', in which might be expressed 'my own experiences as a body', might look like.

Finally in this chapter, I consider Simone de Beauvoir, whose *The Second Sex* (1949) is a pivotal text in any narrative of feminist cultural theory. Through it we can trace backwards, to the work of Wollstonecraft, Gilman and Woolf, and we can also look forward. De Beauvoir foreshadows the work of later cultural theorists in exploring the work of ideology ('myth' in de Beauvoir's terminology) in producing women's 'complicity' in their own subordination, drawing on both Marx and Freud in order to explain the ideological 'overdetermination' of women's subordination. But de Beauvoir offers us not only a theorising of women's position, but also what Judith Okely (1986: 72) calls a sort of 'concealed ethnography', offering herself as a case-study. It is this double aspect of de Beauvoir's theoretical work that I focus on here, arguing that it is not only in her explicit cultural theory that de Beauvoir is a crucial figure. It is also in the contradictions and tensions which her work exhibits: tensions between theory and experience, between her claims about cultural construction and her accounts of the body, between her various accounts of the construction of female subjectivity, and between her claims to philosophical neutrality and her evident situatedness.

In Chapter 3 I turn to the 'daughters' whose work in the 1970s both rejected and re-established (and sometimes ignored) these arguments and contradictions. I begin with an account of the emergence of the Women's Liberation Movement, with its emphasis on the need for a revolution in 'culture and consciousness', an argument found in writers as otherwise different as Betty Friedan, Kate Millett, Cellestine Ware and Sheila Rowbotham. Women's lived experience, argued these writers, had to be wrenched out of the framework of 'common-sense' within which it was habitually understood, and 'made to mean' within a politicized feminist consciousness which would invest it with new cultural meaning. What was needed was not only political activism and the 'naming' of women's immediate and subjective experience, but also a new language of *theory* which would encompass both.

It is this 'new language of theory' which I consider next, examining the work of Betty Friedan and Kate Millett in America, and Juliet Mitchell and Sheila Rowbotham in Britain, before turning to the rather different ways in which this theoretical work entered the academy in the USA and Britain. In America, I argue, feminist cultural criticism tended to find its academic home within literary studies. Thus, although its emphasis on the politics of writing and reading, on the material and ideological embeddedness of texts, and on the embodied nature of gendered identity often moved such work in the direction of cultural studies as it became constituted in Britain, it nevertheless remained – perhaps because of its institutional origins – relatively divorced from work on the texts and readers of popular or 'mass' culture. In Britain, however, the major theoretical developments in feminist writing lay neither in liberal feminism nor in radical feminism as they were defined in the USA, but at the intersection of feminism and socialism/Marxism. Thus from its beginnings, British feminist theory engaged with the issues and concerns which were also central in the founding of academic cultural studies. Writers like Sheila Rowbotham argued, then, for both a revolution in consciousness and a historical analysis of women's oppression within capitalism. Women, she insists, have to struggle for control over both production and reproduction. But Rowbotham also draws substantially on earlier writers like Simone de Beauvoir and Virginia Woolf to argue that what is required is a revolution within language and culture as well as in material structures. Socialist feminists must seek to transform 'the inner world' of bodily experience, psychological colonization and cultural silencing, as well as the outer world of material social conditions.

Finally in this chapter, I turn to the work which feminist academics produced in the 1970s at the Birmingham Centre for Contemporary Cultural Studies. 'From its inception', writes Stuart Hall, 'Cultural Studies was an "engaged" set of disciplines, addressing awkward but relevant issues about contemporary society and culture. . . . This tension (between what might loosely be called "political" and intellectual concerns) has shaped Cultural Studies ever since' (1980a: 17). Thus the concerns of cultural studies, as I have suggested, in many ways *were* the concerns of feminist theory, particularly as it had developed in Britain during the early 1970s. Cultural studies offered an academic and institutional context where feminist research could explore all the complexities of women's positioning in culture. Yet, as the Introduction to the 1978 CCCS publication *Women Take Issue* makes clear, this ground, which should have been so open, was in fact highly problematic for the feminist researchers: constituted around definitions of culture which excluded women and developed through theorists for whom the position for women was a given, not an issue to be contested. The work that emerged is, then, uneasy and unconfident in its straddling of the areas of cultural studies and 1970s feminist theory. Nevertheless, despite its uncertain beginning and its frequently hesitant tone, such work maps out both a set of challenges to existing cultural studies frameworks and a range of issues, methodologies and problems for a feminist cultural studies.

Chapter 4 examines the 'uneasy triangle' of feminism, psychoanalysis and cultural studies. Feminist theorists turned to psychoanalysis for an explanation of women's oppression that would locate it at the level of the ideological, the cultural and the subjective. In doing so, they also *politicized* psychoanalysis. What feminist theory needed, argued Juliet Mitchell in 1975, was an explanation of the processes through which our sexed identities are acquired and maintained, which would both account for the strength and ubiquity of these identities *and* see them as culturally constructed and thus open to change. It was this that she saw psychoanalysis as offering. For Mitchell and for other feminist writers of the 1970s, however, this was not simply a central theoretical issue but an urgent personal and political necessity, and the terminology of psychoanalysis was often juxtaposed with personal history and social analysis in order to open to political analysis that which was experienced as personal and subjective.

I begin with an account of Juliet Mitchell's *Psychoanalysis and Feminism* (1975), in which she challenged what had been the dominant view of psychoanalysis within early second wave feminism. Kate Millett, Shulamith Firestone, Germaine Greer and Eva Figes had all identified Freudian psychoanalysis, with its accounts of 'penis envy' and feminine passivity, as a key agent in the 'counterrevolution' against first wave feminism. For Mitchell, however, 'psychoanalysis is not a recommendation *for* a patriarchal society, but an analysis *of* one. If we are interested in understanding and challenging the oppression of women, we cannot afford to neglect it' (1975: xv). What interests her, therefore, is 'not what Freud did, but . . . what we can get from him, a political rather than an academic explanation'. What we can get from him, she argues, are the concepts with which we can comprehend how ideology functions, principally an account of the unconscious, and, 'closely connected with this, . . . an analysis of the place and meaning of sexuality and of gender differences within society' (1975: xxii). Mitchell seeks, then, a radical historicizing of psychoanalysis, which would locate the origins of what are now symbolic and unconscious structures in material historical practices. Even more important, she wants to argue for their potential overthrow. Ideology may attempt to produce a cultural 'fixing' of sexual identity, she argues, but in the face of the fluidity of sexuality and subjectivity those attempts are bound to fail. A feminist cultural revolution can prize open the laws of patriarchal culture to produce new structures which will in turn take their place in the unconscious.

Mitchell's account of psychoanalysis as the explanation of how human beings learn to occupy – but also resist – their ideologically given roles as men or women within patriarchy was taken up not only by theorists interested in the construction of gendered identity, but also by those seeking to explore how forms of popular culture – films, magazines and popular fiction – construct feminine identities. It was also contested, however, and I turn next to an account of the objections to Mitchell's work and to its defenders.

Elizabeth Wilson offers three objections to what she sees as the 'new orthodoxy' of Mitchell's claims for psychoanalysis. First, Mitchell's replacement of Freud's biologism with an emphasis on the psychological and cultural in the construction of identity, she argues, produces an account which is no less tyrannical and unalterable. To locate the source of women's oppression within unconscious processes, she writes, renders that oppression just as inaccessible to conscious change, and just as impervious to political struggle, as if we locate it within biological differences. Second, she argues that Mitchell's use of Freud locks her into a conception of sexual difference that sees heterosexuality as both arbitrary and inescapable. Feminist psychoanalytic theory, she writes, has had remarkably little to say about homosexuality and lesbianism. Wilson's final objection concerns the usefulness of psychoanalytic theory for a feminist political practice. In referring all social protest to the realm of the psychic, she argues, psychoanalysis reduces revolutionary politics to the status of (futile) rebellion against the 'law of the father'. Feminists should focus their energies on theories of *social* change.

For Jacqueline Rose, however, psychoanalysis is both political *and* centrally concerned with issues of language, representation and the failure of identity. It is difficult but important, unassimilable to the Marxist theory that has underpinned a masculine cultural studies, yet central to any radical social critique. Psychoanalysis is political for feminism, she writes, firstly because it is politically *needed* by feminism as a means of accounting for ideology and subjectivity, and secondly because its 'repeated marginalisation within our general culture' is a result of that culture's refusal to confront the principal concerns of psychoanalysis: sexual identity and the unconscious. That a patriarchal culture should so evade these issues is unsurprising, but for feminism to do so is to play into patriarchy's hands.

For Rose, then, psychoanalysis and feminism are crucially politically linked, not least because together they threaten to de-centre a masculine cultural studies. A Marxist-derived cultural theory can incorporate psychoanalysis as an account of collective fantasy, and it can incorporate a feminism grounded in social critique. Once linked, however, psychoanalysis and feminism together threaten to destabilize a class-based theory of culture and society, and place issues of subjectivity, pleasure and sexual difference at the heart of cultural and political analysis.

The second half of Chapter 3 explores the ways in which psychoanalytic theory has been taken up by feminist cultural critics in the analysis of cinema, art and popular culture, from Laura Mulvey's 'Visual Pleasure and Narrative Cinema', published in 1975, to more recent work by Valerie Walkerdine which brings together psychoanalytic theory and an analysis of the *productivity* of cultural practices drawn from the work of Michel Foucault. Power, argues Foucault, does not simply operate through processes of repression, censorship and denial. It works positively to construct the positions which, as subjects, we inhabit. His work is attractive to feminism because it serves to position female subjectivity *within* culture and history rather than as always the 'other' of male-centred culture. In particular, Foucault argues that *sexuality* is the effect of historically specific power relations. The relationship between power and sexuality is not a negative one, in which power seeks to control an unruly sexuality, he argues. Rather, the production of sexualized subjects is itself a form of regulation.

Forms of popular culture for women, then, operate to produce and regulate female subjectivity within a patriarchal culture. But they also, argues Walkerdine, operate through the mechanism of fantasy. The girls' comics that Walkerdine analyses are, she writes, complex fantasy structures that produce both the resolution and regulation of desire, thus becoming an arena of struggle. But she also argues that such fantasy structures are inseparable from our lived experience. The fantasy structures of popular culture are invested in domestic relations as well as in texts. To understand this we need not only to examine the 'regimes of meaning' constructed within discursive practices, but also to 'go beyond the present use of psychoanalysis', to understand the ways in which fantasies structure not only texts but also lived experience and lived relations.

Chapter 5 picks up the issue of 'lived experience and lived relations', examining the development of ethnographic work within a feminist cultural studies. It begins with an account of 'ethnographic' studies at the CCCS, arguing that such work, whether it was the text-based studies of David Morley or the work on subcultures which grew out of 'culturalist' approaches, offered an inadequate theorizing of women's history and experience. Feminist interest in 'ethnographic' research methods thus developed at least as much from the focus on women's experience as the mainspring for theory, in the 'consciousness-raising' undertaken by Women's Liberation groups of the 1970s.

The chapter moves then to Angela McRobbie's 'The Politics of Feminist Research: between Talk, Text and Action' (1982), which outlines the terms and the issues for such research. The meeting of feminism and ethnography, writes McRobbie, has been by no means unproblematic, and she describes the way in which in her own early research she sought to fit her findings into the class framework dominant within cultural studies. She also challenges the assumptions of 'objectivity' in such work. Feminism, she argues, 'forces us to locate our own autobiographies and our experience inside the questions we might want to ask', so that on the one hand we must recognize the 'resources and capacities of "ordinary" women and girls who occupy a different cultural and political space from us' and, on the other, we can empower their voices by articulating and translating them, using feminist research 'as a weapon of political struggle'.

The chapter then considers three examples of such research in the 1980s: Dorothy Hobson's 'Crossroads': The Drama of a Soap Opera (1982), Janice Radway's *Reading the Romance* (1984), and Ien Ang's *Watching Dallas* (1985). I trace the debates, both explicit and implicit, in such studies: about the status of the text in determining meaning in popular texts; about the importance and meaning(s) of pleasure and fantasy; about the position of the feminist researcher in relation to both the text and the subjects of her research; about the problems of both 'recruitist' and 'redemptive' readings for the politics of feminist research.

From these studies, which begin from specific texts, the chapter moves to work whose focus is more exclusively on the audience itself. Mary Ellen Brown's study of *Soap Opera and Women's Talk* (1994) begins by locating her work within both the tradition of cultural studies audience research and a feminist cultural politics. Soap operas, she argues, are hegemonic texts, designed to reinforce dominant conceptualizations of women, but they are caught up nevertheless in ideological struggle, as their female audiences appropriate them for a critique of these same values. This critique she sees as effected by 'feminine discourse'. Much of women's pleasure in soap operas comes, she argues, through 'feminine discourse' or 'gossip', which may be experienced as freedom from restraint on women's speech, as expression of feelings and as a politicized consciousness-raising about women's oppression. Soap operas actively encourage such gossip, but it is through the production of their own discursive 'texts' that the female audiences of the soap opera are able to activate the 'resistive' meanings available within the soap opera text itself.

Ann Gray's *Video Playtime* (1992) takes as its starting point the rapid take-up of the VCR as home entertainment across the social spectrum in the 1980s, and examines how women use, and what they think about, this piece of entertainment technology. Unlike Brown, Gray is acutely aware of the problems inherent in assuming too easy an identification with the women in her study. The researcher, she writes, 'has access to quite powerful institutions and intellectual capital', which distance her from the women she studies. At the same time, however, she is critical of a 'post-feminist' position, which would assert that no commonalities between women can be assumed. Gray argues, then, that the existence of 'women's genres' is a matter not of essentialized psychic difference but of differing cultural competences and access to cultural capital. For all women this produces contradictory subject positions, since all – including the working-class women in her study – share the dominant cultural evaluation of 'women's genres' as being of a lower order than male-preferred genres. Her study reveals, she argues, that whilst gender rarely reveals itself in 'pure' form but intersects with other determinations such as class, it remains a central duality, not only in dominant discursive categorizations but also in the lived experience of women.

The return to the issue of class in feminist cultural studies, which we can see in the work of Ann Gray, is what concerns the final section of this chapter. Beverley Skeggs' *Formations of Class and Gender* (1997), based on her 11-year study of a group of working-class white women from the north-west of England, seeks, she writes, to 'reinstate class in feminist (and) cultural theory' (1997: 2). For the working-class women in Skeggs' study, femininity is not an identity to be inhabited but a *performance* that can offer a route into respectability. As such it offers the pleasures of shared practices of 'glamour' and dressing up, but also the anxieties produced by (self-)regulation and surveillance. To seek to 'pass' as feminine involves both the work of constructing one's appearance according to ideals found in fashion images, magazines, advertising and other popular texts, and also bodily self-regulation. For the women in Skeggs' study, the body, like the image, is problematic. It must be invested in and regulated because 'letting oneself go' is a marker of non-respectability. But it remains 'the wrong size' for femininity, a source of constant anxiety about not quite 'getting it right'.

Chapters 6 and 7 develop these issues further, focusing on two areas of research, consumption and the body, which have brought together the various theoretical and methodological approaches to be found within a feminist cultural studies and which signal its difference(s) from non-feminist understandings. Chapter 6 is concerned with charting the complex and often contradictory ways in which women are implicated in consumer culture. It begins with an account of the work of the Birmingham CCCS in the 1970s and 1980s on fashion and style. Whereas 'the Fashion System' had been analysed by Roland Barthes as a structure and rhetoric whose codes reproduced dominant cultural stereotypes, 'subcultural style' was seen by CCCS researchers as a mode of working-class *resistance* against dominant structures. Such resistance, however, was seen to be the product of *masculine* subcultures, not simply because these accounts of resistance to 'mass' or 'consumer' culture produced no descriptions of female subcultural resistance. The analyses themselves were founded on a number of unspoken oppositions – between conformity and resistance, passivity and activity, consumption and appropriation – which identified the former with femininity and the latter with masculinity.

For the feminist researchers of the CCCS, the relationship of women to consumer culture was therefore a difficult issue to tackle. Women's identification with consumption positioned them outside the 'relations of production' which were central to the class analysis of the CCCS, yet such exclusion rendered women's oppression doubly invisible. First, it masked the extent to which women have in fact worked outside the home and have suffered oppression in the workplace. Second, it offered no framework for the analysis of consumption itself as a site of women's oppression and/or resistance, at a time when writers within the Women's Movement were arguing that the 'fashion and beauty' system of consumer culture was a form of political oppression in the sphere of the personal. In response, feminist CCCS researchers emphasized consumption as a sphere of women's *work*, both physical – as workers in the domestic sphere – and ideological – in the construction of femininity through the consumption of commodities.

But the growth in practices of consumption, and their separation from processes of production, have also been seen as crucial in the development of modernity as a whole, and the chapter goes on to consider debates about the place of women in this development. For some writers the emergence of the figure of the female shopper, particularly the strolling window-shopper, signalled a new freedom for women in the cities of the late nineteenth century. Others, however, have pointed to the ambiguous status of this figure who, in being invited to purchase sexually attractive images for herself, was uneasily positioned between the roles of consumer and commodity. The chapter traces these debates, before moving on to the emergence of the figure of the 'rational consumer' in descriptions of the twentieth-century shift to a consumer culture. These descriptions, argues Rachel Bowlby, have been marked by the appearance of two quite different models of the consumer, models which are mapped on to ideological assumptions about masculinity and femininity. One, the 'rational consumer', actively pursues and takes possessions, as he actively pursues rational arguments. He may use these possessions to signal his identity, but his identity is not submerged in them. The other, the passive consumer, is linked emotionally rather than rationally to consumption; she is both subject and object in the process of consumption. Like the 'resistant' member of a subculture, however, the rational consumer has a precarious identity, threatening constantly to slip into his feminized 'other'.

The final sections of the chapter examine the areas of fashion, fans and stars. Both fashion and fandom have been seen as areas in which capitalism works through the feminization of mass culture, and they have been linked through the figure of the female star, who acts as an idealized mirror – or shop window – for the female fan. This final part of the chapter examines ways in which this has been theorized, focusing on the contradictions and struggles involved in such identifications. Both fashion and fandom, it has been argued, are contradictory activities, involving both regulation and excess. Fantasy desires and identifications can be acted out through consumption, even though they may simultaneously be contained within the structures that produce them.

Chapter 7 returns to the issue of the body in culture, arguing that it is around this issue that the relationship between feminism and cultural studies has been at its most strained. Whilst the CCCS in the 1970s and early 1980s adopted structuralist frameworks which focused on social structures and texts, the 1970s Women's Movement was characterized by a 'body politics' which argued that the 'woman's body is the terrain on which patriarchy is erected' (Adrienne Rich 1977: 55). The chapter begins, then, with an account of this work with its threefold emphasis: on the constraints on the female body produced by what Sandra Lee Bartky calls 'the fashion–beauty complex'; on the violation of female bodily integrity represented by rape and other forms of sexual violence; and on the medical control of the female sexual and reproductive body. All were to be important for a feminist cultural studies, yet what united them in the 1970s – the desire to reclaim a 'natural' female body, undistorted by patriarchal constraints – sat uneasily within a cultural studies framework which emphasized the dialectic between structure and agency.

It was feminist engagement with the work of Michel Foucault in the 1980s which offered a way of integrating this cultural studies focus with the 'body politics' of feminism. For Foucault, power does not operate through the repression of an 'authentic' body and its sexuality, as feminist writers of the 1970s maintained. Rather, it *produces* the body through its techniques of supervision, discipline and control. In the 1980s and 1990s, then, feminist cultural studies returned to the key issues of the 1970s' 'politics of the body' via an appropriation of Foucault's theories, and it is this which I consider next. Work on eating disorders, on the medicalization of women's sexual and reproductive bodies, and on exercise, body-building and 'working-out' has used Foucault's work to point to the ways in which women's bodies are 'disciplined' in contemporary culture, arguing that discursive practices intersect with social, economic, medical, legal and political structures to produce meanings about the female body which are embodied in both representations and in cultural practices.

Other writers have been more suspicious of Foucault's work, however, arguing that the body about which he writes is often a curiously 'neutral' and abstract body, but one which is always implicitly male. Agreeing with Foucault that the body is always inscribed within culture – never a 'natural' body which can be reclaimed – writers like Elizabeth Grosz and Rosi Braidotti have argued that that body is nevertheless always marked by sexual difference, and have sought to insist on a 'female embodied self'.

The final section of the chapter turns to the debates about the notion of the 'cyborg body' in feminist theory. Arguing that the convergence of communications technologies and biotechnologies means that we simply *cannot* return to a notion of the organic and natural body as a rallying point, Donna Haraway argues that, instead, feminism should welcome the conceptual blurring of boundaries which marks contemporary culture, and embrace a 'cyborg' identity. Western thought has been characterized, she writes, by conceptual dualisms which have served an imperialist project, marking boundaries which have opposed the 'self' (the 'unmarked' white male) against the 'other' (those marked as different by sex and/or race). The cyborg, embodied but not unitary, a figure of blurred boundaries, can help us escape such constricting dualisms. Her vision has proved an attractive one, although other writers have argued that the image of the 'cyborg body' comes already laden with meanings about gendered and racial 'others' and is not so easily reclaimed for feminism. Women's experiences of the blurring of boundaries between the corporeal and the technological have not on the whole been positive, they point out, just as women's experiences of the internet and 'cyberspace' have not matched the visions of 'cyberfeminists' like Sadie Plant who have seen cyberspace as a network of women, computers and communication links which can circumvent the dualism of the sexed body.

The final chapter returns to the issue of stories with which I began, asking questions about the kind of story we might have if feminism were to be the subject – even the hero – of the narrative of 'feminism and cultural studies', and what such a story might mean. In this recentred narrative it would be cultural studies rather than feminism which enters midway through, I argue, offering feminism a space in which to work but at the expense of ceding autonomy and perhaps also the 'signature' of feminist theory. Nevertheless, if, as Elizabeth Grosz argues, the crucial question for feminism is 'What are the costs and benefits of holding such commitments?' (1995: 57), then the 'unsettled relations' which are the result of this meeting are to be embraced.

Note

1. This is a point which Charlotte Brunsdon seems to endorse when she writes that the CCCS Women's Studies Group formed 'one of the bridgeheads into the CCCS of the new social movements of the late 1960s and the 1970s' (1996: 282). My *Webster's Dictionary* offers a definition of 'bridgehead' as 'an advanced position seized in hostile territory as a foothold for further advance'.

2

Thinking Back Through our Mothers: Writing as a Woman and the Politics of Culture

In her 1979 essay on Charlotte Bronte's *Villette*, Mary Jacobus cites Matthew Arnold's dismissal of Bronte's novel. 'Why is *Villette* disagreeable?' asks Arnold. His answer is: 'Because the writer's mind contains nothing but hunger, rebellion and rage, and therefore that is all she can, in fact put into her book' (1979b: 43). For Jacobus the disturbances in the novel's narrative voice which so disquieted Arnold, and which were later noted in a very different way by Kate Millett,[1] are the result of a profound internal struggle. Seeking both to speak – and be heard – within mainstream literary discourse *and* to speak as a woman and a feminist, Bronte experiences a conflict between, on the one hand, her 'revolutionary impulse towards feminism' and, on the other, the tendency of that impulse to, in Jacobus' words, 'confine women within irrationality'. The result is a speaking position marked by 'incoherencies and compromises, inconsistencies and dislocations' (1979b: 58–9). But such disjunctions are characteristic not only of Bronte's writing, she argues. They have also marked the feminist cultural critic and theorist from Mary Wollstonecraft onwards. 'To propose a difference of view, a difference of standard – to begin to ask what the difference might be – is to call in question the very terms which constitute that difference' (1979a: 10): how, then, to write of and from these differences? To seek to argue from within the dominant discourse is not to question the terms of that discourse; to step outside it is to move beyond the terms of 'reason'. This chapter will seek, in Virginia Woolf's terms, to 'think back through' the work of four of the 'mothers' of feminist cultural theory, in order both to trace a narrative of feminist cultural theory and to explore the 'incoherencies and compromises, inconsistencies and dislocations' which mark its progress.

Mary Wollstonecraft (1759–1797) and the Rights of Woman

Mary Wollstonecraft's life reads like a psychiatric case history. So, for that matter, do the lives of many later feminists. . . . [She] was afflicted with a severe case of penis-envy. . . . that she was an extreme neurotic of a compulsive kind there can be no doubt. Out of her illness arose the ideology of feminism, which was to express the feelings of so many women in years to come. (Lundberg and Farnham 1947: 149, 150, 159)

This judgement by Ferdinand Lundberg and Marynia Farnham in *Modern Woman: The Lost Sex* (1947), a judgement which could have been made about any of the women discussed in this chapter, both presents Mary Wollstonecraft as a feminist archetype and employs medical discourse in order to consign her to the feminine 'irrational' – thus forcefully illustrating Jacobus' point. Wollstonecraft's theoretical writing, we are told, is like her life: irrational, lacking restraint, a pathological text whose meaning (a matter of penis-envy) is to be explained by a masculine medical science in terms of its key signifier – her body. Only in the final sentence are there interesting signs of struggle (Marynia Farnham was, after all, a *woman* doctor). The 'ideology of feminism' does indeed 'express the feelings of so many women', but feelings are clearly separated from reason here, so that what seems for a moment to be affirmed – Wollstonecraft's writing, feminism – is after all dismissed. Certainly, *A Vindication of the Rights of Woman* (1792) presents many of the questions that have concerned later feminist cultural theorists: questions about women's relation to (the dominant) culture, to power, to discourse, to identity, to lived experience, to cultural production and to representation. It also manifests all the 'incoherencies and compromises, inconsistencies and dislocations' which, in Mary Jacobus' view, confront the feminist cultural theorist.

For Wollstonecraft, then, seeking to claim access for women to the 'Rights of Man'[2] which eighteenth-century writers like Jean Jacques Rousseau and Thomas Paine were demanding, it was culture not nature – as Rousseau claimed – which determined women's inferior status. It is a matter of 'a false system of education', a system instituted by men who have considered 'females rather as women than as human creatures', and have thus produced a 'partial civilization' in which the 'conduct and manners of women' are constituted so as to render them 'insignificant objects of desire' (1992: 79, 83). The education system, conduct books for women written by men and 'the fanciful female character, so prettily drawn by poets and novelists' all construct norms of femininity which place 'women' as other than 'human', infantilized and confined in a 'female world'. Women are objectified, educated to 'please [the] fastidious eye' (1992: 145, 140–1, 79), and urged to participate in their own objectification:

Taught from their infancy that beauty is woman's sceptre, the mind shapes itself to the body, and roaming round its gilt cage, only seeks to adore its prison. . . . Confined then in cages like the feathered race, they have nothing to do but to plume themselves, and stalk with mock majesty from perch to perch. It is true they are provided with food and raiment, for which they neither toil nor spin; but health, liberty, and virtue, are given in exchange. (1992: 132, 147)

The image here, repeated often in *A Vindication of the Rights of Woman*, simultaneously positions women as *other* than 'the human species', as objectified for the male gaze and complicit in that objectification, and as enslaved. Women's oppression, then – and Wollstonecraft is clear in labelling it oppression – is cultural (constructed and lived out within cultural texts and practices), social (affirmed through social institutions, particularly marriage) and political (enforced through legislation). It is also *embodied*. Anticipating twentieth-century theorists, Wollstonecraft argues here for a continuum of bodily oppression between the Chinese custom of binding girls' feet[3] (1992: 129) and the enforced physical passivity and dependence of European women.

Femininity is thus culturally constructed, and Wollstonecraft seeks, in Jacobus' words, to 'call in question the very terms which constitute . . . difference', arguing that 'the word masculine is only a bugbear', serving merely to 'give a sex to virtue', and that 'the sexual distinction which men have so warmly insisted upon, is arbitrary' (1992: 83–4, 326). As part of its naturalization, however, women are not only deprived of power (economic, social and political); they are offered the *illusion* of power in the personal realm (the 'female world') through sexuality. 'Pleasure is the business of woman's life', writes Wollstonecraft. 'Exalted by their inferiority (this sounds like a contradiction), they constantly demand homage as women, though experience should teach them that the men who pride themselves upon paying this arbitrary insolent respect to the sex, with the most scrupulous exactness, are most inclined to tyrannize over, and despise, the very weakness they cherish' (1992: 146).

Wollstonecraft's analysis sounds remarkably like those of Betty Friedan and Kate Millett in the 1960s and 1970s. Her solution, however, is to argue not for the dismantling of the 'terms which constitute . . . difference', but for an extension of the sphere of the 'masculine' to encompass women. Women, then, should be admitted to the sphere of reason, and with it social and civil responsibility, through education: 'To render women truly useful members of society, I argue that they should be led, by having their understandings cultivated on a large scale, to acquire a rational affection for their country, founded on knowledge' (1992: 324). It is an argument, as Denise Riley writes (1988: 13), which is pitched against the growing sexualization of 'woman', and with it the naturalization of 'separate spheres', which was taking place in the eighteenth century. But it is an argument which, in its demand for access to a 'masculine' public sphere of rationality, also brings with it, as Mary Jacobus argues, 'alienation, repression, division' (1979a: 10) since its price is the rejection of embodied difference.

Wollstonecraft, argues Jacobus, 'speaks not so much *for* women, or *as* a woman, but *against* them – over their dead bodies' (1979a: 14–15). But the body is not so easily expelled. It returns in Wollstonecraft's accounts of prostitution,[4] in her references to the physicality of childhood and in her descriptions of the sweating bodies of working-class women who 'keep together families that the vices of the fathers would have scattered abroad' (1992: 174). And it returns in the appeals to women's – and Wollstonecraft's own – experience. 'I can recollect my own feelings, and I have looked steadily around me', she writes (1992: 130), as she launches an attack on Rousseau's account of femininity – thus aligning rational argument *with* 'feelings', and disturbing the gendered boundary between them which would assign the latter (as in Lundberg and Farnham above) to the *irrational* feminine.[5]

The result is a speaking voice marked by the inconsistencies and dislocations identified by Jacobus. Wollstonecraft's 'rational discourse' places her self-consciously outside the category of 'women in general', for whom she often exhibits a mixture of pity and contempt ('their senses are inflamed, and their understandings neglected', 1992: 153). But this is constantly interrupted by appeals to experience and shifts in tone away from the rational, plain-seeking persona she seeks to adopt ('I aim at being useful, and sincerity will render me unaffected'). Through protest, anger, irony, personal anecdote, through forays into the very use of metaphor and 'flowery diction', which she has explicitly rejected, Wollstonecraft's voice constantly twists and turns and doubles back.

Speaking, then, from an *impossible* position – as a woman, within a public discourse of rationality from which she was excluded by virtue of her sex – Wollstonecraft in the end speaks *both* 'over [women's] bodies' *and* as a woman. The result is an authorial voice that is insistently present yet incoherent as a subject position, neither fully embodied nor 'properly' distanced. Wollstonecraft enacts rather than articulates the impossibility of her position, in sudden shifts and reversals that have been seen as the involuntary eruption of a submerged female identity (Brody 1992). Equally, however, we might – borrowing from Judith Butler – choose to view them as *performance*. Wollstonecraft's questioning of 'the very terms which constitute . . . difference' occurs through the repetition and displacement 'through hyperbole, dissonance, internal confusion, and proliferation' (Butler 1990: 31) of the very constructs by which gender difference – in the discourses available to Wollstonecraft – is established. If, for women, finding a position from which to speak is, as Meaghan Morris suggests, a matter of 'play-acting', of 'developing enunciative strategies . . . precisely in relation to the cultural and social conventions that make speaking difficult or impossible for *women*' (1988: 7), then Wollstonecraft *acts* the impossibility of speaking as a woman. In the process, the discursive boundaries by which in the 1790s gender difference and the privileged position of masculinity were marked out, are constantly subverted.[6]

Women and Economics: Charlotte Perkins Gilman (1860–1935)

Quite simply, how do we analyse the position of women? What is the woman's concrete situation in contemporary capitalist society? What is the universal or general area which defines her oppression? The family and the psychology of femininity are clearly crucial here. However inegalitarian her situation at work (and it is invariably so) it is within the development of her feminine psyche and her ideological and socio-economic role as mother and housekeeper that woman finds the oppression that is hers alone. As this defines her, so any movement for her liberation must analyse and change this position. (Mitchell 1971: 14)

Juliet Mitchell's argument that the key to women's oppression lies in 'her ideological and socio-economic role as mother and housekeeper' was taken up and developed by the CCCS Women's Studies Group in *Women Take Issue* (1978b). Women's subordination, they argue, is secured through a 'masculine hegemony' which operates at the site of 'the family as an *economic* unit' (1978b: 46). It is an argument that is anticipated by Charlotte Perkins Gilman, whose *Women and Economics* was published in 1898. Like Mary Wollstonecraft a century earlier, Gilman appropriates the dominant public discourse of her day – in her case the emerging field of the social sciences – for the analysis of women's position in terms which by definition exclude her. Like Wollstonecraft, her purpose is subversion and change, and like Wollstonecraft, too, her work is marked by an uncertainty – or play – of speaking voice. In her magazine pieces and her fiction, she exploits more fully the possibilities for discursive play in the elaboration of her ideas – as well as for the exploration of psychological conflict and contradiction – but we can find them too in her more explicitly theoretical writing.

Like Juliet Mitchell and the CCCS Women's Studies Group, then, Gilman argues that the key structures that determine women's position are socio-economic, or to use Gilman's term, *sexuo*-economic. 'We are the only animal species', she writes, 'in which the female depends on the male for food, the only animal species in which the sex-relation is also an economic relation. With us an entire sex lives in a relation of economic dependence upon the other sex, and the economic relation is combined with the sex-relation' (1998: 3). Historically, woman's primary 'enslavement' was an economic one, the removal of her freedom to find her own food through the institution of the family as an economic unit. The female was thus made 'dependent upon the male in individual economic relation. She was in a state of helpless slavery' (1998: 64). One result of the institution of this sexuo-economic relation is the exclusion of women from *socio*-economic activity. We have given 'to woman the home and to man the world in which to work', so that 'the whole field of human progress has been considered a masculine prerogative' whilst woman has been 'cut off from personal activity in social economics, and confined to the functional activities of her sex' (1998: 111, 27, 163).

A second result is that the 'sex-relation' has itself become an economic relation. Women must 'obtain their economic goods by securing a male through their individual exertions, all competing freely to this end'. A woman's only saleable commodity is herself as both goods and labour. 'He is the market, the demand. She is the supply'; she herself is 'her only economic goods' – offered in exchange for the lifelong legal guarantee of support which is marriage. Her competitors are both legitimate ('virtuous' women who compete openly on the marriage market) and illegitimate (the 'vicious' woman who offers the same goods at a cut price). Her hatred of the prostitute is no more than the bitterness of the trader who is 'undersold' or the trades-unionist undercut by 'scab labor' (1998: 43–4, 55).

In Carolyn Steedman's (1986) story of 'lives lived out on the borderlands', *Landscape for a Good Woman*, this emphasis on the family as an economic structure emerges as one of the central themes in her analysis not only of her own and her mother's working-class childhood, but also of those marginalized female narratives that appear – to be discounted or reinterpreted – in the work of nineteenth-century male analysts. In the case of the eight-year-old watercress seller interviewed by Henry Mayhew in 1849–50, writes Steedman, what the child emphasized as the central focus of her narrative – her family as a unit whose relationships were all bound by its functioning as an *economic* structure – rendered her story quite simply outside Mayhew's – and perhaps our own – interpretive framework. In the case of Freud's patient Dora, Dora's own interpretation of her story – initially discounted by Freud – was equally clear. 'Dora understood two things about her social and sexual worth. She knew that she was desired and that she might be thought of as an object of exchange between two men. . . . That, in time and place, was Dora's value, what she understood of the world because the world told her so . . .; and it was this knowledge that she tried to repudiate by her hysteria'. Interestingly, Dora's story, as recounted here by Steedman, was also Gilman's own. The work for which she is now most famous, the short story 'The Yellow Wallpaper' (1892), is the semi-autobiographical tale of a woman driven to madness by her confinement within the sexuo-economic structure of marriage and the home. Reinterpreted from within a psychoanalytic framework – the very framework which Gilman was concerned to reject – it has become a literary case-history: a means of returning Gilman – like Dora, or like Mary Wollstonecraft – to the realm of the irrational.

For Gilman, then, woman must produce herself as an object for consumption within the sphere of reproduction. But the sexuo-economic relation also positions her as consumer: she consumes in order to produce herself as object of exchange and display, and the home as (pleasurable) sphere of consumption. Excluded from the wider sphere of production, she becomes 'the priestess of the temple of consumption', her consumption cut off from any relation to what she produces (Gilman 1998: 59–60). On such a sexuo-economic structure, argues Gilman, is built 'a towering superstructure of habit, custom, law': we have 'differentiated our industries, our responsibilities, our very virtues, along sex-lines' (1998: 110, 22). Sex-roles are instilled in childhood through the institution of the family, and reinforced by education, custom and law. But whilst a masculinity thus culturally constructed is accorded all the attributes of humanity, femininity is a matter of reduction and repression. 'Each woman born', argues Gilman, has to be dehumanized and 're-womanized' by 'the same process of restriction, repression, denial; the smothering "no" which crushe[s] down all her human desires to create, to discover, to learn, to express, to advance' (1998: 36). Confined to the private sphere, women have no social relations, merely sexual relations.

Like Simone de Beauvoir 50 years later, then, Gilman argues that femininity is a culturally and ideologically constructed state of oppression. It functions, she argues, to *sexualize* women: ' "the eternal feminine" means simply the eternal sexual' (1998: 23). Writing in 1990, Ann Snitow argues the need for 'an identity not overdetermined by our gender', and adds that 'we all live partly in, partly out of this identity by social necessity' (1990: 9, 13). It is this *overdetermination* of the identity 'woman' about which Gilman is writing. Women, she writes, are 'the sex', they are 'nothing *but* women' (1973: 134), whilst men have appropriated the category 'human'. Within popular discourse – Gilman cites a *Handbook of Proverbs of all Nations* – women are always 'woman', whilst proverbs about men are concerned to 'qualify, limit, describe, specialize' (1998: 26). When women do seek to claim humanity, they are seen as demanding access to masculinity.

For Gilman, however, it was not so easy to 'live partly in, partly out of this identity'. For her, 'social necessity', founded on the sexuo-economic structure and reinforced by a moral and ethical code which is the direct product of that structure (the virtue of a 'virtuous woman' is a *sexualized* virtue; that of a 'virtuous man' is not), fixes women within the bounds of femininity. It is a femininity constructed within discourse (' "to sew" [is] a feminine verb, and "to write" a masculine one'; the 'main avenues of life' are 'marked "male" ') but written on the body. It is manifest in clothing 'whose main purpose is unmistakably to announce . . . sex', in ornament, and in physical and emotional performance – 'overcharged sensibility, . . .

prominent modesty' and a body so disciplined to the performance of the feminine 'as to be grievously deprived of its natural activities' (1998: 27–8).

In her utopian fiction, Gilman imagined a race of women freed – by the absence of men – from the constrictions of femininity. In *Herland* (1915) she has her male narrator reflect:

> [W]e had been cocksure as to the inevitable limitations, the faults and vices, of a lot of women. We had expected them to be given over to what we called "feminine vanity" – "frills and furbelows," and we found they had evolved a costume more perfect than the Chinese dress, richly beautiful when so desired, always useful, of unfailing dignity and good taste.
>
> We had expected a dull submissive monotony, and found a daring social inventiveness far beyond our own, and a mechanical and scientific development fully equal to ours.
>
> We had expected pettiness, and found a social consciousness besides which our nations looked like quarrelling children – feeble-minded ones at that.
>
> We had expected jealousy, and found a broad sisterly affection, a fair-minded intelligence, to which we could produce no parallel.
>
> We had expected hysteria, and found a standard of health and vigor, a calmness of temper, to which the habit of profanity, for instance, was impossible to explain – we tried it. (1979: 81)

In *Women and Economics,* she employs a version of social Darwinism[7] – and a wry humour – to argue for the inevitability of women's economic – and hence social, political and ideological – emancipation. Women's subjection, she argues, however brutal and unjust it may have been, did initially benefit social progress. What it produced was a 'maternalizing' of man. In enslaving woman, he had to provide food and shelter. Thus 'he has been forced into new functions, impossible to male energy alone. He has had to learn to love and care for some one besides himself. He has had to learn to work, to serve, to become human.' With 'a full knowledge of the initial superiority of her sex and the sociological necessity for its temporary subversion', woman should feel only a 'deep and tender pride' in the patience with which she has waited for man to achieve full equality with her (1998: 63–4). This phylogenetic version of the archetypal romance narrative[8] seems consciously used for subversive effect. Like those popular romances, in which the masculine hero is humanized and softened ('maternalized') by love, Gilman's account permits its woman reader a sense of narrative control and agency even in the description of oppression and humiliation. Its story of man's temporary, borrowed supremacy is also a very different account of the origins of patriarchy from the Freudian myth offered in *Totem and Taboo* (1914). There, Freud draws on Darwin's theories to inscribe both patriarchy's origins and its universality in his story of society's Oedipal origins. In his account of the collective killing of the father by the sons which institutes the earliest social structure, the patricide serves both to shift to a symbolic level the previously literal authority of the father, and to institute the exchange of women within the new tribal structure.

Gilman's use of Darwinism, like her myth of origins, is very different, pointing as it does to the end not the universality of women's subordination. The temporary subjection of women has now outlived its usefulness. Its continuation, through the sexuo-economic structure that is the family, fractures the subjectivity of both men and women. Men exhibit both 'the ethics of a free, industrial, democratic age' and the brutal use of power, which characterizes the 'primitive patriarchate' of the family. Women, repressed, denied and confined within the family, find themselves trapped within

> a feverish, torturing, moral sensitiveness, without the width and clarity of vision of a full-grown moral sense; a thwarted will, used to meek surrender, cunning evasion, or futile rebellion; a childish, wavering, short-range judgment, handicapped by emotion; a measureless devotion to one's own sex relatives, and a maternal passion swollen with the full strength of the great social heart, but denied social expression. (Gilman 1998: 166–7)

Gilman's vision of the future, however, is optimistic. The pressure of changing industrial conditions, she writes, is pushing women back into the workplace and breaking up 'that relic of the patriarchal age – the family as an economic unit'. The 'last census', she writes, gives 'three million women workers'; by 1915 she could write that there were 'seven or eight million'. It is this economic independence – not political equality – which should be women's first priority, because it is this which will produce social and political change. The emergence of the 'woman's club movement', she writes, 'is one of the most important sociological phenomena of the century, – indeed of all centuries', because it marks 'the first timid steps toward social organization' resulting from women's economic independence (1998: 76, 81; 1979: 61). Just as she argues that it is shifts in economic structures not ideas that produce social change, she is aligned with Marxist theory in her argument that it is social institutions not individuals which produce ideological change. But individuals, she argues, have agency, and as women are now producing social organizations, they are also producing social movements. The world is being convulsed by a 'twin struggle', she writes: 'the "woman's movement" and the "labor movement" ', the former headed by heroic individuals like Elizabeth Cady Stanton and Susan B. Anthony.

The contradictions in Gilman's argument when she addresses the issue of change foreshadow those in the work of feminists of the 1960s and 1970s. On the one hand she wants to assert the inevitability of change, and to do this she employs a version of social Darwinism. On the other hand, she is acutely aware of struggle, on both the political and the ideological level, and of her own position as an agent in that struggle. In *Herland* she uses irony to reveal the gap between an ideologically constructed 'masculine' and 'feminine' and the actual economic structures of contemporary American society. Terry, one of the three men who find themselves in its all-women country, is speaking to one of Herland's women:

> "Oh, everything," Terry said grandly. "The men do everything with us." He squared his broad shoulders and lifted his chest. "We do not allow our women to work. Women are loved – idolized – honored – kept in the home to care for the children."
>   . . . But Zava begged: "Tell me first, do *no* women work, really?"
> "Why, yes," Terry admitted. "Some have to, of the poorer sort."
> "About how many – in your country?"
> "About seven or eight million," said Jeff . . . (1915: 61)

In *Women and Economics* she argues, firstly, that social and ideological change simply lags behind economic change, but secondly, that social and ideological struggle is necessary to achieve that change. So, for all that she insists that it is women's economic position, rather than women themselves, which is the problem, she is impatient with 'the innumerable weak and little women, with the aspirations of an affectionate guinea pig' (1998: 83). What is needed, she argues – and the whole polemic of her drive to envision a radically *different* economic and social structure is part of the attempt to effect this – is a change in consciousness. 'It is high time', she complains, 'that women began to understand their true position.' Change is already occurring but it 'needs to be made clear to our conscious thought' (1998: 64, 61).

As Alice Rossi points out (1988: 566–7), there are parallels between Gilman's arguments and those of Betty Friedan 65 years later in *The Feminine Mystique*. Like Friedan, she seeks to raise consciousness, to *name* women's problem – for Gilman the 'sexuo-economic relation' – and to locate it in woman's ideological and socio-economic entrapment within femininity. Like Friedan, she seeks to argue that women's liberation will be an inevitable consequence of economic and social change, and she reaches to parallels from nature to reinforce this inevitability. As with Friedan, too, this emphasis sits uneasily with her awareness of the need for ideological struggle. Like Friedan, she wrote popular as well as theoretical works, and she located as a key site of ideological struggle the representations of women within popular culture. 'The Gibson Girl' and the 'honester, braver, stronger' heroines of popular romance and drama, the jokes about the 'new woman', all mark crucial change; but like later analysts she draws attention not only to the narrative centrality and agency of these new heroines ('they are no longer content simply to *be*: they *do*'), but also to the way in which they are persistently restored to femininity at the close of the narrative. Still, she argues, though the heroine may be returned in the end to 'the self-effacement of marriage with economic dependence', nevertheless 'the efforts were there'. It is the move towards transgressive action that is the marker of 'change in circumstances and change in feeling'; it cannot be effaced by even the most 'reactionary' of narrative closures (1998: 75).

Gilman, however, is a far more radical writer than Friedan. As both a feminist and a socialist, she is well aware that the changes she demands cannot be encompassed within existing social structures. If the ethical public sphere has been constructed through the 'maternalizing' of man, then its re-opening to women will demand both the destruction of the family as a socio-economic unit and – in any conventional terms – the 'masculinization' of women. Writing as a woman, however, Gilman's discursive freedom was limited. Like Mary Wollstonecraft, moreover, she was a woman whose actions had already doubly marginalized her within the realm of the feminine/feminist irrational: after the period of depression recounted in 'The Yellow Wallpaper', she had 'abandoned' both husband and child. For the most part, then, her theoretical writing treads warily. She may urge the freeing of women's bodies from the constraints of femininity, and insist that sexuality is culturally not biologically produced, but she is nevertheless careful to conclude that 'true marriage' (as opposed to 'the sexuo-economic relation') belongs to evolutionary development. As the 'personal union for life of two well-matched individuals', she reassures her readers, it can only be improved by women's independence (1998: 107). Her concern to occupy a position within dominant scientific discourse in order to argue that women's liberation is not simply just or desirable but *inevitable*, also leads her into an often uncomfortable use of social Darwinism. As a rhetorical strategy, this appropriation of evolutionary theory enables Gilman to effect smooth transitions between what Teresa de Lauretis terms the two poles of feminist thought: the 'critical negativity' of her social and ideological analysis and the 'affirmative positivity' of her political goals (1990: 266). But it jars uncomfortably with both her emphasis on conscious agency as the means of change and her concern, as a socialist, for the liberation of all.

What, finally, can we conclude about her speaking position? Her concern to occupy a position that will be *taken seriously* leads in *Women and Economics* to an emphasis on rational argument that is careful to avoid the inconsistencies and digressions of Wollstonecraft's writing. The appropriation and subversion of a masculine discourse is a common device in Gilman's fiction, from the ironic undercutting of the male narrators of her Utopian novels[9] to her short story, 'If I Were a Man' (1914), where she imagines the transformation of 'true woman' Mollie Mathewson into her husband Gerald. What results for Mollie/Gerald is 'a new and delightful feeling of being *the right size*' in what s/he now recognizes as 'the world as it [is] – man's world, as made, lived in, and seen, by men'. From within 'this large dominant masculine consciousness . . . this serene masculine preoccupation with the male point of view', however, the 'submerged' Mollie learns – like Gilman herself – to appropriate its discourse for her own purposes (1981b: 33–6). In *Women and Economics* this discursive play, though more muted, is still in evidence. It is to be found in the ironies, the sudden changes of direction, the unexpectedly radical conclusions to which the careful accumulation of logical argument is made to lead, the rhetorical flourishes and bursts of irritation and impatience, and in the way in which Gilman's own terms – the 'sexuo-economic relation', the 'maternalizing of man' – are inserted into, and so subvert, the dominant discourse which she has appropriated.

Like Mary Wollstonecraft, then, Gilman writes as a cultural outsider, inside and outside both femininity and the masculine discourse which for her is both constraint and weapon. But, unlike Wollstonecraft, she has access both to an idea of female embodiment which is not dependent on femininity and to an 'imagined community'[10] of women/feminists. Her voice can therefore be less insistent in its claims, less concerned to say 'I', but it is always careful above all – with its ironies, subversions and rhetorical play – not to render itself vulnerable to relegation to the no-place of discourse, the feminine irrational.

Virginia Woolf (1882–1941): Writing as Women Write

With Virginia Woolf we arrive at a theorist whose central concerns can be identified squarely with those of feminist cultural studies. Michele Barrett makes such a case in her discussions of Woolf's *A Room of One's Own* (1929). Woolf's central concern, she argues, is with the restricted access of women to the means of literary production. But she is also concerned with issues of representation and reception, 'with the fabric and texture of the writing, psychological aspects of the creative process, and issues of consciousness and identity. Woolf wanted to discuss not only the *production* of literature, but the ways in which the social context of its *reception* influenced the writing itself.' Woolf's strength as a feminist cultural theorist, argues Barrett, 'is that her discussion of representation is located in an analysis of both the historical production and distribution of literature and its social consumption and reception' (1993: xv–xvi; 1988: 104). But like that of Wollstonecraft and Gilman, Woolf's writing also embodies the contradictions inherent in her enterprise: that of writing theoretically as a woman. It embodies them in a far more self-conscious way. Woolf's writing constantly draws attention to itself, playing across the surface of language and with discursive forms, in order to write about women and as a woman whilst simultaneously refusing, in Ann Snitow's words, 'an identity . . . overdetermined by [her] gender' (1990: 9). But it remains caught in these contradictions nevertheless. A passage from her 1931 lecture, 'Professions for Women' sums up her difficulties. Writing for a female audience, Woolf insists on the necessity for the woman writer to 'kill' that internalized self-censor, 'the Angel in the House', if she is to be able to write. With the destruction of this image of an idealized femininity, the woman writer has now only to 'be herself':

> Ah, but what is 'herself'? I mean, what is a woman? I assure you, I do not know. I do not believe that you know. I do not believe that anybody can know until she has expressed herself in all the arts and professions open to human skill. That indeed is one of the reasons why I have come here – out of respect for you, who are in process of providing us by your experiments what a woman is, who are in process of providing us, by your failures and successes, with that extremely important piece of information. (PW: 358)[11]

This is very close to contemporary feminist arguments about the constructed nature of the category 'woman' such as those of Denise Riley (1988): 'To put it schematically: 'women' is historically, discursively constructed, and always relative to other categories which themselves change' (1988: 13). Certainly the passage pulls in this direction: we can not, after all the qualifying and problematizing, believe in this 'extremely important piece of information', so neatly tied up – or believe that Virginia Woolf believes in it. Nevertheless, there is still the *desire* to believe in a self beyond contradiction, a fully human self that might – at some point in the future – be 'expressed' and 'known'. Lurking here, despite all Woolf's attempts to unravel and undermine patriarchy's assumptions, is the suspicion that all the instabilities around the category 'woman' are the result of her being not-quite, or not-yet 'human'.

Woolf's argument, argues Michele Barrett, is 'strongly materialist' (1993: xiv). The most famous expression of her insistence that cultural production depends on material conditions is her proposition in *A Room of One's Own* that 'it is necessary to have five hundred a year and a room with a lock on the door if you are to write fiction or poetry' (*ROO*: 94). Women have been denied education and the ability to earn money, and, had it been possible to earn money, 'the law denied them the right to possess what money they earned' (*ROO*: 20). It is 'the right to earn one's living', she argues in *Three Guineas* (1938), that will give women 'that weapon of independent opinion which is still their most powerful weapon' (*TG*: 180–1). Like Charlotte Perkins Gilman she argues that it is economic freedom not the vote which will liberate women, and like Gilman she produces a powerful attack on women's poverty, and on the hypocrisy of arguments that claim women are partners in their husbands' earnings. She also attacks sex discrimination in employment and makes a powerful plea for women's rights. Women, she argues, have been treated as slaves, denied education, ownership and citizenship (*TG*: 170–80, 234).

It is the results of these exclusions that concern Woolf, however. It is not simply that women have been debarred from cultural production, or that they have internalized the ideological assumptions about their incapacity ('Outwardly, what obstacles are there for a woman rather than for a man?

Inwardly, I think, the case is very different; she has still many ghosts to fight, many prejudices to overcome', PW: 360). Women's exclusion from the material structures that confer citizenship places them outside the forms of cultural identity which come with that citizenship. The story Woolf tells in *A Room of One's Own* of being expelled from the 'Oxbridge' turf by a College Beadle and refused entry to the library unless 'accompanied by a Fellow of the College or furnished with a letter of introduction' (*ROO*: 7), is, then, at once a very material exclusion ('he was a Beadle; I was a woman') and an exclusion from the symbolic community which confers legitimacy of identity.

Women, Woolf argues, are both inside and outside all the symbolic structures which construct identity. A woman is outside nation because she can not herself lay claim to national identity: 'for her there are no "foreigners", since by law she becomes a foreigner if she marries a foreigner' (*TG*: 233). She is outside class because she has no access to the markers of class: education, income, profession, possessions. She is outside history because she is invisible within the 'historian's view of the past' as a series of 'great movements'. History, writes Woolf, is at present 'unreal, lop-sided'; to include women would be to rewrite it, shifting the margins – the 'glimpse of [women] in the lives of the great, whisking away into the background' – into the centre (*ROO*: 41–2). And she is outside science: 'Science, it would seem, is not sexless; she is a man, a father, and infected too' (*TG*: 267). What Woolf is arguing here is the power of discursive structures – themselves rooted in structures of material power – to define as well as to exclude. In material terms, women have been confined to the private sphere, excluded from social power, but the ideological damage has been far greater. In a 'purely patriarchal society' the discourses of history, science, philosophy, literature all 'celebrate male virtues, enforce male values and describe the world of men' (*ROO*: 68, 92). 'Woman' is constructed by and within these discourses, a 'very queer, composite being . . . an odd monster', at once worshipped and reviled, 'imaginatively . . . of the highest importance; practically . . . completely insignificant' (*ROO*: 39–40).

Women, however, must *live* these discursive contradictions, and it is here that Woolf's technique, moving between observation, analysis and anecdote, (fictional) autobiography and fantasy, works so powerfully. Her argument about the politics of dress, for instance, is anchored – as Barthes was later to anchor his similar arguments about ideology and myth – in photographs which she includes, and accompanied by descriptions of 'tiptoeing' into a public building. In her analysis she points to the function of male dress as public, hierarchical code ('every button, rosette and stripe seems to have some symbolical meaning'). But her ridicule also points out the deadly logic of this marking of rank and status: 'your finest clothes are those that you wear as soldiers' (*TG*: 133–7). For a woman, she argues, to whom such public display is forbidden, dress advertises her position within the *sexual* economy. But it also renders her of no status, hence invisible in the public sphere. Woolf's image here is of the veil; elsewhere she writes of women's 'desire to be veiled', to conceal the 'inner strife' which accompanies their forays into the public sphere, by adopting the mask either of femininity or – in the case of the male pseudonyms adopted by women writers – of masculinity (*ROO*: 46). Women become visible, however, when they transgress, and Woolf's narratives of exclusion – from the College library and turf, from education, from the world of professional life – make it clear that this is a lived, material exclusion, a matter of embodied experience as well as of symbolic identity.

What this exclusion produces, argues Woolf, is a difference in what she elsewhere calls the 'angle of vision' (1993: 166): 'though we see the same world, we see it through different eyes' (*TG*: 133). Women 'see' differently as cultural producers and as readers, and the representations of the world that they produce are also different. This is a matter of cultural construction not of essential sexual difference, but it *is* an embodied difference. In an interesting phrase, Woolf argues that the 'book has somehow to be adapted to the body'. Here she comes close to later theorists like Luce Irigaray (1985), who argues that in Western patriarchal society, representation is the product of the 'male imaginary', so that its structures and rhythms are always implicitly male. Like Irigaray, Woolf speculates on what a *female* 'imaginary', in which might be expressed 'my own experiences as a body' (*PW*: 360), might look like.

For the present, she points to two consequences of this masculine hegemony which are important theoretically. The first is that woman's consciousness, and her identity, are split. Characteristically, Woolf describes this in terms that anchor it as experience and that link individual subjectivity to public identity: 'if one is a woman one is often surprised by a sudden splitting off of consciousness, say in walking down Whitehall, when from being the natural inheritor of that civilization, she becomes, on the contrary, outside of it, alien and critical' (*ROO*: 88). The second, in one of Woolf's most famous formulations, is that '[w]omen have served all these centuries as looking-glasses possessing the magic and delicious power of reflecting the figure of man at twice its natural size' (*ROO*: 32). This image embodies a number of ideas. It positions woman as man's 'other' – marginal, invisible as herself. It also makes clear that the existence of this 'other' to man's 'self', this private 'looking-glass vision', is what *enables* the public dominance not only of Western patriarchy but also of imperialism: '[h]ow is he to go on giving judgement, civilizing natives, making laws, writing books, dressing up and speechifying at banquets, unless he can see himself at breakfast and at dinner at least twice the size he is?' (*ROO*: 330). It clarifies, too, the difficulties of women's access to representation. For man, representation is always self-representation; the mirror always shows him himself. For woman, there is no such guarantor of identity, no Lacanian 'mirror phase' through which to imagine the self. What there is instead seems to be the 'Angel in the House', that phantom of the male imagination which blocks woman's attempts to see, and to write, herself. For woman, representation involves the repression not the reflection of the body.

When Woolf writes that 'we think back through our mothers if we are women' (*ROO*: 69), then, she is arguing for an act of retrieval, and through it the construction of new structures of representation, and new reading positions for women. About fathers and their power, literal and symbolic, she is scathing in her condemnation. 'Society it seems', with its institutions (its 'societies'), is 'a father' (*TG*: 263). The patriarch who inspires fear in the home finds his ideal image – medals, uniforms and all – in the figure of the fascist dictator. Anticipating later feminist arguments, Woolf insists that 'the public and the private worlds are inseparably connected; that the tyrannies and servilities of the one are the tyrannies and servilities of the other' (*TG*: 270). Destroying fascism means destroying patriarchy: the battle is 'of the daughters against the fathers', between the 'victims of the patriarchal system' and 'the patriarchs' (*TG*: 189). Typically, her examples link public tyrannies with institutionalized patriarchy (the practices and discourses of medicine, politics, the Church) and private oppressions. What makes Woolf very different from her predecessors in this is that she is not simply arguing that women are oppressed; she sets out to analyse the desires and fears of the patriarch, asking, 'what possible satisfaction can dominance give to the dominator?' (*TG*: 257). Patriarchy, she argues, oppresses women but also needs, hates and fears women. The patriarch and the society he has produced suffer – and here she appropriates that most patriarchal of discourses, Freudian psychoanalysis – from 'infantile fixation'. But he erects ideological structures ('unwritten laws') to protect his position. It has been the task of the daughters to uncover these 'laws': 'it is beginning to be agreed that they were not laid down by 'God', who is now very generally held to be a conception, of patriarchal origin, valid only for certain races, at certain stages and times; nor by nature, who is now known to vary greatly in her commands' (*TG*: 319).

Virginia Woolf argues, then, that identity is culturally constructed but always embodied. Society's 'unwritten laws', constructed within culture, are 'to some extent the product of our bodies, and there are two kinds of body, male and female' (*TG*: 319). For women, for whom the body is repressed by and within patriarchal discourse, identity is experienced as fractured. It is in this context that what Elaine Showalter (1977) calls Woolf's 'flight into androgyny' should be viewed. Women, argues Woolf, must write differently from men: the 'book has somehow to be adapted to the body' (*ROO*: 70). In 'Professions for Women', however, she confesses that neither she nor any other woman has yet succeeded in 'telling the truth about my own experiences as a body' (*PW*: 360). When she asks herself in *A Room of One's Own* whether there might be 'two sexes in the mind corresponding to the two sexes in the body, and whether they also require to be united in order to get complete satisfaction and happiness' (*ROO*: 88), it is as a fantasized solution to the fracturing of consciousness which she has just described. The image she employs is of sexual union, and she invokes this image again when she describes the ideal writing process:

> [I]t is fatal for anyone who writes to think of their sex. It is fatal to be a man or woman pure and simple; one must be woman-manly or man-womanly. . . . Some marriage of opposites has to be consummated. The whole of the mind must lie wide open if we are to get the sense that the writer is communicating his experiences with perfect fullness. There must be freedom and there must be peace. Not a wheel must grate, not a light glimmer. The curtains must be close drawn. The writer, I thought, once his experience is over, must lie back and let his mind celebrate its nuptials in darkness. (*ROO*: 94)

In this passage the body, so difficult to express, returns, but, as Stephen Heath has pointed out (1982: 114), it returns as *male*. The only image available to Woolf to describe the androgyny she seeks to invoke returns her to the masculine discourse that she is trying to circumvent, a discourse in which the subject can only be male.

In the later *Three Guineas*, she is more inclined to emphasize difference, arguing that to seek to 'merge identity' (*TG*: 230) could only return women to patriarchal dominance. The difficulty here, however, is familiar: to write from a position of difference is to write from no position at all. Like Mary Wollstonecraft and Charlotte Perkins Gilman before her, Woolf is aware of how perilously close to the irrational place outside discourse she finds herself. She found herself repeatedly placed there in her life.[12] Her most characteristic solution is neither the attempt to 'write the body' nor the 'flight into androgyny', but the refusal to adopt any fixed writing position at all. She refuses the identity 'feminist', arguing that it is too limited; she refuses also 'Miss' and 'Mrs' ('a contaminated word; an obscene word', *TG*: 174); she refuses to be 'Virginia Woolf'. In *A Room of One's Own* she is 'Mary Beton, Mary Seton, Mary Carmichael or . . . any name you please'; ' "I" is only a convenient term for somebody who has no real being. Lies will flow from my lips . . .' (*ROO*: 4). We do not know whether we are reading autobiography or fantasy, fictional narrative, observation or metaphor. What Elaine Showalter describes with some irritation as *A Room of One's Own*'s 'strenuous charm, its playfulness, its conversational surface', its use of 'repetition, exaggeration, parody, whimsy, and multiple viewpoint' (1977: 282), is described by Gillian Beer as the 'attempt to rupture the continuities of language by fixing our attention on them' (1979: 90). It is, that is to say, *performance*. Virginia Woolf writes 'as women write' (*ROO*: 68), which means that though she may dream of a transparent self-expression and an androgynous writing, what she actually offers us is the constant construction and dismantling of identity, both that of patriarchy in its many aspects and her own.

Simone de Beauvoir (1908–1986):
The Personal and the Philosophical

Simone de Beauvoir's *The Second Sex*[13] (1949) is a pivotal text in any narrative of feminist cultural theory. Through it we can trace backwards: to Mary Wollstonecraft, with her appropriation of a philosophical discourse which is constantly interrupted and dislocated by the pressure of what it is unable to contain; to Charlotte Perkins Gilman, with her attempts to construct a social and economic history of women's oppression together with a utopian vision of a liberated future; and to Virginia Woolf, with her exploration of women as culturally situated subjects and as cultural producers. Through it we can also look forward. Toril Moi points out that de Beauvoir belonged to the first generation of European women to be educated as men's equals. It was the attempt to fully realize her position as intellectual *woman* that produced *The Second Sex* (Moi 1994: 67). For Moi, de Beauvoir thus became 'the greatest feminist theorist of our century. Long before the emergence of the Women's Movement *The Second Sex* posed every one of the problems feminists today are still working to solve' (1994: 3). Michele Barrett makes similar claims for her as originator, writing that de Beauvoir 'argues fundamentally for a cultural and ideological perspective', foreshadowing the work of later cultural theorists in exploring the work of ideology ('myth' in de Beauvoir's terminology) in producing women's 'complicity' in their own subordination (Barrett 1988: 52, 110). De Beauvoir, she points out, draws on both Marx and Freud in order to explain the ideological 'overdetermination' of women's subordination. Finally, Judith Okely adds to this emphasis on de Beauvoir as cultural theorist by pointing out a further, far less explicit way in which she anticipates later issues within feminist cultural studies. 'A paradoxical strength' of *The Second Sex* is, she suggests, 'the hidden use of herself as a case study' (1986: 72). De Beauvoir, she argues, offers us not only a theorizing of women's position but also a sort of 'concealed ethnography':[14] though she studiously avoids the first person in her examples, her presence can be felt throughout in the 'girl' and 'woman' whose attempts to live out the contradictions of femininity she records. It is this double aspect of de Beauvoir's theoretical work that I want to focus on here, since it seems to me that it is not only in her explicit cultural theory that de Beauvoir is a crucial figure. It is also in the contradictions and tensions which her work exhibits: tensions between theory and experience; between her claims about cultural construction and her accounts of the body; between her various accounts of the construction of female subjectivity; and between her claims to philosophical neutrality and her evident situatedness.

If we turn to de Beauvoir's account of the inception of *The Second Sex*, we get some idea of these tensions. Thinking about writing her memoirs,

I realized that the first question to come up was: What has it meant to me to be a woman? At first I thought I could dispose of that pretty quickly. I had never any feeling of inferiority, no one had ever said to me: 'You think like that because you're a woman'; my femaleness had never been irksome to me in any way. 'For me,' I said to Sartre, 'you might almost say it just hasn't counted.' 'All the same, you weren't brought up in the same way as a boy would have been; you should look into it further.' I looked, and it was a revelation: this world was a masculine world, my childhood had been nourished by myths forged by men, and I hadn't reacted to them in at all the same way I should have done if I had been a boy. I was so interested in this discovery that I abandoned my project for a personal confession in order to give all my attention to finding out about the condition of woman in its broadest terms. I went to the Biblioteque Nationale to do some reading, and what I studied were the myths of femininity. (Quoted in Moi 1994: 66–7)

The account slips constantly between recognition and non-recognition of de Beauvoir's own lived experience as female: the sudden 'revelation' that the world is masculine and that 'I hadn't reacted . . . in at all the same way I should have done if I had been a boy' – a revelation which has to come to her via Sartre's logic; the negativity and circumlocution of this statement (her reaction is presented only in negative terms: it wasn't that of a boy); the perception that 'femaleness' could only be – but hadn't been – experienced as 'irksome'; the disappearance of the personal (the 'revelation' which inspired the project) so soon after its acknowledgement – the 'personal confession' 'abandoned' in favour of a scholarly work on 'the condition of woman in its broadest terms'.

All of these position her, in Toril Moi's words, as 'at once . . . accept[ing] and deny[ing] the implications of being born a woman' (1994: 67). The tension evident here between accepting the identity 'woman' and, in investigating the *meaning* of that identity, wishing to refuse it as 'hopelessly compromised', is a tension which Ann Snitow (1990) sees as fundamental to contemporary feminist theory (1990: 17). Charlotte Brunsdon, writing from the Birmingham CCCS in *Women Take Issue* (1978), makes a similar argument: 'We have somehow to hold the necessary articulation of female experience (our oppression lies partly in the invisibility of this experience) with the struggle to understand the determinants on this experience to allow us to change it at a more than individual level' (1978: 31). *The Second Sex*, with its division into two parts, 'Facts and Myths' ('the determinants on [women's] experience') and 'Woman's Life Today' (the 'articulation of female experience'), seeks to do this. In the process, it anticipates in a number of ways later writing within feminist cultural studies: in its attempts to bring together arguments from history, sociology and psychoanalysis; in its bringing together issues of the body and of ideology; in its explorations of the ways in which ideology invades subjectivity and of the construction of gendered subjectivities; in its registering of the historical specificity of the construction of subjectivity; in its teasing out of the ambiguities of women's acceptance of and resistance to the imposition of norms of femininity; and in its attempts to hold together the 'critical negativity' of feminist cultural analysis with the 'affirmative positivity' of its political vision (de Lauretis 1990: 266).

Before turning in more detail to aspects of *The Second Sex*, there is one further tension that runs throughout de Beauvoir's analysis of the different 'determinate moments' of women's oppression (to borrow Stuart Hall's phrase),[15] which I should like to consider here: that between the analysis of *oppression* and the emphasis on *choice*. Sartrean existentialism, which underpins the arguments of *The Second Sex*, states that human freedom is attained in moving from the inert or fixed state of 'Being-in-Itself' (*en soi*), or what de Beauvoir calls 'immanence', into 'Being-for-Itself' (*pour soi*) or in de Beauvoir's terms, 'transcendence'. This movement from facticity into freedom is achieved through consciously undertaken actions in the world. Thus there is no pre-given human identity, or essence; individuals create themselves (become 'existents') in specific and changing situations through consciously made choices. If they fail to do this, they are guilty of 'bad faith'. Clearly these concepts give force to the utopian aspects of *The Second Sex*: whatever the existing limitations on women's freedom, this is not a matter of *essential* differences. Woman, in 'beginning to exist for herself' can create her own freedom: 'the future remains largely open' (*SS*: 739, 723). Nevertheless, this emphasis on individual choice is at odds with a theory of oppression. Women, argues de Beauvoir, have been *confined* to immanence by men, who have claimed the quality of transcendence for themselves: 'This is the lot assigned to woman in the patriarchate; but it is in no way a vocation, any more than slavery is the vocation of the slave' (1988: 284). How optimistic can we be, then, about *woman's* power to choose 'existence' or 'transcendence' in the light of such a history? Either there is something in the nature of *being a woman* which has meant that she has been unable to grasp her freedom, or she has been prevented from achieving freedom by men, whose 'transcendence' has (as Virginia Woolf argued, though in different terms) depended on the 'immanence' of women. The tension between these two explanations, which runs throughout *The Second Sex*, and the way in which they intersect with de Beauvoir's attempt to produce an account of women's lived experience, are what make the book both theoretically important and a complex and contradictory work.

De Beauvoir begins her account of 'Facts' with 'The Data of Biology' – 'data', however, which are far from neutral in their presentation. Although she begins her explanation by rejecting the argument that, in their relative passivity/activity, the female ovaries can be 'likened to immanence, the sperm to transcendence' (*SS*: 44), in fact this comparison of female sexuality to immanence and passivity, and male sexuality to activity and transcendence, runs throughout the book. For de Beauvoir, then, life itself is a matter of both the perpetuation of the species and its transcendence, but these two essential elements 'are separately apportioned to the two sexes'. Woman is 'more enslaved to the species than is the male, her animality is more manifest' (*SS*: 51, 285); it is *harder* for her to achieve transcendence. Through both motherhood – which de Beauvoir sees as turning the woman from 'a human being, a conscious and free individual, [into] life's passive instrument' (*SS*: 513) – and through heterosexuality, woman is alienated from herself. Her description of the (hetero)sexual act is particularly disturbing. Whilst for man the sexual act is self-expression, a laying claim to individuality, his 'living transcendence', the female is first violated, then alienated: 'she *submits* to the coition, which invades her individuality': 'Woman, like man, *is* her body; but her body is something other than herself' (*SS*: 54, 55, 61). The following, from the chapter on 'Sexual Initiation', is the most extended of her descriptions of female sexuality. Whereas the male adolescent, writes de Beauvoir, 'assumes his [body] easily and with pride in its desires', for the female 'it is a strange and disquieting burden':

> Feminine desire is the soft throbbing of a mollusc. Whereas man is impetuous, woman is only impatient; her expectation can become ardent without ceasing to be passive; man dives upon his prey like the eagle and the hawk; woman lies in wait like the carnivorous plant, the bog, in which insects and children are swallowed up. She is absorption, suction, humus, pitch and glue, a passive influx, insinuating and viscous: thus, at least she vaguely feels herself to be. Hence it is that there is in her not only resistance to the subjugating intentions of the male, but also conflict within herself. To the taboos and inhibitions contributed by her education and by society are added feelings of disgust and denial coming from the erotic experience itself: these influences are mutually reinforced to such an extent that after the first coition a woman is often more than ever in revolt against her sexual destiny. (*SS*: 406–7)

Male sexuality in this account is assertive, self-realizing – elsewhere de Beauvoir consistently describes man's transcendence in sexual terms ('he burst out of the present, he opened the future', *SS*: 95). Woman, however, is profoundly self-alienated, and the speaking position adopted in the passage shifts in the attempt to register this. It is now outside female embodiment ('She is absoption, suction . . .'), now inside. But inside, speaking *as* woman, the text becomes uncertain. The woman 'vaguely feels herself to be' passive, insinuating and viscous, but then – apparently drawing back – she is prisoner of the 'inhibitions and taboos' supplied by education and society (on the previous page de Beauvoir has written that woman 'is thoroughly indoctrinated' with these notions). Confronted with erotic experience, she feels 'disgust and denial', but whether against her 'sexual destiny', which is one of subjugation, against the man who thus subjugates her (elsewhere de Beauvoir writes of the 'indissoluble synthesis of attraction and repulsion' which characterizes heterosexual female desire), or against the viscous passivity of her own desire, is unclear.

This sense of internal conflict and contradiction is continued in the chapter on 'The Psychoanalytic Point of View'. Here de Beauvoir's purpose is to insist that 'the body as lived in by the subject' is no more *determining* of woman's destiny than is the body itself: 'Woman can be defined by her consciousness of her own femininity no more satisfactorily than by saying that she is a female, for she acquires this consciousness under circumstances dependent upon the society of which she is a member' (*SS*: 80). If de Beauvoir argues that psychoanalysis is wrong in mistaking the historically specific for the universal, and in thus denying *choice* to the individual, however, she nevertheless returns us constantly to the body in her explanations of subjectivity. Drawing on Lacan, she argues that, following separation from the mother, the infant's identity is affirmed through identification with its own mirror-image: 'his ego becomes so fully identified with this reflected image that it is formed only in being projected' (*SS*: 296–7). For the male infant, however, the penis then assumes this function of 'double'. At once 'himself and other than himself', it can be his *alter ego*. Thus 'the little boy can boldly assume an attitude of subjectivity; the very object into which he projects himself becomes a symbol of autonomy, of transcendence, of power' (*SS*: 306). Not having this *alter ego,* the girl 'is led to make an object of her whole self, to set up herself as the Other' (*SS*: 80).

What we have here, as in all de Beauvoir's descriptions of female subjectivity as embodied ('the body as lived in by the subject'), is a painful sense of contradiction. On the one hand we have the female body, with its sexuality, experienced as vulnerable (possessing 'a disturbing frailty'). It slips back into immanence, makes woman 'the prey of the species' and tempts her into self-objectification. Only after the menopause, argues de Beauvoir, are woman and her body one (*SS*: 63). On the other hand, there is an equally powerful, and contradictory, sense that the male's phallic power is *symbolic*. The penis is *not* equivalent to transcendence; it is merely a symbol convenient to a patriarchal society. In a society organized differently, other symbols of the alienated self – other *alter egos* – could be found. The problem, in this analysis, is not the body experienced as female, but the body experienced as female in a patriarchal society. For the woman of today, the outcome is a divided subjectivity, a slipping in and out of the identity 'woman'. Adopting an identity means for her a form of masquerade: she may 'play at being a man', or 'play at being a woman' (*SS*: 82). But de Beauvoir is clear that the emancipated woman of the future will possess a distinctively female and fully embodied subjectivity: 'Man is a human being with sexuality; woman is a complete individual, equal to the male, only if she too is a human being with sexuality' (*SS*: 691–2). What this will *mean* – how different this free woman will be from man – remains to be seen.

It is in the chapters on 'Myths' that de Beauvoir most clearly anticipates later cultural theory, not only in her account of the functioning of 'myth' (or ideology), which anticipates the writing of Roland Barthes,[16] but also in her analysis of how cultural representations work to reproduce social relations of power and to produce individual subjectivities. It is here that she most fully transforms a 'gender-neutral'[17] existentialist philosophy, with its emphasis on individual choice, into a theory of gender oppression. Drawing on Lévi-Strauss (1949), she argues that human culture is marked by the construction of binary oppositions, with the valorized term acquiring meaning only with reference to its opposite. Thus the human subject can construct his sense of self only in opposition to that which is Other. 'The category of the *Other*' is 'as primordial as consciousness itself'. Man, however, has assigned to himself the category of Subject, and confined woman to the status of Other: 'She is defined and differentiated with reference to man and not he with reference to her; she is the incidental, the inessential as opposed to the essential. He is the Subject, he is the Absolute – she is the Other' (*SS*: 16). In order to see himself as transcendent, he projects on to woman all the properties of immanence, the body and sexuality: 'she appears as the dark chaos from whence life wells up, as this life itself, and as the over-yonder towards which life tends' (*SS*: 176). At the same time, however, the recognition that woman is, like himself, a potentially free individual is important to him. His victory is the greater if the woman seems free to resist; only as his potential equal can her recognition of his superiority have value.

De Beauvoir's analysis of woman's function as both object and reflection for man is reminiscent of Virginia Woolf's account in *A Room of One's Own*. Woman, she argues, is 'the mirror in which the male, Narcissus-like, contemplates himself'; through her 'he will experience the miracle of seeming to himself to be another, another who is also his profoundest ego' (*SS*: 217). On to her image he therefore projects both fantasies of transcendence and fears of carnality. The fantasy of the 'Eternal Feminine' is elaborated in myths of unattainable and ideal beauty and self-sacrifice, but also in stories of devouring female flesh: 'The womb . . . becomes a pulp of humours, a carnivorous plant, a dark, contractile gulf, where dwells a serpent that insatiably swallows up the strength of the male' (*SS*: 223). What is so powerful about de Beauvoir's analysis here is that she links representation both to individual subjectivity and to social power. 'Representation of the world, like the world itself,' she writes, 'is the work of men; they describe it from their own point of view, which they confuse with absolute truth' (*SS*: 175). Dominance – and here she extends her analysis to include imperial and racial dominance – is maintained through 'such intermediaries as religions, traditions, language, tales, songs, movies'. Myth, she argues,

> had roots in the spontaneous attitude of man towards his own existence and towards the world around him. But going beyond experience towards the transcendent Idea was deliberately used by

patriarchal society for purposes of self-justification; through the myths this society imposed its laws and customs upon individuals in a picturesque, effective manner; it is under a mythical form that the group-imperative is indoctrinated into each conscience. (*SS*: 290)

Woman, too, having no myths of her own, must frame her experience 'through men's eyes'. Indeed, if she is not to contest her positioning as inci-dental, inessential Other, object rather than subject, it is vital for man that she *make herself* object, or Other: 'in order that all reciprocity may appear quite impossible, it is necessary for the Other to be for itself an other, for its very subjectivity to be affected by its otherness' (*SS*: 288). Part Two of *The Second Sex*, 'Woman's Life Today', therefore comprises a detailed account of woman's lived experience in all its contradictions and painful compromises.

I have dealt already with the tensions that run through de Beauvoir's discussion of female sexuality. It is here that her prose is at its most strained, as it struggles with the disjuncture between what she sees as the inherent passivity of female sexuality and her insistence on woman as subject. But this sense of contradiction can be felt throughout her account of women's lived experience. If we turn to her discussion of women as cultural produc-ers, we find her echoing Virginia Woolf as she argues that 'one is not born a genius: one becomes a genius; and the feminine situation has up to the present rendered this becoming practically impossible' (*SS*: 164). But like Woolf, when she comes to describe the process of cultural production, it seems *inherently* male. Women, she writes, 'have erected no virile myth in which their projects are reflected; they have no religion or poetry of their own'. They will need 'an apprenticeship in abandonment and transcen-dence' before they can produce art, literature or philosophy (*SS*: 174, 720). This model of a transcendent subjectivity, producing art or philosophy through a process of self-reflection, seems unattainable for her divided woman, caught in the contradictions of female desire.

Women, then, can produce 'sincere and engaging' autobiographies and clear-sighted reporting, but, '[s]till amazed at being allowed to explore the phenomena of this world', they can not produce art. They 'take inventory without trying to discover meanings' (*SS*: 719). Throughout Part Two of *The Second Sex*, therefore, we find her using women's writing, whether autobiography or fiction, as *evidence* – as a transparent recording of women's lives equivalent in status to the case histories by male writers which she also cites. Yet her concept of culture as 'myth' – as a framing of lived experience serving the interests of a patriarchal society – suggests a quite different valuation. Women's writing, like women's friendships and, indeed, like the stubborn hostility of women's bodies to male sexual demands and fantasies, acquires the force of resistance. Running through Part Two of the book, then, is a sense of woman's lived experience as resis-tant – as living within, but as negotiating with and refusing to be subjugated by, the male universe which everywhere encloses, limits, dominates (*SS*: 291).

In this valuation – and it is one that de Beauvoir offers, though only intermittently – women's fractured and resistant experience under patriarchy can be viewed as more authentic or truthful than that of men.[18] Duped by the ease with which he can elide the symbolic and the literal functions of the penis, man fails to recognize his split nature as at once body and consciousness, and constructs myths to preserve his identity as subject. Woman, however, must live out the contradictions between myths of femininity, propounded within both 'high' and popular culture, and the realities of her experience. De Beauvoir thus argues that popular culture for women – magazines, fashion and popular fiction – is an ambiguous space. Produced by men, it instructs women about femininity ('the art of preserving . . . sexual attractiveness while washing dishes', *SS*: 541), and women are complicit in their identification with its objectified images, but it also offers a space in which a genuine and shared anxiety can be expressed. The women's culture thus produced is 'a kind of counter-universe', a genuinely supportive community operating within the bounded space of femininity and characterized by localized rebellions and collective resistances. But, characteristically, de Beauvoir adds that, unlike relationships between men, it rarely 'rises to genuine friendship' (*SS*: 556–60).

We find throughout this part of the book, then, on the one hand a utopian vision of a transcendent female subjectivity, to be achieved only when woman is truly free and, running alongside it, an understanding of women's lived experience under patriarchy as fractured, compromised, but resistant. De Beauvoir's rhetoric of emancipation is thus disconnected from her account of women's opposition to patriarchy in the present. The first will be a product of a free subjectivity not yet in existence; the second is bound up irredeemably with a compromised femininity whose oppositional strategies are simultaneously complicit with a masculine hegemony.[19] Even the newly emerged 'independent woman' is thus divided, torn between past and future, 'a "true woman" disguised as a man, . . . ill at ease in her flesh as in her masculine garb' (*SS*: 734). The truly free woman of the future can be scarcely imagined; her identity is not rooted in the woman of today.

Finally, there is the question of the speaking position constructed in *The Second Sex*. Unlike Mary Wollstonecraft two centuries earlier, Simone de Beauvoir's command of philosophical discourse is assured. We do not find here the structural disorganization and violent shifts in tone which characterize *A Vindication of the Rights of Woman*. Nevertheless, the tension between the personal and the philosophical which marks its inception is present throughout. Writing about 'the condition of woman in its broadest terms', de Beauvoir, despite her insistence on an embodied female subjectivity, does not speak – at least officially – *as* a woman. Yet in her often violent imaging of women's bodily experience (the 'bloody strawberry that inside the mother is transformed into a human being'; the 'rifled and bleeding womb' with its 'shreds of crimson life', *SS*: 609, 510), the generalized 'woman' she describes has the quality of the real – and of the personal. Moreover, Part Two of *The Second Sex* is marked by a multiplicity of voices, as de Beauvoir cites novels, (auto)biographies, case histories, personal anecdotes and contemporary news reports extensively. No less than Mary Wollstonecraft, then, she is engaged in 'developing enunciative strategies . . . precisely in relation to the cultural and social conventions that make speaking difficult or impossible for *women*' (Morris 1988: 7), and like Wollstonecraft she *enacts* the impossibility of speaking – at least philosophically – as a woman. Later feminists have tended to reject her assumed philosophical neutrality and her idealization of an implicitly male 'transcendence', but, like the other women discussed in this chapter, she anticipates both the arguments and the contradictions within contemporary feminist cultural analysis. In the following chapter, then, we shall turn to the 'daughters' whose work in the 1970s both rejected and re-established (and sometimes ignored) these arguments and contradictions.

Notes

1. See Kate Millett's *Sexual Politics* (1970: 146). See also Virginia Woolf's comments on *Jane Eyre* in *A Room of One's Own* (1993: 62–3).
2. See Jean Grimshaw's discussion (1986: 9–11). Wollstonecraft had herself written a defence of the ideals of the French Revolution, *A Vindication of the Rights of Men* (1790).
3. See Millett's *Sexual Politics* (1970: 46).
4. This is even stronger in Wollstonecraft's posthumously published novel *The Wrongs of Woman: or, Maria* (1798).
5. In Wollstonecraft's fiction, however, she is much more inclined to acknowledge not only the interdependence of but also the conflict between 'understanding' and 'feelings'. In *Mary: A Fiction* (1788), for example, we find:

   Neglected in every respect, and left to the operations of her own mind, she considered every thing that came under her inspection, and learned to think. . . . In this manner was she left to reflect on her own feelings; and so strengthened were they by being meditated on, that her character early became singular and permanent. Her understanding was strong and clear, when not clouded by her feelings; but she was too much the creature of impulse, and the slave of compassion. (Wollstonecraft 1976: 4, 7)

6. Jane Moore makes a very similar point, arguing that it is the boundary between the 'philosophical' (masculine) and the 'literary' (feminine) – 'the extant binarism of genre and gender difference of the 1790s' – which Wollstonecraft subverts (1989: 167). It seems to me, however, that the range of tone that she employs is broader than this, encompassing as it does outbursts of anger, humour and satire.
7. Ann J. Lane describes Gilman's relation to social Darwinism thus:

   One view [of social Darwinism], formulated by English theorist Herbert Spenser, and defended in the United States by William Braham Sumner, was that society's laws are irrevocably rooted in the evolutionary process, and that there is no way to interfere with the struggle for existence and the survival of the fittest. Lester Frank Ward, an American sociologist, rejected this interpretation of Social Darwinism. . . . He insisted that it was possible for humans, who, unlike other animals, possess a Mind and therefore a Culture, to shape the social laws under which they operate. Gilman early identified herself with the ideological camp of Ward in believing that human beings were the key to determining their own destinies and in using evolutionary theory as a weapon in the movement for social change. (1979: ix–x)

Nevertheless, the most difficult aspect of *Women and Economics* for a modern reader is Gilman's use of the word 'race'. She uses it to distinguish human attributes from those which are sex-specific: 'To teach, to rule, to make, to decorate, to distribute, – these are not sex-functions: they are race-functions' (1998: 27). At times, however, these references to the 'human race' can tip into a much more uncomfortable version of social Darwinism, as when, for example, black servants are described as being 'alien in race' – though it should be added that Gilman's concern in this passage is to condemn the practice of maintaining servants in this way (1998: 127). Compare Darwin's own view of the parallels between women and 'the lower races':

It is generally admitted that with women the powers of intuition, of rapid perception, and perhaps of imitation, are more strongly marked than in man; but some, at least, of these faculties are characteristic of the lower races, and therefore of a past and lower state of civilization. (Quoted in Beer 1979: 83)

8. See Janice Radway (1987) for an account of the 'ideal hero' of the popular romance novel. Within the romance narrative, she writes, it is the heroine's love that will 'magically remake a man incapable of expressing emotions or admitting dependence. As a result of her effort, he will be transformed into an ideal figure possessing both masculine power and the more "effeminate" ability to discern her needs and to attend to their fulfillment in a tender, solicitous way' (1987: 128).
9. *Moving the Mountain* (1911), *Herland* (1915) and *With Her in Ourland* (1916). Extracts from *Moving the Mountain* and *With Her in Ourland* can be found in Gilman (1981).
10. The quotation is from Stuart Hall (1991). The concept of 'imagined communities' is drawn from Benedict Anderson (1983).
11. The references which follow are to the 1993 Penguin edition of *A Room of One's Own* (*ROO*), *Three Guineas* (*TG*) and 'Professions for Women' (PW).
12. Woolf had experienced her own bouts of 'madness' and like Gilman had found herself committed by a loving husband to the 'rest-cure' developed by American doctor Silas Weir Mitchell. Elaine Showalter (1977: 274) describes this form of 'therapy' as 'a sinister parody of idealized Victorian femininity: inertia, privatization, narcissism, dependency'.
13. The references that follow are to the 1988 Picador edition of *The Second Sex* (*SS*).
14. The phrase is Toril Moi's. See Moi (1994: 67).
15. See Hall (1980b: 130).
16. See Roland Barthes, *Mythologies* (1973), first published in Paris in 1957.
17. In fact, as Toril Moi points out (1994), the 'existent' of existentialist theory is always implicitly male.
18. Toril Moi points out (1994: 284) that what in Parshley's translation is rendered

as 'Woman lives her love in a more authentic fashion' should in fact be translated as 'Woman has a more authentic experience of herself.'

19. Her account of women's resistance as the construction of 'a set of "local rules"' within '*the* world, which is [men's] world' strikingly anticipates Stuart Hall's (1980a) description of the operations of cultural hegemony.

|3|

The 1970s:
'A New Consciousness
Among Women'[1]

> An underground revolution is taking place today in major cities and
> small towns, on campuses and in living rooms everywhere. The new
> feminists, women young and old, are meeting to demand complete
> equality: social, political and economic. To get it, they intend to fight.

So announces the book-jacket of Cellestine Ware's *Woman Power: The
Movement for Women's Liberation* in answer to its own rhetorical demand:
'Who are the new feminists? What do they want?' Like Kate Millett's
Sexual Politics, Eva Figes' *Patriarchal Attitudes* and Germaine Greer's *The
Female Eunuch*, Ware's book was published in 1970. Seven years earlier,
Betty Friedan, in *The Feminine Mystique*, had felt no such confidence. For
her, feminism was 'dead history. It ended as a vital movement in America
with the winning of that final right: the vote' (1965: 88). Ware's designation of the newly emergent Women's Liberation Movement as the 'new
feminism' is of course double-edged, serving not only to emphasize continuity with 'the first phase of feminism' but also – in a now familiar use of
the adjective ('New Daz', 'the New Left', 'New Labour') – to insist on
difference.[2] For some writers of the early 1970s, it was this difference which
was most apparent. As Sheila Rowbotham argued, whilst 'women's liberation does have strands of the older equal-rights feminism, . . . it is something more': it is the product of a changed social and political context and
possesses a sharper and far more radical feminist consciousness (1973: ix).
Whilst 'old feminism' was individualist and reformist, she argued, 'women's
liberation' was collective and revolutionary. Others, particularly those identifying themselves as radical feminists, chose to assimilate the two, reclaiming as the first wave of 'the most important revolution in history' earlier
feminist writing and activism.[3] Temporarily halted by a 50-year counter-
offensive, the 'onslaught' of feminism was now resurgent; it could, in Kate
Millett's words, 'at last accomplish its aim of freeing half the race from its
immemorial subordination' (1977: 363).

This difference of emphasis signals both the complex origins of the 1970s Women's Liberation Movement and its internal divisions. In America two major strands can be distinguished. Following the impact of *The Feminine Mystique*, Betty Friedan had herself founded NOW (National Organization for Women) in 1966. Formed as a direct result of the failure of America's Equal Employment Opportunity Commission (EEOC) to take seriously the issue of sex discrimination, NOW's aims were reformist, lying very much within a liberal Equal Rights tradition. It sought 'to bring women into full participation in the mainstream of American society now, assuming all the privileges and responsibilities thereof in truly equal partnership with men' (cited in Freeman 1975: 55). Its Board members included two former EEOC commissioners and three trades union representatives, and at its first conference, in October 1967, it formally adopted a Bill of Rights for women.

In contrast, the origins of radical feminist groups[4] in 1970s America lay in the civil rights, anti-Vietnam War and student movements of the 1960s. As participants within these various left-wing activist groups, women found, in Juliet Mitchell's words, 'the attitude of the oppressor within the minds of the oppressed' (1971: 19), an attitude most famously expressed in Stokeley Carmichael's 1964 comment that 'the only position for women in SNCC (Student Non-violent Coordinating Committee) is prone'. 'Movement women' began to defect to a range of localized, non-hierarchical women's liberation groups. Unlike NOW, these groups had no national organization; instead they drew on the infrastructure of the radical community, the underground press, and the free universities. In a speech given at the Free University in New York City in February 1968, Anne Koedt describes this development:

> Within the last year many radical women's groups have sprung up throughout the country. This was caused by the fact that movement women found themselves playing secondary roles on every level – be it in terms of leadership, or simply in terms of being listened to. . . . As these problems began being discussed, it became clear that what had at first been assumed to be a personal problem was in fact a social and political one. . . . And the deeper we analyzed the problem and realized that all women suffer from this kind of oppression, the more we realized that the problem was not just confined to movement women. (Koedt *et al.* 1973: 318)

Koedt's description here includes two concepts which are key within the body of writing emerging from the developing Women's Liberation Movement. The first, 'consciousness-raising', describes the move to transform what is *experienced* as personal into *analysis* in political terms. 'Women's oppression', argued Juliet Mitchell, 'is hidden far from consciousness'. 'Consciousness-raising' – the speaking or naming of the previously unspoken, unnameable – was the process of 'transforming the hidden, individual fears of women into a shared awareness of the meaning of them as social problems, the release of anger, anxiety, the struggle of proclaiming the painful and transforming it into the political' (1971: 62). The resultant recognition that 'the personal *is* political' – that not only is male power exercised and reinforced through 'personal' institutions such as marriage, child-rearing and sexual practices, but that the very concept of a separate realm of 'the personal' which is *outside* politics serves political and ideological purposes – constituted a second key concept within the Women's Liberation Movement. Both concepts emphasized the extent to which Women's Liberation was seen as above all a revolution in 'culture and consciousness', an argument found in writers as otherwise different as Betty Friedan, Kate Millett, Cellestine Ware and Sheila Rowbotham. Women's lived experience – and this included their subjective and sexual experience – had, as the quotation above from Juliet Mitchell emphasizes, to be wrenched out of the framework of 'common-sense' within which it was habitually understood, and 'made to mean' within a politicized feminist consciousness which would invest it with new cultural meaning.

Commitment to a female revolution in consciousness via the process of consciousness-raising became a defining characteristic of women's liberation groups. Sheila Rowbotham describes the excitement of this process as she experienced it in Britain in the late 1960s:

> The atmosphere around '68 was very much one in which culture and consciousness were emphasized at the expense of the objective circumstances in which we found ourselves. . . . The rediscovery of our early perception of ourselves and our own sexuality entered politics – not as a theoretical question but as a passionate and practical demand scrawled on a bog wall in a sit-in. 'Give me back my past, my childhood, my body, my life.' This helped us to connect a sense of femaleness to our sense of ourselves as political animals. Our bodies at least were female. (Rowbotham 1973: 23)

The same impetus underlay the first major public actions of the Women's Liberation Movement. In September 1968, American feminist groups organized a demonstration against 'the sexual sell' of the Miss America contest. For the demonstration's organizers, the contestants epitomized 'the role all women are forced to play in this society, one way or another: apolitical, unoffending, passive, delicate (but delighted by drudgery) *things*' (Morgan 1993a: 26). Among the demonstrators' actions was the creation of a 'Freedom Trash Can' into which were thrown 'objects of female torture' such as dishcloths, high heels, bras and girdles – and the media myth of 'bra-burning' was born.

In Britain, the political and intellectual context in which the Women's Liberation Movement emerged was somewhat different. Here, too, the 1960s saw the appearance of Equal Rights groups, but these were identified not with an organization of professional women, but with the industrial militancy of working-class women like the sewing machinists at Fords in Dagenham, who in 1968 went on strike for equal pay. In Britain, too, there were American women working against the Vietnam War, and this provided another strand. The biggest impetus, however, came from women active in radical left-wing politics, and this gave the British Women's Liberation Movement, in common with its European counterparts, a Marxist-socialist inflection rather different from the division into liberal/reformist or radical/revolutionary commonly used to describe feminist groups in the USA. Nevertheless, feminists in Britain followed their American counterparts in demonstrating against the 1970 Miss World competition in London, and in February 1970 the first national Women's Liberation conference was held at Ruskin College, Oxford, with over 500 participants. Twenty years later Juliet Mitchell could reflect that, despite the different strands making up the movement, 'In 1970, at Ruskin, we felt we had one goal, we were unified. . . . [we] could have one feminism. One "women's liberation" ' (Wandor 1990: 111). The four demands formulated by the conference, for equal pay, equal education and opportunity, 24-hour nurseries, and free contraception and abortion on demand, signal again the double focus which marked second wave feminism: on women as an oppressed *social* group and on the female *body* with its need for sexual autonomy as a primary site of that oppression.

The 'second wave' feminism of the Women's Liberation Movement, then, sought both to voice or 'name' women's immediate and subjective experience and to formulate a political agenda and vision. To connect the two, what was needed was a new language of *theory* that would encompass both. As Sheila Rowbotham argued, 'Ultimately a revolutionary group has to break the hold of the dominant group over theory. . . . We can't just occupy existing words, we have to change the meanings of words even before we take them over' (1973: 33).

USA: From Activism to Theory

1970 is the year that marks an explosion of feminist theoretical writing. Kate Millett's *Sexual Politics*, Shulamith Firestone's *The Dialectic of Sex*, Cellestine Ware's *Woman Power* and Robin Morgan's edited collection *Sisterhood is Powerful* were all published in the USA, and in Britain Germaine Greer's *The Female Eunuch* and Eva Figes' *Patriarchal Attitudes* appeared. All drew, though often in an unacknowledged way,[5] on Simone de Beauvoir's *The Second Sex* (1949); it is de Beauvoir's account of the cultural construction of woman as 'Other' which laid the foundations for much of the theoretical work of the 1970s. The bridge, however, was provided by Betty Friedan's *The Feminine Mystique* (1963). Indeed, Juliet Mitchell, writing in 1971, argued that '[i]f a single inspiration for the [Women's Liberation] movement is to be cited, it was the publication in 1963 of Betty Friedan's *The Feminine Mystique*' (1971: 52).

Friedan's book, based on the results of a questionnaire she circulated among her former Smith College classmates in 1957, 15 years after their graduation, set out to analyse the profound but apparently unnameable dissatisfaction felt by these educated American housewives. As such, it was a key contributor to the emphasis on consciousness-raising within second wave feminism. 'The problem', writes Friedan, 'lay buried, unspoken, for many years in the minds of American women. It was a strange stirring, a sense of dissatisfaction, a yearning that women suffered in the middle of the twentieth century in the United States. Each suburban wife struggled with it alone' (1965: 13). She identifies it as 'the problem that has no name' and the cause as the 'feminine mystique':

> The feminine mystique says that the highest value and the only commitment for women is the fulfilment of their own femininity. . . . It says that this femininity is so mysterious and intuitive and close to the creation and origin of life that man-made science may never be able to understand it. . . . The mistake, says the mystique, the root of women's troubles in the past is that women envied men, women tried to be like men, instead of accepting their own nature, which can find fulfilment only in sexual passivity, male domination, and nurturing maternal love. (1965: 38)

The definition clearly draws on de Beauvoir's 'myth of the Eternal Feminine' and, like de Beauvoir, Friedan calls for a 'drastic reshaping of the cultural image of femininity that will permit women to reach maturity, identity, completeness of self' (1965: 318). At present, she writes, women are offered 'the mistaken choice between femaleness and humanness that is implied in the feminine mystique' (1965: 264). Friedan's account lacks both the theoretical complexity and the acute sense of lived contradiction of de Beauvoir's work, however, and its radical potential is too easily dissolved. Neither her account of women's oppression nor her call for liberation are rooted in an analysis of material circumstances, and she seems unaware of material differences between women's lives: her suburban housewife stands in too readily for all women. As a result, her call for change in culture and consciousness shifts easily into a demand for 'self-actualization', the 'becoming complete' which will result from women throwing off the 'mistaken ideas and misinterpreted facts' (1965: 28) which currently entrap them. The metaphor she chooses to describe such liberation, indeed, renders it not as material struggle but as natural process, a matter of the 'strange breath-holding interval before the larva breaks out of the shell into maturity' (1965: 330). Elsewhere her demand for cultural change shifts into the argument that 'the feminine mystique' is a matter of 'cultural lag' (1965: 131): since culture *reflects* social change, what is needed is for it to 'catch up' with changes in post-war American society. For Friedan, the solutions can be found within existing social structures. Since American society already espouses the goal of individual fulfilment, all that is needed for the release of women's potential is their admission into full participation in that society.

Above all, Friedan's account lacks any concept of *ideology* which might both account for the power of the cultural discourses and representations she describes within the consciousness and lived experience of her women respondents, and link them to material structures. At times she struggles towards such a concept. Thus her comparison of the suburban housewife to the inmate of a Nazi concentration camp, in which she argues that 'not the S.S. but the prisoners themselves became their own worst enemy' (1965: 265), manifests at once a disturbing inability to register the actualities of material oppression and an attempt to register the very real power of ideology as an agent of that oppression.

It is in her account of popular cultural texts addressed to women that Friedan's account acquires both its greatest complexity and its force as cultural analysis. As Rachel Bowlby argues, in dealing with the relations between consumption and femininity, Friedan also suggests how 'these issues are in turn connected to questions of female subjectivity' (Bowlby 1992: ix). Against the background of the post-war changes in American women's lives, she traces the shifts in the image of 'American woman' to be found in women's magazines, cinema stars and advertising images. Arguing that the madonna/whore split characteristic of the 'myth of the Eternal Feminine' finds its redefinition in contemporary culture as the division between 'the feminine woman, whose goodness includes the desires of the flesh, and the career woman, whose evil includes every desire of the separate self' (1965: 40), she traces this shift within both the narrative structures and heroine figures of popular fiction for women, and in the non-fiction content of women's magazines. It is at this point, she argues, that

> [t]he line between mystique and reality dissolves; real women embody the split in the image. In the spectacular Christmas 1956 issue of *Life*, devoted in full to the 'new' American woman, we see, not as women's magazine villain, but as documentary fact, the typical 'career woman – that fatal error that feminism propagated' – seeking 'help' from a psychiatrist. She is bright, well-educated, ambitious, attractive; she makes about the same money as her husband; but she is pictured here as 'frustrated', so 'masculinized' by her career that her castrated, impotent, passive husband is indifferent to her sexually. (1965: 51–2)

Women, that is, live out the contradictions to be found in popular cultural representations. At the same time, such 'documentary' representations serve as powerful ideological tools. '[P]layed back as the ideal, the way women should be', these 'images of real women who devote their lives to children and home' operate by feeding on 'the very facts that might contradict' them (1965: 53). The strength of her analysis, then, lies in its account of the relationship between popular culture aimed at women, shifting ideologies of the feminine, and women's everyday lives. Imperfectly theorised, her book nevertheless had a huge impact, not least because she, unlike Simone De Beauvoir, wrote not just about but quite clearly *from* the personal and everyday experience of women. As Sheila Rowbotham described it in 1973: 'Her book was a revelation to many women because it was so determinedly about everyday matters. And most of our lives are "everyday" ' (1973: 5). *The Feminine Mystique* thus engages with both the politics of the popular and the politics of everyday experience.

In contrast, both Kate Millett's *Sexual Politics* and Shulamith Firestone's *The Dialectic of Sex* (both 1970) were hugely ambitious theoretical works that emerged from the radical feminist movement. Millett's book popularized both the term 'sexual politics' and the broadening of the term 'patriarchy' beyond its original definition as the rule of a dominant elder male within a traditional kinship structure, to mean the institutionalized oppression of all women by all men. Patriarchy, argues Millett, is a *political* institution, the 'institution whereby that half of the populace which is female is controlled by that half which is male', and sex is a 'status category with political implications' (1977: 24). Moreover, patriarchy is the *primary* form of human oppression, without whose elimination other forms of oppression – racial, political or economic – will continue. Patriarchal domination is maintained principally, though not exclusively, through *ideological* control:

> one is forced to conclude that sexual politics, while connected to economics and other tangibles of social organization, is, like racism, or certain aspects of caste, primarily an ideology, a way of life, with influence over every other psychological and emotional facet of existence. It has created, therefore, a psychic structure, deeply embedded in our past, capable of intensification or attenuation, but one which, as yet, no people have succeeded in eliminating. (1977: 168)

Evident throughout history, patriarchal ideology has been all-pervasive. Most recently it has been 'legitimized' by the pseudo-science of psychoanalysis, especially during the period of the 'counterrevolution' (1930–60), which in Millett's account followed the 'first phase' of the feminist sexual revolution (1830–1930). Freud, argued Millett, was 'beyond question the strongest individual counterrevolutionary force in the ideology of sexual politics during the period'. Making 'a major and rather foolish confusion between biology and culture, anatomy and status', Freud saw his patients' symptoms not

> as evidence of a justified dissatisfaction with the limiting circumstances imposed on them by society, but as symptomatic of an independent and universal feminine tendency. He named this tendency 'penis envy,' traced its origin to childhood experience and based his

theory of the psychology of women upon it, aligning what he took to
be the three corollaries of feminine psychology, passivity, masochism,
and narcissism, so that each was dependent upon, or related to, penis
envy. (1977: 178–9)

Like Simone de Beauvoir, then, Millett accuses Freud of confusing the
culturally produced with the biologically determined, but her attack –
though gloriously vituperative – lacks the complexity of de Beauvoir's
often painful descriptions of an embodied, but internally divided, female
subjectivity. For Millett, patriarchal ideology is a matter of false representations institutionally deployed against women, who are its political
victims. Women are socialized into accepting the ideology of femininity,
and with it their inferior status. In instances of failure of ideological
control, however, patriarchy will also, in common with other 'total ideologies' like racism or colonialism, call on force. Such force may be institutional, from legal penalties for women's adultery to the lack of abortion
rights, but it may equally be enacted in the sphere of the personal: in rape
or its cultural equivalent, pornography. This emphasis on the cultural and
ideological as the primary means through which patriarchy maintains its
'merciless, total, and seemingly irrefutable control' (Millett 1977: 233)
finds its strongest expression in Millett's scathing critique of the work of
novelists D.H. Lawrence, Henry Miller and Norman Mailer. Insisting that
their work be read *ideologically* – as a discourse which speaks from and
for their social and cultural positioning within patriarchy – Millett's book,
as Cora Kaplan indicates, shifted the terrain of literary criticism. 'Since
Sexual Politics', writes Kaplan, 'it has been difficult for critics to ignore the
wider social and political implications of the representation of sexual practice in fiction. . . . [Critics] have been forced on to her ground, made to
admit that the depiction of sex in literature is an ideological issue for
author, reader and critic' (1986a: 16).

It is Kate Millett's *voice* that is in many ways the most striking aspect of
Sexual Politics. As Dale Spender notes approvingly, the force of Millett's
analysis 'lies not just in what she says, but in how she says it'. Her anger,
her tone of *certainty*, themselves constitute 'an act of insurrection against
male rule' (Spender 1985: 38–9). It is a certainty, however, which is bought
at the expense of a complexity of analysis, a recognition of historical specificity, and an attention to contradictions within subjectivity and lived experience. When she turns to the analysis of fictional representations, it is to
male writers as 'cultural agents' (1977: 233) of patriarchy: author, protagonist and point of view are unproblematically identified. As readers,
women are not complicit; their *subjectivity* is not engaged. Rather, they
have been duped. Subordinated within a political relationship which has
been 'relatively constant throughout history' (1977: 211), they have been
victims of patriarchal ideology as false consciousness. 'The hope of seeking
liberating radical solutions of their own seems too remote for the majority

to dare contemplate and remains so until consciousness on the subject is raised' (1977: 38). Millett's own polemic is clearly designed to bring about such consciousness-raising.

There is thus very little attention given in *Sexual Politics* to women's actual lives, either in the form of lived experience – as readers, consumers of popular culture or participants in cultural practices – or as explored within women's writing. Millett's discussion of Charlotte Bronte's *Villette* stands out as an exception. Here too she identifies author, character and point of view. Lucy Snowe is invested with Charlotte Bronte's own 'revolutionary' consciousness. The 'great exception' to women of the period, Lucy 'has watched men look at women, has studied the image of woman in her culture' (1977: 140, 143). When Millett describes Lucy's 'inner conflict', then, she is clear that it is a choice between the true and the false, between 'her newness, her revolutionary spirit, and the residue of the old ways which infects her soul' (1977: 144). On the one side are the 'bogs of sentimentality which period feeling mandates she [Lucy/Bronte] sink in'; on the other 'the ambition of every conscious young woman in the world': the desire 'to be free . . . to escape, to learn, to work, to go places'. Lucy's internal conflict is a direct reflection of the exterior conflict 'between her ambitions and desires and the near impossibility of their fulfillment' (1977: 146, 144).

The conclusion of *Sexual Politics* calls for a cultural revolution:

> The enormous social change involved in a sexual revolution is basically a matter of altered consciousness, the exposure and elimination of social and psychological realities underlining political and cultural structures. We are speaking, then, of a cultural revolution, which, while it must necessarily involve the political and economic reorganization traditionally implied by the term revolution, must go far beyond this as well. (1977: 362)

The terms are seductive, and recall those of Raymond Williams' (1961) description of the three aspects of *The Long Revolution* in contemporary life: the economic/industrial, the political/democratic and the communicative/cultural (see pages 61–2). But in Millett's account the revolution in consciousness is primary. This means on the one hand that for Millett, it seems, consciousness-raising can *accomplish* revolution. On the other hand, however, since patriarchal ideology is global and transhistorical, manifest in literature, myth, religion and popular culture alike, unanchored and uncontested in material practices and lived experience, and since it has so thoroughly succeeded in subordinating women in the past, it is difficult to see how such a revolution is to come about. Certainly Millett cites few examples of women's resistance in the past or present and offers no ground for resistance or agency in cultural production, cultural practice or in the structures and circumstances of everyday life.

USA: Feminism in the Academy

Literary Studies

Cora Kaplan's (1979) 'rethinking' of *Sexual Politics* argues that one effect of Millett's success in placing literary analysis in the context of ideologies of gender difference found elsewhere in contemporary discourses and practices, was to push American feminist cultural criticism in the direction of *literary* criticism, within an academic context defined as literary rather than cultural studies (1986a: 16).[6] Elaine Showalter, herself a key figure in the development of feminist literary criticism, describes this development. Feminist criticism in the United States, she writes, 'was created by literary and academic women – editors, writers, graduate students, university instructors and professors – who had participated in the women's liberation movement of the late 1960s and who shared its polemical force, activist commitment, social concern, and sense of communal endeavor'. It has its strongest institutional base in departments of literature (1986: 5, 8). This political history has meant, as Elspeth Probyn (1993) has argued, that American feminist literary criticism has retained an emphasis on the gendered experience of writing *and reading,* insisting on situating women's writing and reading within the context of a politics of identity and lived (historical) experience, and pushing out beyond the disciplinary boundaries of the literary text. Indeed, Showalter's 1977 study of British women novelists, *A Literature of their Own,* argues that women writers and their readers can be best understood using a subcultural model. Women, she argues, 'have constituted a subculture within the framework of a larger society, and have been unified by values, conventions, experiences, and behaviors impinging on each individual' (1977: 11). When we look at the beginnings of Black American feminist cultural criticism, we find it too drawing on this framework. Barbara Smith's 1977 manifesto, 'Towards a Black Feminist Criticism', is a blueprint for what she terms a black feminist *literary* criticism.[7] Such a criticism, writes Smith, would begin 'with a primary commitment to exploring how both sexual and racial politics and Black and female identity are inextricable elements in Black women's writings' and 'work from the assumption that Black women writers constitute an identifiable literary tradition' (1986: 174). It is the task of the black feminist critic, she argues, to recover this tradition with its common language and cultural experience, and, writing out of her own identity within such a tradition, to make explicit the ideas and political implications expressed within its writings in a way that will be useful to a black feminist movement.

This institutionalization of American feminist cultural criticism within literary studies also meant, however, what Cora Kaplan describes as an 'overemphasis . . . on high culture as a leading influence, benign or vicious, on women's subordination or struggle' (1986a: 30). If, in its emphasis on the politics of writing and reading, on the material and ideological embeddedness of texts, on the embodied nature of gendered identity, such criticism seems to move in the direction of cultural studies as it became constituted in Britain, it nevertheless remained – perhaps because of its institutional origins – relatively divorced from work on the texts and readers of popular or 'mass' culture. Janice Radway, whose study of popular romance novels and their readers, *Reading the Romance* (1984), is now seen as a key text within feminist cultural studies, describes this institutional separation when she outlines the origins of her own study in the contested terrain between 'literary studies' and 'the social sciences' in America:

> Writing within the framework prescribed by the social sciences and preoccupied therefore with questions of evidentiary validity and statistical representivity, my future colleagues (who were not, for the most part, literary critics) argued that while 'elite' literature might be taken as evidence for the beliefs of a particular section of the American population, assertions based upon it could not easily be extrapolated to wholly different classes or ethnic groups. (1987: 3)

She herself occupied the difficult role of 'student of popular culture but also ... literary critic' (1987). When, in her 1986 survey of international feminist criticism, Elaine Showalter came to describe British work in the field, she identified it as having an analytic focus on 'the connection between gender and class' and 'an emphasis on popular culture', but she positioned it still within the field of *literary* criticism (1986: 8–9).

'Mass Communication'

When we turn to American academic feminist research on the mass media in the 1970s, we find it rooted within the social science methodologies that Radway critiques. The focus was on 'the portrayal of sex roles in the mass media', with media representations being seen as false – or at least limiting – images of women, whose effect is to damage women's self-perceptions and narrow their social roles. If feminist literary criticism in the USA took its impetus from Millett's *Sexual Politics*, then the origins of feminist work within the study of 'mass communications' lie far more in Friedan's *The Feminine Mystique*[8] with its assumption that such stereotyping is a problem *for* rather than fundamentally *of* American society. Like Friedan's work, these 1970s American studies concentrate for the most part on 'sex-role stereotyping' within media images, and to demonstrate such stereotyping they apply the quantitative survey methods of mainstream American mass communication research.

The 1978 collection *Hearth and Home: Images of Women in the Mass Media*, edited by Gaye Tuchman, exemplifies such work. The volume, which contains contributions from both male and female academics, offers a range of political perspectives. At one extreme is Carol Lopate's class-based analysis of the representation of Jackie Kennedy Onassis within American women's magazines, in which she argues that the true function of Friedan's 'feminine mystique' is to obscure women's role as a reserve labour force within capitalist society (1978). At the other is Sprafkin and Liebert's study of 'Sex-typing and Children's Television Preferences', which concludes that television's 'confining and outmoded sex roles' may *perhaps* undermine – but more probably simply 'retard' – American society's inevitable progress towards the liberation of *both* sexes (1978b: 239). Throughout the book, however, the dominant research methods, as in other contemporary 'sex-role research' on the mass media (Busby 1975, Janus 1977), are the quantitative survey methods of 'content analysis' and 'effects studies'. The theoretical assumptions underlying such research methods are outlined in Tuchman's introductory chapter. The mass media, she argues, firstly *reflect*, in the form of images or representations, society's dominant values. Hence content analyses can be used to reveal a predominance of traditional and stereotypical images of women across all media forms. Secondly, they act as agents of *socialization*, transmitting stereotyped images of sex-roles, particularly to young people. Hence effects studies reveal that children exposed to such stereotypes have a more restricted view of appropriate sex-roles than those exposed to counter-stereotypical representations. Despite Tuchman's own trenchant criticism of the media's treatment of women as a form of 'symbolic annihilation', therefore, what such criticism suggests is a problem whose solution lies within the existing social structure. What is occurring, she argues, is a 'culture lag' (the term is borrowed from Friedan) between media images and the real roles of women in a changing society (1978a: 37). Since 'the expansion of the American economy depends upon increasing the rate of female employment', such rigid stereotyping represents 'an anachronism we [American society] can ill afford' (Tuchman 1978a: 37–8).

In a 1979 review article Tuchman was herself to attack the theoretical and political assumptions behind such approaches. 'Perhaps because the media associated with the 'mass' were insistently differentiated from high culture and intellectual substance', she writes, researchers had approached their study not from the theoretical perspectives found within literary theory, but as 'scientists'. Simultaneously, they had 'hired themselves out as media consultants'. Armed with 'the sophisticated techniques of modern social science', they had carried out empirical studies for 'both Madison Avenue and the media conglomerates'. It was not surprising, she concludes, that research on *women* and the media – including her own – had become 'theoretically stalled', bound within the functionalist perspective that underlay its research methods – finding 'practical answers to seemingly practical questions' (1979: 528). She summarizes its 'naive' conclusions, with their assumption of a direct relationship between media organization, content and social effects, as follows.

1. Few women hold positions of power in media organizations, and so:
2. The content of the media distorts women's status in the social world. The media do not present women who are viable role models, and therefore:
3. The media's deleterious role models, when internalized, prevent and impede female accomplishments. They also encourage both women and men to define women in terms of men (as sex objects) or in the context of the family (as wives and mothers). (1979: 541)

Such arguments, she suggests, offer neither analytic purchase nor radical critique. If research is really to offer any understanding of the relationship between women and media, it must address the issue of the *ideological* hegemony of the media by adopting a theoretical framework capable of analysing media as text, as discourse and as *myth*. Tuchman's definition of myth follows that of Roland Barthes.[9] Myths, she writes, are bearers of ideology, 'ways of seeing the world that resonate with the conscious mind and the unconscious passions and that are embedded in, expressive of, and reproductive of social organization' (1979: 538, 541).

Britain: Theory and Activism

In Britain, Germaine Greer's *The Female Eunuch* was published in 1970, proclaiming its radical feminist credentials with its opening sentence, 'This book is a part of the second feminist wave' (1971: 11). Like Millett's *Sexual Politics*, it had its academic base in literary studies, though it drew far more eclectically on a range of literary and mass media texts, and its call for revolution was based less on a systematic analysis than on a condemnation of all women who did not adopt Greer's individualistic definition of sexual revolution as revolution through sex.[10] The major theoretical developments in British feminist writing, however, lay neither in liberal feminism nor in radical feminism as they were defined in the USA. Olive Banks, writing in 1981, gave an American view of the difference: 'The main difference between the United States and Britain . . . is the closer link in Britain between socialism or Marxism and feminism. . . . There was never the deep rift between radical men and women that occurred, and indeed persisted, in the United States and kept the two groups not only apart but hostile to each other' (1981: 238, cited in Showalter 1986).

In 1966, Juliet Mitchell's essay 'Women: the Longest Revolution' appeared in *New Left Review*. Predating by some two years both Mitchell's own feminist activism and the founding of Britain's first Women's

Liberation groups, the essay was a response to the publication in 1961 of Raymond Williams' *The Long Revolution*. Williams' work, which will be returned to in this chapter, had argued that we are living through a 'long revolution', a 'genuine revolution, transforming men and institutions; continually extended and deepened by the actions of millions, continually and variously opposed by explicit reaction and by the pressure of habitual forms and ideas' (1965: 10). It had, argued Williams, three aspects, the 'democratic revolution', the 'industrial revolution' and the revolutionary expansion of communication technologies, but to understand the process of change we must see these strands not as separate but as profoundly interactive and as productive of a 'deeper cultural revolution'. This last, he argues, 'is a large part of our most significant living experience, and is being interpreted and indeed fought out, in very complex ways, in the world of art and ideas' (1965: 12). Nowhere in Williams' 'inclusive' account, however, do women appear. But if Mitchell's essay is a response to Williams' analysis and its omissions, it is also important to note that she follows his methodological emphasis in insisting on the complex origins (the 'overdetermination') and historical specificity of any revolutionary change.

In both this essay and her 1971 book *Woman's Estate*, Mitchell attacks Marxism's failure to offer any materialist analysis of women's oppression. The issue, she writes, has become 'a subsidiary, if not an invisible element in the preoccupations of socialists. Perhaps no other major issue has been so forgotten' (1984: 19). Marxist/socialist theory, she argues, sees women's liberation as merely an adjunct to class analysis, where it considers it at all. But Mitchell also critiques what she sees as the over-simplistic and transhistorical accounts of 'patriarchy' offered by radical feminists like Kate Millett and Shulamith Firestone. Like them, she sees women's oppression as operating largely through ideology, an ideology manifest in the 'psychology of femininity' and lived out in women's roles within the 'personal' sphere of sexuality and the family. But women's oppression, she argues, takes place always in *specific* historical circumstances; its forms will alter with changes in economic and social organization. To describe patriarchy as omnipresent and universal, as Millett does, is to accept its own ideological formulations: 'Patriarchy may seem universal, but in the first place this universality is part of the ideology by which it maintains itself, and in the second where it does indeed have common factors through different political systems these common factors find themselves in different combinations in all specific instances' (1971: 83). What is needed in its analysis, therefore, is both a radical feminist consciousness and the tools of historical materialism.

For Mitchell, such an analysis involves 'differentiating woman's condition, much more radically than in the past, into its separate structures; which together form a complex – not a simple – unity' (1984: 26). Woman's condition, she argues, is the product of four distinct but overlapping ('overdetermining') structures: those of production (woman's position in the workplace), reproduction (her positioning in the family), sexuality (woman's appropriation as sexual object) and the socialization of children (her function in bringing up children). If the movement towards women's liberation is to succeed, transformation of *all four* structures must be achieved since the 'four elements of women's condition cannot merely be considered each in isolation; they form a structure of specific interrelations' (1984: 50). Transformation of only one aspect – as, for example, in the 'wave of sexual liberalization' of the 1960s – may simply open the way to a shift in the *form* of women's oppression – in this case to women's *increased* sexual objectification as capitalism shifts its focus from production to consumption.

A similar analysis was offered by Sheila Rowbotham in *Woman's Consciousness, Man's World* published in 1973. Like Juliet Mitchell, Rowbotham was active in the organization of the 1970 Women's Liberation Conference at Ruskin College, coming to feminist activism from an involvement in Marxist politics. She too argues for both a revolution in consciousness and a historical analysis of women's oppression within capitalism. Oppression, she insists, 'is not an abstract moral condition but a social and historical experience. Its forms and expression change as the mode of production and the relationships between men and women, men and men, women and women, change in society' (1973: xi). Women, she argues, have to struggle for control over both production and reproduction. What is vital therefore is the emergence of a movement of *working-class* women, since their experience 'spans production and reproduction, class exploitation and sex oppression' (1973: 124). But Rowbotham also draws substantially on earlier writers like Simone de Beauvoir and Virginia Woolf to argue that what is required is a revolution within language and culture as well as in material structures. Socialist feminists must seek to transform 'the inner world' of bodily experience, psychological colonization and cultural silencing, as well as the outer world of material social conditions.

Woman's Consciousness, Man's World is an uneven book, often showing the strain of its attempt to realize in practice its argument that 'the things which were called political' must not be 'dissociated from personal life' (1973: xi), and of its twin origins in feminist and Marxist theory. At its best, however, its juxtaposition of personal history and theoretical analysis enacts the coming to political consciousness which Rowbotham describes as inevitably 'at first . . . fragmented and particular' and which she elsewhere characterizes as 'the struggle between the language of experience and the language of theory' (1973: 27, 33). It is a juxtaposition which can bring into productive relationship texts as different as Betty Friedan's *The Feminine Mystique* and Raymond Williams' *The Long Revolution*. For Williams, the language of experience or 'practical consciousness' of an era is what he calls its 'structure of feeling', a 'kind of feeling and thinking' which, social rather than individual, represents the expression of the era's lived experience rather than its officially articulated beliefs (1977: 131). As such, this 'emergent experience' is often at odds with the consciously held

ideology of the period. It is frequently felt first as 'a certain kind of disturbance or unease, a particular type of tension' which arises from 'the endless
comparison that must occur in the process of consciousness between the
articulated and the lived' (1979: 168).

Here, more fully theorised – as Rowbotham argues – is Betty Friedan's
'problem that has no name', the everyday lived experience of women which
found no articulated expression in contemporary ideologies of the feminine,
so that to attempt to see it as *political* seemed like trying to 'organize round
a sense of emptiness' (1973: 5). Rowbotham's description of her own
coming to awareness of 'the depth and extent of my colonization' presents
it both as personal history and, in Williams' terms, as precisely the kind of
'disturbance' – in Rowbotham's terms, 'electric shock' – which produces the
'fissure in consciousness' through which new structures can arise. Her
evidence is drawn from her own experience and from that of other women
either personally recounted or recorded in Women's Liberation publications
like *Shrew*,[11] but her analysis seeks to offer a new *theoretical* articulation
of that experience. Like Williams too, then, she sees revolution as also a
'matter of language'. For Williams, argues Terry Eagleton, words were
'condensed social practices, sites of historical struggle, repositories of political wisdom or domination' (1989: 8).[12] Whereas for Williams, however, it
was a matter of tracking 'the long revolution' through the history of
language change, Rowbotham's analysis is more radical. Just as Williams'
'disturbance and unease' becomes her 'electric shock', so she argues that
women's experience of struggle within language has parallels with, but is in
the end fundamentally different from, the experience of other oppressed
groups:

> Although we share the same analysis, the same estrangement from the
> world we do not control, the peculiar difficulties we encounter in
> making words which can become the instruments of our own theory
> differ. Our oppression is more internalized – the clumsiness of women
> penetrates the very psyche of our being. It is not just a question of
> being outside existing language. We can never hope to enter and
> change it from inside. We can't just occupy existing words. We have
> to change the meaning of words even before we take them over. ...
> The exclusion of women from all existing language demonstrates our
> profound alienation from any culture which can generalize itself.
> (1973: 34)

'Women', she writes, 'have only myths made by men. ... All conceptions of
female 'nature' are formed in cultures dominated by men, and like all
abstract ideas of human nature are invariably used to deter the oppressed
from organizing effectively'. All revolutionary movements 'create their own
ways of seeing' (1973: 117, 27). The terrain that Rowbotham stakes out for
her own 'long making of a new society' (1973: xiii) combines social and
material change, a 'conscious relationship to other women which will

encourage us to trust our own isolated, atomized and fragmented sensations' (1973: 37), the learning to take control over our own bodies and their sexuality, and the coming to (self) consciousness. This last represents the making of a new culture through learning *not* to see ourselves through men's eyes, the painful recovery of a lost identity from 'the darkness of our unremembered childhood', and the exploration of fantasy in order to understand 'the relationship between our experience in fantasy, dream and ecstasy and the experience which is intelligible to us in terms of political strategy' (1973: 35, 44).

In her bringing together of socialist and feminist theory, in her emphasis on the social and material *and* on embodied subjectivity, on culture as lived experience *and* representation, on the personal *and* the theoretical, Rowbotham clears the ground for the development of a feminist cultural studies. Her argument that women must together move 'through the looking-glass' of male ways of seeing draws on both Virginia Woolf and Simone de Beauvoir, but places both within a new political framework. As a result she can offer an analysis of media images of women which sees them as agents of 'masculine cultural hegemony', both engaged in the commodification of women and responding 'however bizarrely', to changes in women's social role and consciousness (1973: 110). She can also trace the processes of resistance in women's everyday lives and can argue, like Raymond Williams,[13] that media images, despite their status as hegemonic texts, also offer spaces of contradiction which can be exploited. In responding as they must – since it represents a shift in the market – to the changing consciousness of women, they also serve to 'make explicit areas of experience which have previously existed only in our subterranean selves. The very act of communication makes these sensations and experiences assume a shape, whereas before they were only implicit' (1973: 110). In thus making *visible* a previously privatized female experience, they offer themselves for re-appropriation by women themselves.

What, finally, of the voice, the 'enunciative position' (Probyn 1993: 11) from which Rowbotham articulates this complex analysis? She is acutely aware of the difficulties for women in saying 'I'. 'We are oppressed', she writes, 'by an overwhelming sense of not being there' (1973: 35). She seeks, therefore, to place herself and other women as *present* in the text, by anchoring analysis in personal history and by exploring the subjective and the fantasized as well as the social and political. It is an uneasy balance, however, in which a male-voiced socialist theory can seem at odds with the 'new female consciousness' which seeks to transform it. In the end, Rowbotham is unsure about her intended audience. From the women who have shared her experience and might share her consciousness, it shifts to become the women and men of the socialist movement, to whom she urges that the analysis of women's position must become 'part of the general theory and practice of the Left' (1973: 124). Later she was to describe her movement out of 'women's groups and . . . into more general socialist politics' during the course of the 1970s, as she sought to 'ensure that the experience of an autonomous movement contributed to a better socialist movement' (Wandor 1990: 41).

The Birmingham CCCS

If the work of Raymond Williams was both infuriating and inspirational for British feminist theorists in the 1970s, it was central in the founding of the Centre for Contemporary Cultural Studies at Birmingham University. Stuart Hall cites *Culture and Society* and *The Long Revolution,* along with Richard Hoggart's *The Uses of Literacy* and E.P. Thompson's *The Making of the English Working Class* as 'originating texts' for the Centre, 'the original "curriculum" of the field' (1980: 16). Hall describes *The Long Revolution* as shifting 'the whole ground of debate from a literary-moral to an anthropological definition of culture. But it defined the latter now as the "whole process" by means of which meanings and definitions are socially constructed and historically transformed, with literature and art as only one, specially privileged, kind of social communication' (1980: 19). For Williams, echoing Marx,[14] '[p]articular cultures carry particular versions of reality, which they can be said to create', but at the same time, 'the individuals who bear these particular cultural rules are capable of altering and extending them' (1965: 34). In his insistence on the interrelationship of the economic, the political and the cultural, in his redefinition of 'culture' to include not only 'texts and representations' but also 'lived practices, belief systems and institutions' (Hall 1980a: 23), in his insistence on the importance of 'the experiential moment', and in his *engagement* in the process by which 'the long revolution' is 'being interpreted and indeed fought out, in very complex ways, in the world of art and ideas' (Williams 1965: 12), Williams was crucial to the foundation of cultural studies. 'From its inception', writes Stuart Hall, 'Cultural Studies was an "engaged" set of disciplines, addressing awkward but relevant issues about contemporary society and culture. . . . This tension (between what might loosely be called "political" and intellectual concerns) has shaped Cultural Studies ever since' (1980a: 17).

All of these concerns are also, as we have seen, those of feminist theory as it developed, with its own 'continuities and breaks' (Hall 1980a: 16), from Mary Wollstonecraft onwards. Williams' analysis, however, like that of the other founding 'fathers' of cultural studies, has no place for women. That his account of culture as an evolving 'whole way of life' ignored the struggle between conflicting or dominant/subordinate *ways* of life is a point made by critics from E.P. Thompson onwards (see Hall 1980a: 20). But his omission of women seems symptomatic of a larger problem in the founding conceptions of 'culture' within cultural studies. At one point in *The Long Revolution,* Williams names *four* interlocking strands in cultural change,

'the system of decision [politics], the system of communication and learning, the system of maintenance [economics] and the system of generation
and nurture' (1965: 136). As the editors of *Politics and Letters* point out,
however, the fourth system – the private sphere of the family that Juliet
Mitchell was to explore so fully in her response to Williams – disappears
immediately from his analysis. Interviewed in 1979, Williams is at a loss to
explain the omission:

> I wish I had [explored these issues] in *The Long Revolution,* and I also
> wish that I understood what prevented me from doing so, because it
> wasn't that I was not thinking about the question. I think that the like-
> lihood is that I had such a comparatively unproblematic experience
> both in my home and in my own family, which were very good ones,
> that I was not as intensely aware of disorder and crisis in the family
> as I was in other areas. (1979: 149–50)

The response suggests the limitations of too great a reliance on 'the experiential moment' in prompting radical analysis! As Williams continues,
however, it is clear that the structural oppression of women is unthinkable
within the outline of cultural change that he proposes. In *The Long
Revolution* he argues that the separation of 'our family and personal life
from the life of society' was an understandable but mistaken response to the
growing dehumanization of working conditions, but for Williams it was a
response that 'we' – the inclusive 'parents and children, brothers and sisters,
husbands and wives' – made (1965: 135). In *Politics and Letters* the family
is seen as less of a safe haven, but this is because of the penetration into it
of social and economic pressures from elsewhere, so that 'women and children' are no longer safe there. He cites 'frequent evidence of the break-up
of relations under the strain of poverty and unemployment, and of the very
ugly reproduction inside certain families of the repression and cruelty and
frustration of the work situation, of which women and children are the
primary victims', and speaks of 'the unfinished attempt to liberate women
and children from the traditional controls of extreme brutality and from the
reproduction of brutality within the family' (1979: 148–9). Despite his
welcoming of the emergence of 'a movement for women's liberation', therefore, since the family is not *in itself* seen as a source of oppression, women's
history can safely be subsumed within that of men, and the fact that
Williams has recorded a wholly *masculine* history of cultural change
remains unacknowledged.

Stuart Hall's (1980a) account of the origins of cultural studies cites
approvingly E.P. Thompson's replacement of Williams' 'rather evolutionary
approach' to cultural change with an insistence on 'the historical specificity
of culture, on its plural, not singular, definition – cultures, not "Culture":
above all, on the necessary struggle, tension and conflict between cultures
and their links to class cultures, class formations and class struggles' (1980a:
20). It was this shift, together with Williams' stress on lived experience and

'structures of feeling', which made possible the Birmingham Centre's work on subcultures in the 1970s, work which in turn 'posed the question of the experiential moment in any project of research in "lived" cultures as an irreducible element of any explanation' (1980a: 24). The resulting research explored social issues – youth cultures, the study of deviance, schooling and relations of the workplace – but using qualitative methods which sought to give weight to the ways in which the participants themselves gave value and meaning to their activities.

Hall's description of the institutional effects of this research employs a curious metaphor. The Birmingham Centre, he writes, at this point 'began to desert its "handmaiden" role and chart a more ambitious, properly integrated territorial space of its own' (1980a: 22). This description of the 'masculinization' of cultural studies through the carving out of 'territorial space' finds its echo in the definition of subcultures to be found in the Centre's (Hall and Jefferson 1976) edited collection, *Resistance Through Rituals*. Subcultures, argue Hall *et al.*, 'must exhibit a distinctive enough shape and structure to make them identifiably different from their "parent" culture. They must be focussed around certain activities, values, certain uses of material artefacts, *territorial spaces* etc. which significantly differentiate them from the parent culture' (1976: 14, my emphasis). It is little wonder, then, that Angela McRobbie and Jenny Garber's contribution to the volume begins by remarking on the 'absence of girls from the whole of the literature in this area' and continues, in words familiar from all areas of 1970s feminist research, 'The difficulty is, how to understand this invisibility' (1976: 209). Their conclusion, tentatively expressed, attempts to stay within the terms of Hall *et al.*'s definition, but in so doing has to wrest the definition of 'space' from its literal meaning and, even so, has to conclude that the definition, and the theoretical assumptions on which it is based, simply do not work for women: 'We feel that when the dimension of sexuality is included in the study of youth subcultures, girls can be seen to be negotiating a different space, offering a different type of resistance to what can at least in part be viewed as their sexual subordination' (1976: 221).

In her other publications of the late 1970s, McRobbie explores these issues further. In 'Working Class Girls and the Culture of Femininity' (1978) she distinguishes three levels of oppression experienced by these girls. There are, first, the 'material limitations placed upon the girls': working-class girls did not have the opportunities available to their middle-class counterparts, but equally, restricted to home, school and youth club, they did not have access to 'territorial space' in the same ways as their brothers. As she put it in a later article (1991a: 29), 'It has always been on the street that most subcultural activity takes place'; but 'the street remains in some ways taboo for women'. Second, there are 'the ideological apparatuses they inhabit (family, education, media, etc.)' through which these limitations are understood (as 'feminine' spaces and occupations). Finally, there is 'an invisible level of oppression which stems directly from their explicit experience of sexual relationships': they are subject to the 'brutally sexist attitudes' of their male peers (1978: 106–7). Both the 'oppression' and the 'resistance' of these girls cannot be understood, then, within the terms of a male-defined model of subcultures. The very 'culture of femininity' into which the girls retreat, as a response to the material restrictions of working-class life, itself reconfirms their position as *women*; they are 'both saved by and locked within the culture of femininity' (1978: 108).

Despite the efforts of Stuart Hall in 1980 to align the work on subcultures of the Birmingham Centre with the feminist research into women's history being carried out by Sheila Rowbotham (1980a: 24), the two fields remain very separate. It is notable, for example, that Dorothy Hobson's early writing on her ethnographic studies of young working-class housewives sits uneasily within the Centre's ethnographic work on subcultures. The 1980 'Introduction to Ethnography at the Centre', co-written by Hobson (with Roger Grimshaw and Paul Willis) begins with the curious disclaimer that 'this whole section should not be taken as a guide to the current state of ethnographic work at the Centre nor to the form of its theoretical/methodological integration in current projects' (Grimshaw *et al.* 1980: 73). The paragraph introducing Hobson's own work traces its origins not to earlier work on subcultures but to the Women's Liberation Movement: 'The privileging of "the personal" was first developed in the Women's Liberation Movement through small-group consciousness-raising, where women learned to talk about personal experiences and to recognize that their experiences were shared by other women. Part of the ethnographic project for feminists has been to give a voice to the personal experience of the women and girls who are studied in the research' (1980: 75–6). The significance of this last point is emphasized by Angela McRobbie when in her 1980 article, 'Settling Accounts with Subcultures', she contrasts the personal investment – and the personal *voice* – of the feminist researcher with the 'absence of self' in men's writing on (male) subcultures.[15] Both, it can be argued, could be included within the central problematic of ethnographic work within cultural studies as described in the Grimshaw, Hobson and Willis 'Introduction': that of the analysis 'of the complex relations between representations/ideological forms and the density or "creativity" of "lived" cultural forms' (1980: 74). Yet for the feminist researcher, the 'experience' being investigated always to some extent implicates her; she is herself, as Sheila Rowbotham points out, caught in the contradictions she explores. For her, the 'struggle between the language of experience and the language of theory' (Rowbotham 1973: 33) is both a gendered and an internal struggle; it is not merely a matter of analysis. In the early work of Dorothy Hobson, indeed, we find almost a refusal of analysis as the researcher refuses to speak *for* her interviewees in the language of theory: 'What I have felt is that in many ways the words spoken by the women are more forceful when left to stand on their own. For this reason this article is concluded with a long extract, spoken by one woman, left without detailed comment because I think the woman speaks her own oppression . . .' (1978: 92).

Women Take Issue

In 1980 Stuart Hall states that '[a] theory of culture which cannot account for patriarchal structures of dominance and oppression is, in the wake of feminism, a non-starter. . . . Feminism has . . . radically altered the terrain of Cultural Studies' (1980a: 39). The concerns of cultural studies, as I have suggested, in many ways *were* the concerns of feminist theory as it had developed before and after the 'ruptural moment' (to borrow from Stuart Hall) of the early 1970s. This was an academic – and institutional – context where feminist research could explore all the complexities of women's positioning(s) in culture(s). Yet, as Hall's statement actually makes clear, this ground, which should have been so open (to borrow again), was in fact constituted around definitions of culture which excluded women and developed through theorists – including the 'structuralist' theorists whose influence was to become so important in the late 1970s – for whom the position for women was a given, not an issue to be contested. As the Women's Studies Group wrote in the Introduction to the 1978 CCCS publication, *Women Take Issue*, 'To intervene effectively . . . it seems we would have to conquer the whole of cultural studies, in itself multi-disciplinary, and *then* make a feminist critique of it' (1978a: 10). They did not, it is clear, belong.

The volume that emerged is, then, uneasy, unconfident, straddling the areas of cultural studies and 1970s feminist theory. Its contributors reach constantly across to the work of Juliet Mitchell and Sheila Rowbotham in particular – though also to other 1970s feminist theorists – in order to drive a wedge into the theoretical frameworks that seem to be constricting them. They locate their most challenging insights within 'Women's Studies' rather than cultural studies, and they often adopt a half-apologetic tone. In 'Women "inside and outside" the Relations of Production', for example, the writers (Lucy Bland, Charlotte Brunsdon, Dorothy Hobson and Janice Winship) begin: 'We have attempted here to work on the articulation of sex/gender and class in an understanding of women's subordination. We have tried to hold on to "the two-fold character" of "the materialist conception" of the "production and reproduction of immediate life" which is posed, though inadequately developed, by Engels . . .'. They *begin*, that is, from accepted/acceptable Marxist theory before moving to 'What we have learnt through feminism' (1978: 35). Despite its uncertain beginning (the group cannot agree on a conclusion to their introductory chapter), and its frequently hesitant tone, however, the volume does map out both a set of challenges to existing cultural studies frameworks and a range of issues, methodologies and problems for a feminist cultural studies.

'Women's studies, like black studies, as a subject or discipline, has political not academic roots', argues the group (1978a: 9), and it is on these grounds that it challenges a male-centred cultural studies. The focus on class, then, is challenged using a range of feminist writing, particularly the work of Juliet Mitchell and Sheila Rowbotham, and the historical/theoretical 'originating texts' of cultural studies' founding fathers contested. Janice Winship, for example – implicitly taking issue with Raymond Williams as well as with later writers – argues that 'the potential "split" that has developed under capitalism: production/consumption; work/leisure; work/personal life; work/everyday life . . . is a split which operates for *men* but which is dependent on women's patriarchal subordination – their confinement to family, home, personal and everyday life' (1978: 136–7). Rachel Harrison's study of Charlotte Bronte's *Shirley* takes a novel published during the period – the 1840s – which Williams takes as his 'case-study' in *The Long Revolution*, but subjects it to analysis in terms of 'the ideology of romance, an ideology which operates to 'secur[e] patriarchal relations of reproduction' (1978: 192).

At the same time, theoretical concepts drawn from a class analysis – Louis Althusser's definition of ideology as 'the imaginary relation of . . . individuals to the real relations in which they live', Antonio Gramsci's concept of hegemony as the process by which dominant groups win the consent of the subordinate – are appropriated for a feminist analysis of 'patriarchal ideology' and 'masculine hegemony'. But they are also supplemented, though with some hesitation, by concepts drawn from psychoanalysis, in the search for a theorisation of sex/gender identity, which will have as its focus individual subjectivity as well as social relations. Finally, through work like Angela McRobbie's study of girls and 'subcultures' and Charlotte Brunsdon's exploration of theoretical issues raised by the Women's Liberation Movement's emphasis on 'the personal' as 'political', we find a challenge to the definitions of culture offered by a developing cultural studies. Sheila Rowbotham had written, 'We are oppressed by an overwhelming sense of not being there' (1973: 35). Women, as McRobbie argues, are 'not there' in subcultures; equally, argues Charlotte Brunsdon, they are 'not there' in culture. Drawing on Rowbotham's work and on other writing from the WLM, Brunsdon demonstrates that the argument that women are 'somehow, outside history, and both central to, and absent in, culture' (1978: 20) is one that cannot be contested from within existing cultural studies paradigms. Her conclusion that 'We have somehow to hold the necessary articulation of female experience (our oppression lies partly in the invisibility of this experience) with the struggle to understand the determinants on this experience to allow us to change it at a more than individual level' (1978: 31) offers a framework for a feminist cultural studies.

Within this framework, a number of key issues and methodologies can be seen to emerge. In addition to the political/historical analysis of women's position already being developed by Mitchell, Rowbotham and others,[16] we find an exploration of theories of subjectivity using psychoanalysis. This development, inaugurated by Juliet Mitchell's (1975) *Psychoanalysis and Feminism* (see Chapter 4), and later described by Stuart Hall as 'the "re-opening" of the closed frontier between social theory and the theory of the unconscious' (1992a: 282), is a key, though contested, element of a feminist cultural studies. As Burniston, Mort and Weedon write in *Women Take Issue*, without a focus on sexual ideologies and the subjective, 'the feminist element' in any materialist analysis 'is always in danger of being lost'. Freud, as 'the first theorist to bring the question of sexuality to the fore and to show that sexual identity is socially constituted rather than biologically innate', can be used 'politically, in the move towards a theorization of sexuality and sex-oppression' (1978: 109), though the writers – seeking always to remain within accepted cultural studies paradigms – insist that psychoanalytic concepts must be 'transformed and integrated into material and concrete analyses of the construction of sexuality and the forms of sexual oppression' (1978: 128).

In the work of Janice Winship, Angela McRobbie and Dorothy Hobson, we can see these shifts in theoretical framework translated into key methodological developments. In these chapters are brought together the analysis of ideologies of femininity within popular culture and the exploration of women's lived experience – what Charlotte Brunsdon calls 'the "intimate oppression" of femininity as lived' (1978: 19). Winship and McRobbie also explore the theoretical complexities that such work suggests. McRobbie, as we have seen, explores the complex relations between class and gender oppression in the girls' culture she examines. For Winship the focus is the ideological contradictions within the text–reader relationship in the women's magazines she analyses. If we deconstruct the representations within these magazines, argues Winship, 'we can begin to reveal some of the important contradictions of women's patriarchal subordination under capitalism with which the magazine . . . must necessarily engage' (1978: 133). In the 'ideal images' of women that we find presented, we can trace the positioning of women as 'feminine subjects'. Like earlier feminist theorists, she describes the kind of mirror that this image offers its female viewers: 'the woman is not simply an "ideal" woman but also *not* a woman: it is not her as a live, fluctuating and enigmatic *person* that is represented, but her as a *thing*. She is constructed from commodities: make-up by . . ., clothes by. . . . She is also *the* commodity – the magazine itself which is to be consumed' (1978: 134). What appears to be so central within the magazine, 'the relation of women to women – is simultaneously defined in relation to absent men/masculinity – they are feminine; and in relation to an absent reality of capitalist production – they are consumers to be themselves consumed as commodities' (1978: 134).

As a feminist, however, the analyst is not *outside* such constructions:

> Our femininity is not something any of us can escape. All of us as
> women 'achieve' our subjectivity in relation to a definition of women
> which in part is propounded by women's magazines. We may be strug-
> gling against such a definition, but none of us, though we might like
> to, can eliminate the modes of subjectivity in their patriarchal form by
> disparagingly ignoring them; as if we too do not live within them,
> having to find our place within the parameters they set. (1978: 134)

Here, then, we find an account of experience as 'epistemologically productive', as productive of but also in tension with theory, which is both within
and outside cultural studies' frameworks. Within, because from the work of
Raymond Williams onwards (see Probyn 1993: 14–26) such tensions had
been 'a pivotal site of Centre theorizing and debate' (Hall 1980a: 24);
outside, because this positioning of the researcher as both 'subject and
object of [her] study' (Women's Studies Group 1978a: 13) – as both the
'absent' feminine (object) and the 'present' feminist (researcher); as seeking
to 'give voice to' women's experience and to theorise it; as implicated in,
even complicit with, the modes of subjectivity she seeks to expose to analysis – is something derived from the politics of the Women's Liberation
Movement. In place of 'the authorial "I" or "we"' which nevertheless
signals an 'objective' 'absence of self' (McRobbie 1991a: 19), we find the
inclusive 'we' of 'a subordinate group defining ourselves through our
absences' (Winship 1978: 136).

That this 'we' is a tentative collectivity is, however, perhaps the dominant impression left by *Women Take Issue*. The theoretical concepts drawn
from or provoked by the WLM often sit uneasily against the 'weighty' theorizing within and against which the writers seek to position themselves.
There is a clear sense – articulated most strongly in the Introduction – that
whilst cultural studies *should* be the academic and institutional context in
which feminism can produce its most important theoretical and methodological developments, the 'masculine hegemony' theorized by the group
and analysed in the lives of its research subjects, operates here too,
constricting analysis within a framework which amounts to a kind of silencing. Finally, there is the persistent threat of an internal fracturing of the
'we'. The group themselves, as the Introduction makes clear, were often
divided. In addition, there is a recognition – only at times acknowledged
here, but later to become so important – that the 'making of a feminist
consciousness in the finding of a *common* oppression is a labour which
must recognize the *different* oppression of black women, lesbians, of older
women, working class women, as well as those women most articulate
within the dominant culture, young, straight, white middle class women'
(Brunsdon 1978: 30). In the following chapters, then, I shall trace the ways
in which the questions, issues, approaches and debates begun in this work
of the 1970s were taken up and developed over the next 25 years.

Notes

1. Rowbotham (1973: ix).
2. Ware herself is somewhat tentative about this designation. 'Throughout this book,' she writes, 'I have used the terms Women's Liberation Movement and feminism interchangeably. I took this freedom even though there are women radicals within the WL Movement who are not ready to be called feminists.' Nevertheless, she continues, 'references to the WL Movement as the new feminism are steadily receiving more acceptance' (1970: 108).
3. Firestone (1979: 23). See also Germaine Greer (1971: 11), 'This book is part of the second feminist wave.'
4. The boundaries between these two strands were not always clear-cut, however. The 1969 Congress to Unite Women, for example, contained representatives both from NOW groups and from radical feminist groups – as well as from groups like the Socialist Workers Party (see Koedt *et al.* 1973: 302–17). Moreover, one of the most radical of the feminist groups, The FEMINISTS, founded in 1968 by Ti-Grace Atkinson, had begun within the New York chapter of NOW (see Ware 1970: 24).
5. Greer's title seems to be drawn from de Beauvoir's comment, 'No biological, psychological, or economic fate determines the figure that the human female presents in society; it is civilization as a whole that produces this creature, intermediate between male and eunuch, which is described as feminine' (de Beauvoir 1988: 295). Both the structure of Millett's *Sexual Politics* and individual pieces of analysis seem directly drawn from de Beauvoir's work. In the section titled 'Anthropological: Myth and Religion', for example, we find the following passage, its derivation in de Beauvoir's work unacknowledged:

   > As both the primitive and the civilized worlds are male worlds, the ideas which shaped culture in regard to the female were also of male design. The image of women as we know it is an image created by men and fashioned to suit their needs. These needs spring from a fear of the 'otherness' of woman. (1977: 46)

6. Shulamith Firestone's *The Dialectic of Sex*, also published in 1970, which also argued that women's oppression under patriarchy, founded on reproductive difference, is 'the oldest, most rigid class/caste system in existence' (1979: 23) pre-dating oppression based on race or class, gave a larger role to popular culture as both representation and lived experience. Urging, like Millett, a complete cultural revolution, she nevertheless argued that spaces for women's resistance have always existed in the margins and interstices of mainstream patriarchal culture. See my comments in *Passionate Detachments* (1997: 10–11).
7. It was not until 1991 that Jacqueline Bobo and Ellen Seiter sought to extend this work to the study of television texts and their audiences. See Bobo and Seiter (1991). bell hooks begins explicitly locating herself within a cultural studies framework in her 1990 *Yearning: Race, Gender and Cultural Politics*.
8. Gaye Tuchman's 1979 attack on such research cites Friedan's book and the work of NOW as important influences (Tuchman 1979: 530).
9. See Barthes, 'Myth Today' in *Mythologies* (1973: 109–59).
10. In an early review of *The Female Eunuch* reprinted in Anne Koedt *et al.*, *Radical Feminism* (1973), Claudia Dreifus argued that Greer had no real links with radical feminism, and 'consistently takes a view that is not merely male but inimical to women' (1973: 360).
11. The founding of *Shrew* is described by Sheila Rowbotham in 1972:

> The first [Women's Liberation] newsletter came out in May [1969]. The next issue was called *Harpies Bizarre* and reported response from leafletting the equal pay demonstration, and the formation of a group in Peckham. . . . The third newsletter was called *Shrew* and the name stuck, with the principle established that the editing should pass from group to group. (Wandor 1990: 20)

It was published regularly until 1973, but by 1974 its publication schedule is listed as 'occasional' in Allen *et al.*, *Conditions of Illusion*.

12. Cited in Probyn (1993: 17). Probyn discusses Williams' use of the category of experience in her rethinking of 'the category of the self' within feminism and cultural studies.

13. See Williams, *Problems in Materialism and Culture* (1980).

14. 'Men make their own history, but they do not make it just as they please; they do not make it under circumstances chosen by themselves, but under circumstances directly encountered, given and transmitted from the past' (Marx 1977, *The Eighteenth Brumaire of Louis Bonaparte*: 10).

15. This avoidance of the personal, she argues, goes hand in hand with a refusal to deal with the gender implications of the 'resistant' cultural forms being analysed, a refusal which often masks an identification on the part of the researcher with the working-class youth groups he is studying.

16. See also, for example, the 1976 collection edited by Juliet Mitchell and Ann Oakley, *The Rights and Wrongs of Women*, and Annette Kuhn and AnnMarie Wolpe's (1978), *Feminism and Materialism*.

4

'Unsettled Relations': Psychoanalysis, Feminism and Cultural Studies

It's hard to describe the import of the opening of that new continent in cultural studies, marked out by the relationship – or rather, what Jacqueline Rose has called the as yet "unsettled relations" – between feminism, psychoanalysis, and cultural studies, or indeed how it was accomplished. . . . The interrelations between feminism, psychoanalysis, and cultural studies defines a completely and permanently unsettled terrain for me. (Hall 1992a: 282, 290)

[I]t was the Women's Movement of the sixties and early seventies, with its emphasis on the *ideological* forms of sexual subordination, and the development of strategies for ideological struggle, which utilized psychoanalysis politically, in the move towards a theorization of sexuality and sex-oppression. (Burniston, Mort and Weedon 1978: 120)

Our oppression is more internalized – the clumsiness of women penetrates the very psyche of our being. It is not just a question of being outside existing language. . . . The exclusion of women from all existing language demonstrates our profound alienation from any culture which can generalize itself. (Rowbotham 1973: 33–4)

In Stuart Hall's 1992 narrative of cultural studies, psychoanalysis enters the story via the 'interruption' of feminism. The metaphors he chooses for his account are suggestive. He describes 'the "re-opening"' of a 'closed frontier', the 'opening' of a 'new continent', and the uneasy occupation of a new and unsettled 'terrain'. In the first two descriptions it is not clear from the account who is doing the (re)opening, but in the third it is clear that Hall himself is occupying the terrain. The description recalls Freud's own metaphor of the 'dark continent' to describe female sexuality. For Freud, the psychoanalyst was both explorer and archaeologist, clearing away psychic material 'layer by layer' in a manner analogous 'with the technique of excavating a buried city'.[1] Hall's relationship to the 'new terrain' is altogether more uncertain. Nevertheless, in his account feminism joins femininity as the object of analysis, with cultural studies/Hall as the exploring subject.

The account by Burniston, Mort and Weedon, which appears in the 1978 CCCS collection *Women Take Issue*, is one which occurs frequently in descriptions of the emergence of Hall's uneasy 'triangle' of feminism, psychoanalysis and cultural studies. As Robert Young, who makes a similar argument, summarizes, 'One of the forms of the oppression of women is that the personal, the domestic, sexuality, the family, and so forth are denied political, or even "serious" status of any kind' (1991: 152). Feminism, he writes, turned to psychoanalysis in order to explain this oppression, but in so doing it also *politicized* psychoanalysis. The bridge between the two was provided by the reformulation of the concept of ideology by Marxist philosopher, Louis Althusser, a reformulation which had also been a key influence (Hall 1980a) in moving cultural studies away from its early focus on culture as an unproblematically understood 'whole way of life' (see Chapter 3). Ideologies, argued Althusser, provide 'the frameworks of understanding through which men interpret, make sense of experience and "live" the material conditions in which they find themselves' (Hall 1980a: 32). He therefore not only emphasized the representational aspects of ideology (ideology as imposed through education, religion, the mass media), but also argued that our subjectivities, rather than being whole and autonomous, are fractured and constructed *in* ideology. Ideology, he argued, 'has very little to do with "consciousness". . . . It is profoundly *unconscious*' (Althusser 1977: 233). For feminism, attracted to theories of ideology in order to explain the longevity of the oppression of women, Althusser's work seemed to offer powerful explanatory tools. Moreover, because he drew on psychoanalytic accounts of subjectivity, particularly those drawn from Jacques Lacan's rereading of Freud, in order to explain how the individual accepts his/her place within ideology, his work could also be seen as giving a central place to issues of sexual difference.

The final quotation from Sheila Rowbotham makes clear, however, that this is not simply a central *theoretical* issue for the feminist theory that emerges from the 1970s, but an urgent personal and political necessity. When in *Woman's Consciousness, Man's World* (1973) Rowbotham seeks to bring together personal history ('woman's consciousness') and social analysis ('man's world'), it is not only the 'language of experience' (1973: 33) on which she draws for her account of the former; it is also the terminology of psychoanalysis. When she writes of seeking to grasp 'the depth and extent of my colonization', with its roots in 'the darkness of our unremembered childhood', and of the necessity of understanding 'the relationship between our experience in fantasy, dream and ecstasy and the experience which is intelligible to us in terms of political strategy' (1973: 39, 35, 44), she is both drawing on and seeking to transform psychoanalytic understandings of femininity, of (sexed) identity, and of the unconscious. Her description of the 'looking glass' world of her childhood evokes Lacan's account of the child's acquisition of a sense of self through identification with its own mirror-image. This identification, argues Lacan, is with an *idealized* self-image, since the mirror image is always more co-ordinated, more unified and in control than is the child itself. To this extent its self-recognition as discrete individual is always a *mis*recognition. Later, this sense of identity and separation will make possible the individual's entry into language and culture, able to operate as a subject – an 'I' – within language. Rowbotham's description, however, is of the *absence* of identity that haunts the little girl. Women are oppressed, she writes, 'by an overwhelming sense of not being there' (1973: 35):

> When I was a little girl I was fascinated by the kind of dressing-table mirror which was in three parts. You could move the outer folding mirrors inwards and if you pressed your nose to the glass you saw reflections of yourself with a squashed nose repeated over and over again. I used to wonder which bit was really me. Where was I in all these broken bits of reflection? The more I tried to grasp the totality, the more I concentrated on capturing myself in my own image, the less I knew who I was. (1973: 26)

For Rowbotham, women's 'entry into language and culture' is an entry into dislocation, masquerade and silencing. When, therefore, she recounts her own 'venturing' into the theoretical ground of the 'New Left' from which British cultural studies was emerging in the 1960s and 1970s (Hall 1980a: 17), her description recalls Stuart Hall's account of feminism's 'intervention' into cultural studies as 'unseemly' interruption. For Rowbotham, however, this is neither 'new continent' nor 'unsettled terrain', but firmly occupied 'territory':

> We lumbered around ungainly-like in borrowed concepts which did not fit the shape we felt ourselves to be. Clumsily we stumbled over our own toes, lost in boots which were completely the wrong size. We struggled to do our/their flies up for us/them. We clowned, mimicked, aped our own absurdity. Nobody else took us seriously, we did not even believe in ourselves. We were dolly, chick, broad. We were 'the ladies', 'the girls'. Step forward now dears, let's see you perform. Every time we mounted the steps of their platforms we wanted to run away and hide at home. We had a sense of not belonging. It was evident we were intruders. Those of us who ventured into their territory were most subtly taught our place. (1973: 30)

When Sheila Rowbotham mounts her critique of a Marxist social and cultural analysis which ignores 'the most hidden part of our secret selves' (1973: 124), then, she draws on the concepts and terminology of psychoanalysis in order to do it. But she also filters this use through a politicized autobiographical narrative that places her accounts of fantasy, dream and representation firmly within a specific historical and cultural context. Even so, the two strands sit uneasily together. The question she raises, of how exactly an account of subjectivity which draws on psychoanalytic concepts can be brought together with a social and political analysis, is one which will be posed again and again in feminist cultural studies. The structuring device of autobiography, which she chooses in order to juxtapose and inter-twine history and fantasy, the social and the psychic, will also recur as we shall see, to be both advocated and critiqued.

Juliet Mitchell: Psychoanalysis and Feminism

The gestures towards psychoanalysis made by Sheila Rowbotham were taken up in a far more systematic and clearly articulated way by Juliet Mitchell in her (1974) *Psychoanalysis and Feminism*. In this book Mitchell challenged the dominant view of psychoanalysis within early second wave feminism. Kate Millett, Shulamith Firestone, Germaine Greer and Eva Figes had all identified Freudian psychoanalysis, with its accounts of 'penis envy' and feminine passivity, as a key agent in the 'counterrevolution' against first wave feminism. Yet the theories of ideology on which Millett in particular drew in her explanation of the power of patriarchy, depend on some notion of unconscious processes if they are to have any force. What feminist theory needed, argued Mitchell, was an explanation of the processes through which our sexed identities are acquired and maintained which would both account for the strength and ubiquity of these identities *and* see them as culturally constructed and thus open to change. It was this that she saw psychoanalysis as offering. Her account of psychoanalysis as the theoriza-tion of how human beings learn to occupy – but also resist – their ideolog-ically given roles as men or women within patriarchy was thus to be taken up not only by theorists interested in the construction of gendered identity, but also by those seeking to explore how forms of popular culture – films, magazines and popular fiction – construct feminine identities.

Mitchell begins, then, with an uncompromising assertion. 'However it may have been used,' she argues, 'psychoanalysis is not a recommendation *for* a patriarchal society, but an analysis *of* one. If we are interested in understanding and challenging the oppression of women, we cannot afford to neglect it' (1975: xv). What interests her, therefore, is 'not what Freud did, but . . . what we can get from him, a political rather than an academic explanation'. What we can get from him are 'the concepts with which we can comprehend how ideology functions', principally an account of the unconscious, and, 'closely connected with this, . . . an analysis of the place and meaning of sexuality and of gender differences within society' (1975: xx, xxii). Her book is concerned to distinguish, therefore, what Freud *actu-ally* wrote – in a rereading heavily influenced by the work of Jacques Lacan – from the uses made of his work by both radical post-Freudians (Reich and

Laing) and feminist critics from de Beauvoir to Millett. The final section offers her own summary of the usefulness of psychoanalysis to a feminist analysis of both the present patriarchal system and the prospects for a 'cultural revolution'.

We can identify a number of key features in her account. Feminism, she argues, needs an account of subjectivity which can explain ideology and hence the oppression of women. 'The longevity of the oppression of women *must* be based', she argues, 'on something more than conspiracy, something more complicated than biological handicap and more durable than economic exploitation' (1975: 362). This 'something' is the concept of the unconscious. It is in the unconscious that 'we live as "ideas" the necessary laws of human society' (1975: xvi). The unconscious is 'why ideology persists through changing cultures, changing economic modes, while having also to be altered. If you like, it is why women are everywhere within civilization the second sex, but everywhere differently so' (1975: 381). That these 'laws' are unconscious does not make them any the less social or historical, however. Freud's analysis is of the human being *in culture*. 'Man and woman', argues Mitchell, once again echoing de Beauvoir, 'are *made* in culture' (1975: 131).

Mitchell is concerned first, then, to render women, in Jane Gallop's words, 'fully human', to refuse a biological essentialism which would position them at 'the outskirts of culture, kept close to nature, in biology, trapped in unwitting reproduction' (Gallop 1989: 36–7), even when such an essentialism would see itself as 'feminist'. Women in her account are firmly located in history, and this is the case whether or not they can be identified within the class structure which is the object of a Marxist analysis, because the personal and subjective are as much a matter of cultural construction as is the public and social. Second, she is concerned to produce a non-essentialist account of sexuality and sexual identity that would emphasize the *fluidity* of these terms.

Freudian theory, argues Mitchell, places sexuality and sexual identity as central in its account of the human being in culture, but it is an account, above all, of the *failure* of identity. Freud, she writes, insists on the original bisexuality of the human infant. Both sexes, then, begin by desiring to be the object of desire of the mother. It is with the Oedipus complex – which Mitchell, like Lacan, identifies with the infant's entry into culture, and which she describes as 'a patriarchal myth' (1975: 403) – that the child learns its sexed identity. At this point the boy 'enters into the prospect of his future manhood'. The girl, however, 'has almost to build her Oedipus complex out of the impossibilities of her bisexual pre-Oedipal desires. . . . Not being heir to the law of culture, her task is to see that mankind reproduces itself within the circularity of the supposedly natural family. The family is, of course, no more "natural" than the woman, but its place within the law is to take on "natural" functions' (1975: 405). Both the 'naturalness' of femininity and the identification of femininity with 'the natural' are, then, ideological constructions. Mitchell, indeed, seems to argue that not only is femininity a constructed position; it is also a *non-position*. The girl's submission to the 'law of the father' which is patriarchal culture lies 'in establishing herself as its opposite – as all that is loving and irrational' (1975: 405). It is no wonder, then, that femininity is a profoundly unstable position.

In order to explain how this came about, Mitchell turns to the account of kinship structures given by Lévi-Strauss. For Lévi-Strauss, the distinguishing feature of human kinship structures is the exchange of women. It is this material social practice which is responsible for the incest taboo (women must be exchanged *outside* the family if the tribal structure is to be established), and it is this which institutes patriarchal human culture. Mitchell, then, wants to locate the origins of what are now symbolic and unconscious structures in material historical practices. But even more important, she wants to argue for their potential overthrow. In analysing contemporary Western society, she argues, 'we are . . . dealing with two autonomous areas: the economic mode of capitalism and the ideological mode of patriarchy' (1975: 412). Patriarchal structures have served capitalism well, but their contemporary form of the nuclear family has become less and less able to bear the weight of the unconscious structures (the Oedipus complex) which were developed to preserve much earlier forms of kinship structure. But the nuclear family not only threatens to explode under the weight of its own contradictions, she argues. It is also no longer functional for a capitalism that needs women in its workforce. The laws of patriarchal culture are now potentially redundant. A feminist cultural revolution can prize them open to produce new structures which will in turn take their place in the unconscious.

What Mitchell seeks to produce, then, is a radical historicizing of psychoanalysis, which will preserve the force of the Freudian concepts of the unconscious and of the fragility and fluidity of sexual identity, whilst still insisting on the power of conscious agency for change. Ultimately, it remains unconvincing. As Jane Gallop points out (1982: 12–13), Mitchell's own analysis has posited Freudian structures as so essential to the foundation of human culture, and so embedded in the unconscious, that her argument for the imminence of revolution can be made only at the expense of ignoring her earlier claims and arguing for a rational (non-divided) self which can somehow evade the effects of its own unconscious.[2] It is made at the expense too – as Jane Gallop points out[3] – of omitting any discussion of Lacan's views on language in Mitchell's extensive use of his work. For Lacan, the infant's entry into culture was also his/her entry into language, and language was itself constituted around the dominance of the phallus as the ultimate marker of difference. It is difficult to see how a feminist cultural revolution could liberate women from their inscription within *language* as easily as Mitchell suggests they can be liberated from patriarchal culture. Nevertheless, in its account of a psychoanalysis which is a theory of patriarchal culture, of the attempts of ideology to produce a cultural 'fixing' of sexual identity, and of the inevitable failure of those attempts in the face of the fluidity of sexuality and subjectivity, *Psychoanalysis and Feminism* offered a theoretical framework – however contested – with which a feminist cultural studies could work.

Elizabeth Wilson: Questioning the 'New Orthodoxy'

It is this aspect of Mitchell's argument that Elizabeth Wilson stresses in the critical analyses of Mitchell's work that she produced in the early 1980s. The importance of Mitchell's appropriation of psychoanalytic theory, she writes, lies in its claimed centrality for a feminist cultural studies. Claiming to elucidate the workings of ideology, it can therefore argue 'that it is the account we need of how the dominant ideologies become "lived experience" or "lived relations"'. In the 1980s, she continues, this has 'widened into a cultural enterprise of the exploration of popular culture as it constructed femininity, and in recent years interesting work has been done on girls' and women's magazines and "pulp romances", on pornography, and on fashion, as well as on film and the novel' (1986a: 126). I shall return to some of this 'interesting work' later in this chapter, but what concerns me here is the nature of the claims Wilson feels are being made for psychoanalysis, and the nature of her reservations about these claims.

It was 'natural', she argues, that what began as an enquiry into ideology should look again at psychoanalysis (1986a: 123). Juliet Michell, using the work of Louis Althusser and Jacques Lacan, 'sought to retrieve Freud from biologism', effecting 'the rehabilitation of Freud by presenting him as the theorist of the way in which the human infant, "a small animal", achieves the entry into *culture*' (1986b: 157). Unlike theories which emphasize 'conditioning' or 'socialization', however, what such an approach stresses is the *failure* of gendered identity. Women do not become 'feminine' naturally, easily or indeed successfully. Once femininity is seen as 'a structure as flawed and unstable as the ego itself' (1986a: 124), then the possibilities for subverting that structure are clearly greatly increased.

Whilst Wilson accepts both 'the psychoanalytic account of the way in which sexual identity gets constructed – haltingly and with difficulty', and the fact that it is 'constructed in the context of male power', however, she offers a number of objections to what she sees as 'this new orthodoxy' (1986b: 166, 149). The first is that the psychological 'imperative' with which Mitchell replaces 'the tyranny of biology' is, in Wilson's view, no less tyrannical and unalterable. Once 'human culture' and 'patriarchal culture' are equated – and Mitchell argues that historically they have been the same thing – then the 'entry into culture' seems tied inescapably to constricting structures of 'masculinity' and 'femininity'. To locate the source of women's oppression within unconscious processes, after all, renders that oppression just as inaccessible to conscious change, and just as impervious to political struggle, as if we locate it within biological differences. Psychoanalytic arguments can argue about the 'success' or 'failure' of feminine identity; what they cannot do, argues Wilson, is conceive of a radically *different* identity.

This psychological determinism, argues Wilson, is a result of the fact that psychoanalysis moves between a focus on the highly particular (the individual psyche and its unconscious processes) and on the universal (the 'law of the father' and the Oedipus complex). What is missing is an analysis of the historical and the social. In separating as she does the structures of capitalism and patriarchy, and arguing that the first operates in the economic and the second in the cultural sphere, Mitchell in effect abandons any consideration of the material basis of the oppression of women. Social policy, child-rearing practices, income distribution: all may be specific determinants of conceptions of the 'feminine' role at a particular historical moment, a role which women may adopt for economic rather than psychological reasons. Moreover, because Mitchell's prediction of the imminence of a feminist 'cultural revolution' depends on the argument that the patriarchal nuclear family is out of step with the needs of capitalism, argues Wilson, she cannot deal with the interaction of the two structures. Family structures continue to serve the needs of capitalism, she argues, and patriarchy may be mediated by public institutions (education, the law, the media) as well as the private institution of the family.

Mitchell's use of Freud also locks her into a conception of sexual difference, argues Wilson, which sees heterosexuality as both arbitrary (the human infant is originally bisexual) and inescapable (we must all adopt an identity which is on one side of the line masculine/feminine). Feminist psychoanalytic theory, she writes, has had 'remarkably little to say about homosexuality and lesbianism' (1986b: 164). Yet its focus on sexual *difference*, on the 'having' or the 'lacking' of the phallus which determines our positioning in (patriarchal) culture, is an implicit argument for the inevitability of heterosexuality. Anything else would constitute a denial of such difference.

Wilson's final objection concerns the usefulness of psychoanalytic theory for a feminist political practice. Feminine identity may never, according to Mitchell, be 'successfully' imposed, but the concept of the 'fractured self' which replaces it calls into question the very existence of the identity 'woman', around which women might unite as a distinctive and oppressed social group. Moreover, in referring all social protest to the realm of the psychic, psychoanalysis reduces revolutionary politics to the status of (futile) rebellion against the 'law of the father' – which indeed Freud did in his own discussions of feminism.[4] 'Feminists should know better', she concludes, than to be taken in by a theory 'that teaches them only to marvel anew at the constant recreation of the subjective reality of subordination and which reasserts male domination more securely than ever within theoretical discourse' (1986b: 168). They should focus their energies on theories of *social* change.

Jacqueline Rose: A Subjectivity at Odds with Itself

The question of identity – how it is constituted and maintained – is . . . the central issue through which psychoanalysis enters the political field. This is one reason why Lacanian psychoanalysis came into English intellectual life, via Althusser's concept of ideology, through the two paths of feminism and the analysis of film (a fact often used to discredit all three). (Rose 1986: 5)

For Rose, responding to Elizabeth Wilson's critique, psychoanalysis is both political *and* centrally concerned with issues of language, representation and the failure of identity. It is difficult but important, unassimilable to the Marxist theory that has underpinned a masculine cultural studies, yet central to any radical social critique. Far from being, as Wilson suggested, a 'new orthodoxy', it is more usually – as the above quotation suggests – discredited. Moreover, to question, as Wilson does, the political implications of psychoanalysis for feminism is 'to pose the problem the wrong way round. Psychoanalysis is already political for feminism' (1986: 84). It is political firstly because it is politically *needed* by feminism as a means of accounting for ideology and subjectivity, and secondly because its 'repeated marginalisation within our general culture' is a result of that culture's refusal to confront the principal concerns of psychoanalysis: sexual identity and the unconscious. That a patriarchal culture should so evade these issues is unsurprising, but for feminism to do so is to play into patriarchy's hands.

For Rose, then, psychoanalysis and feminism are crucially politically linked, not least because together they threaten to de-centre a masculine cultural studies. A Marxist-derived cultural theory (Rose cites Perry Anderson, Fredric Jameson and Terry Eagleton) can incorporate psychoanalysis as an account of collective fantasy, and it can incorporate a feminism grounded in social critique. Once linked, however, psychoanalysis and feminism together threaten to destabilize a class-based theory of culture and society, and place issues of subjectivity, pleasure and sexual difference at the heart of cultural and political analysis. It was to this tension that Stuart Hall referred in 1992, when he spoke of the 'unsettling' effect of feminism and psychoanalysis on cultural studies. 'The gains of understanding cultural questions in and through the insights of psychoanalytic work, especially as those have been reread through the political practices of feminism, opened up enormous insights for me', he states. 'Psychoanalysis completely breaks that sociological notion of socialization; I'll never use it again. . . . But I cannot translate the one onto the other. I have to live with the tension of the two vocabularies, of the two unsettled objects of analysis . . .' (1992a: 290–1). For Cora Kaplan, however, writing from within *both* cultural studies and feminism, there is no such splitting. A 'psychoanalytic understanding of the construction of sexual difference does not turn feminism or socialism away from a political practice of resistance but consistently informs and enriches theory and practice', she writes. Appropriating Raymond Williams' phrase for her de-centring of his conception of culture as an ungendered 'whole process', she adds: 'Without an analysis of the *structure of feeling*, it is hard to get below the surface of sexual differentiation and subordination' (Kaplan 1986b: 4–5, my emphasis).

For Jacqueline Rose, feminism's 'affinity with psychoanalysis rests above all . . . with [the] recognition that there is a resistance to identity at the very heart of psychic life' (1986: 91). What the concept of the unconscious suggests is that there is no stability of sexual identity because the unconscious always undermines any apparent identity. Femininity, then, is a position that is *never* achieved. That this was and still is of political importance to feminism is clear, Rose argues, if we look at the cultural context of the nineteenth century into which Freud introduced psychoanalysis. The control of women's sexuality, both within marriage and as sexualized bodies outside marriage was (and arguably still is) a principal form of social regulation – Rose cites as evidence the Contagious Diseases Acts of the 1860s and the nineteenth-century debates about the educability of women, which hinged on whether educating young women would damage their reproductive capacity. Women were to be guardians of the nation's social and moral health; failure or deviation in this role was a matter of individual perversion or pathology. Psychoanalysis, with its insistence that sexual identity is *never* achieved, radically subverts this agenda – and indeed *any* social agenda that is based on gender identity. Only 'the concept of a subjectivity at odds with itself', argues Rose, 'gives back to women the right to an impasse at the point of sexual identity', refusing any construction of gender norms (1986: 15).

Unlike Juliet Mitchell in 1975, then, Jacqueline Rose is not concerned to integrate psychoanalysis into a Marxist teleology. For her there is no progression to maturity, whether biological or psychological, and no possibility of a 'whole' identity in the future. The concept of ' "male" and "female" as complementary entities, sure of each other and of their own identity' (1986: 56) is a regulatory fantasy, designed to 'guarantee' the identity of the male subject. Femininity, as an identity that is not only fantasized, but fantasized from the male position, can therefore be no more than a masquerade. In pursuing these arguments, Rose, unlike Mitchell, firmly embraces Lacan's arguments about language.

For Lacan, as we have seen, the child's initial recognition of itself in its own mirror image both gives it its first sense of itself as a coherent identity, and at the same time splits its identity in two, between the imaged and the imaging self. This is a self, then, constructed in representation and through identification. It is also a fiction. This realm, the pre-linguistic, Lacan termed the imaginary. The order of language and culture, for which the imaginary identification was a preparation, is the symbolic. Here the subject is both constituted and also further split. We enter culture, that is, by learning to say 'I'; in so doing we 'become' a subject – the subject of our own utterances – but we are also subjected. Language is a structure that precedes us and places us; we can operate only according to its rules, and we are objects as well as subjects in it. 'I', moreover, is an unstable position, occupied only momentarily, at the point of speech; like language itself, it can designate only an absence. Language, after all, is a structure of symbols that stand in for the real. It is at heart metaphorical, so that whilst as 'subjects in language' we persist in our fantasy that somewhere there is a point of 'truth', of perfect correspondence between language and the real, it is a belief endlessly frustrated.

Constituted as speaking subjects within language, we have to occupy one or other of the positions 'man' or 'woman'. These are regulatory positions, but they are also fictions: there is no such thing as an essence to 'feminine identity' that precedes language. But not only is there, according to Lacan, no 'feminine' outside language; the feminine as a position *within* language is constituted always as the negative term. It is the 'phallic term' which is the privileged term within language (Rose 1986: 80). This positioning of femininity is, as we have seen, a matter of fantasy, a projection on to 'woman' of the 'lack' which is actually at the centre of all identity. 'If *she*, who is different from me, is lacking,' runs the masculine logic, 'then *I* am whole'. This does not mean, however, that we can counter it by reference to a 'real' essence of femininity, a place outside language to which the feminine, and through that, women, might escape (1986: 81). We are all caught up in language; the appeal to a reality outside it can only position us outside culture and the symbolic altogether.

What, then, are the implications for feminism of these arguments? If we accept such an analysis, there can be no throwing off of ideology in favour of the real, as Kate Millett proposes, nor any reconstituting of the unconscious in line with historical change, as Juliet Mitchell suggests. In Rose's reading of Lacan there is no historical origin of the patriarchal unconscious in the exchange of women, as Mitchell proposed; rather, it is the constituting of femininity as 'Other' within language which produces women's subjection. Equally, then, there can be no 'restoration' of women's position through social change in the future. Instead Rose argues, first, that the recognition that 'there is a resistance to identity at the very heart of psychic life' allows feminism to bring into the political arena the issue of subjectivity. If there is no secure and knowing subject, and if the categories on which our identities are based are a matter of fantasy, conflict and desire, then the regulatory structures and institutions which are founded on such categories, and which are the basis for traditional political analysis, must also be brought into question.

Second, feminism can expose to analysis the 'phallic imposture' through which femininity is always assigned the place of 'Other' within language and culture – an imposture in which Lacan himself is implicated, argues Rose – and thus give women a place from which to speak. Such a position accepts the divided, unfinished and contradictory nature of female subjectivity, but uses this awareness to expose the fantasy of identity which underpins *any* claim to psychic wholeness.[5] Third, if we accept that our sexuality and sexual identity are constituted in and through *representation*, and that for women such representations – and the identifications through which they work – are constructed within the terms of a masculine fantasy, then we begin to have the tools with which to analyse them. This – the material of a feminist cultural studies – will not be a matter of uncovering a patriarchal ideology which can then be overthrown, as Kate Millett, for example, suggests. Rather, it will be the analysis of a particular structure of fantasy or 'logic of desire' (1986: 219) which, in soliciting our identification, seeks to conceal the non-identity at its own centre.

None of this, however, answers Elizabeth Wilson's objection that psychoanalysis offers feminism tools for analysis but not for change. Rose accepts that the concept of the unconscious does not 'sit comfortably with the necessary attempt by feminism to claim a new sureness of identity for women, or with the idea of always conscious and deliberate political decision-making and control' (1986: 103). Yet as Robert Young points out, whilst 'the question of identity remains one of the major problems in the relation of psychoanalysis to the political', those who, like Wilson, argue for the political necessity of a notion of a coherent subject, are relying on 'a fairly crude theory of intentionality, which imagines that you need a totally unified subject to be able to have any form of will or agency at all' (1991: 155). Moreover, the psychoanalytic insistence on the failure of sexual identity is of use, argues Rose, not only *to* feminism, in its struggle against patriarchal culture, but also *within* feminism. We should, she suggests, 'open up a space' between the concepts of a political and a psychic identity. The first would be an identification embraced consciously and for political ends by *feminists*; the second assumes a psychic identity between *women*. If we confuse the two we gloss over too easily not only the fracturing within individual subjectivities, but also the *different* ways in which women may be subjected to/within patriarchal culture. To hold on to the insights into subjectivity, sexual difference and fantasy which psychoanalysis can offer, whilst simultaneously pursuing a fully political programme, is, she argues, the challenge for a feminist politics.

Visual Pleasures?

Women are constantly confronted with their own image in one form or another, but what they see bears little relation or relevance to their own unconscious fantasies, their own hidden fears and desires. They are being turned all the time into objects of display, to be looked at and gazed at and stared at by men. Yet in a real sense, women are not there at all. (Mulvey 1989a: 13)

Laura Mulvey's comments come from the conclusion to her 1973 review for *Spare Rib* of an exhibition of sculptures by Allen Jones. The essay thus pre-dates by some two years the publication of her more famous essay on film, 'Visual Pleasure and Narrative Cinema', but makes the same use of psychoanalytic theory in its analysis. The exhibition, called 'Women as Furniture', featured 'life-sized effigies of women, slave-like and sexually provocative' which doubled as hat-stands, tables and chairs (Mulvey 1989a: 6). For Mulvey, Jones' work, with its fetishistic images of women, reveals 'the contradiction between woman's fantasy presence and real absence from the male unconscious world' (1989a: 7). In these images of women made by and for men, women are displayed 'as figures in an amazing masquerade, which expresses a strange male underworld of fear and desire'. As 'signs', they have no reference to real women; they are 'simply the scenery' on to which is projected the 'narcissistic wound' of man's castration anxiety. These are images, she adds, which 'pervade not just specialised publications but the *whole of the mass media*' (1989a: 13, original emphasis).

In 'Visual Pleasure and Narrative Cinema' she was to further develop this argument. 'Woman', she writes there, 'stands in patriarchal culture as a signifier for the male other, bound by a symbolic order in which man can live out his fantasies and obsessions through linguistic command by imposing them on the silent image of woman still tied to her place as bearer, not maker, of meaning' (1989b: 15). Cinema offers the male spectator erotic pleasure in looking, the fulfilment of desire (and the warding off of anxiety) through fantasy, and a return to the pleasures of imaginary self-identity which, following Lacan, she identifies with the 'mirror phase' of infancy. In the figure of the male movie star, she argues, the spectator is offered identification with his 'ideal ego', that 'more perfect, more complete, more powerful ideal ego conceived in the original moment of recognition in front of the mirror' (1989b: 20). But patriarchal culture and the cinema it has produced is 'a world ordered by sexual imbalance', in which 'pleasure in looking has been split between active/male and passive/female':

> The determining male gaze projects its fantasy onto the female figure, which is styled accordingly. In their traditional exhibitionist role women are simultaneously looked at and displayed, with their appearance coded for strong visual and erotic impact so that they can be said to connote *to-be-looked-at-ness*. Woman displayed as sexual object is the *leitmotif* of erotic spectacle: from pin-ups to strip-tease, from Ziegfeld to Busby Berkeley. (1989b: 19)

This active/passive division, argues Mulvey, also structures film narrative, so that the image of woman as erotic spectacle interrupts the flow of narrative, whilst the central male figure advances the story and, as the ideal ego of male fantasy, controls events, the woman, and the erotic gaze.

Mulvey, then, seeks to use psychoanalytic theory as a 'political weapon, demonstrating the way the unconscious of patriarchal society has structured film form' (Mulvey 1989b: 14). 'Visual Pleasure and Narrative Cinema' was to be a hugely influential essay, grounding feminist discussions of a range of images of women in both 'high' and 'popular' culture. But whilst her account offers the analysis of the structures of masculine fantasy which Rose suggests as one outcome of a feminist politics of representation, her description of the perfect fit between cinematic structures and patriarchal fantasy (she writes of the 'beauty in [the] exact rendering of the frustration experienced under the phallocentric order') seems to offer women little room for change, and none at all for pleasure – she writes of the need to destroy 'visual pleasure'. There seems no space here for the concept of a *failure* of identity and there is no discussion of *female* subjectivity. Thus the feminists who must wield the 'radical weapon' of psychoanalytic theory seem to have to make their politics not, as in Rose's account, from a split subjectivity but from a point of total absence. As B. Ruby Rich complained, although Mulvey 'does show that psychoanalysis provides a useful tool primarily for analyzing the status quo, which is patriarchal', the problem is that 'there don't seem to be any women there' (Rich in Citron *et al.* 1978: 87). Mulvey herself was later to comment on the way her 'either/or binary pattern seemed to leave the argument trapped within its own conceptual frame of reference, unable to advance politically into a new terrain or suggest an alternative theory of spectatorship in the cinema' (1989c: 162).

Mulvey's arguments were taken up elsewhere in feminist analyses of visual representation. Griselda Pollock's (1977) 'What's Wrong with Images of Women?', for example, addresses the inadequacy of any analysis of media images of women which treats them simply as reflections (true or false) of a pre-existing 'reality' of women's lives. The idea that 'images of women' merely *reflect* meanings which originate elsewhere (in the intentions of media producers, or in social stuctures), she writes,

> implies a juxtaposition of two separable elements – women as a gender or social group versus representations of women, or a real entity, women, opposed to falsified, distorted or male views of women. It is a common misconception to see images as merely a reflection, good or bad, and compare 'bad' images of women (glossy magazine photographs, fashion advertisements, etc.) to 'good' images of women ('realist' photographs, of women working, housewives, older women, etc.). This conception . . . needs to be challenged and replaced by the notion of woman as a signifier in an ideological discourse. (Pollock 1987: 41)

In her 1987 introduction to the collection *Looking On*, which brings together feminist writing on images of femininity in fine art, fashion, advertising, magazines and pornography, and which includes Pollock's article, Rosemary Betterton both endorses and questions this view. Critics like Mulvey, she argues, 'have pointed out that many of the pleasures offered by dominant visual culture are connected to the ways in which it addresses a heterosexual *male* spectator' (1987: 11). If the analysis of how 'definitions of femininity are produced and articulated in cultural forms' is vital for feminism, however, the task of the feminist critic is not simply to elucidate these structures, but to 'identify . . . with the *woman* who looks' (1987: 6–7, my emphasis). Once women are positioned as active and investigative viewing subjects, questioning what is 'normal' in representation, two crucial questions are raised. The first concerns the supposed inevitability (and pretended neutrality) of the dominant male gaze. If meaning, like subjectivity, is neither fixed nor innate, but subject to struggle and contestation, then, as feminists, we might 'actively intervene to change the meaning of cultural artefacts' (1987: 6).

The second question concerns the issue of pleasure. Mulvey's 'radical weapon' was to be the destruction of visual pleasure and the substitution of the alternative pleasure (the 'beauty') of analysis. But this is to deny any space to female fantasy, indeed to deny altogether the space of the unconscious to women. Yet any account of women's subjectivity as split, as, in Cora Kaplan's words, 'structured, divided and denigrated through the matrices of sexual difference' (1986c: 227), has to deal with the contradictory ways in which *women* experience pleasure, and power, in looking. As Betterton asks, 'if the voyeuristic gaze of the male spectator does not exhaust possible ways of seeing, what other ways might there be? In particular, what kind of power (or powerlessness) do women have in looking?' (1987: 13). One way in which this question has been explored, she adds, has been to look at cultural forms which are addressed to women, since these are areas where pleasure is constructed primarily *for* women. But, she adds, often 'these pleasures are contradictory, since they are bound up with the way in which femininity is defined' (1987: 13). It was the exploration of these contradictions that became central to a psychoanalytically informed feminist cultural studies.

Recognizing Ourselves

The signifier 'woman' always signifies woman: we recognize ourselves in *any* representation of woman . . . because we are always already defined by our gender. Having recognized ourselves . . ., we are then 'freshly' positioned as specific feminine subjects in an identification achieved through a misrecognition of ourselves – the signifier 'woman' can never in fact represent us as individual women. (Winship 1980: 218–9)

Janice Winship's work on advertisements and women's magazines offers a rather different use of Lacanian psychoanalytic theory from that of Laura Mulvey or Griselda Pollock, cited above. Her insistence on going beyond the text in her analysis, and on implicating herself as caught up in the contradictions of feminism and femininity, has its origins, as I argued in Chapter 3, partly in cultural studies' use of the category of 'experience', but even more in the kind of self-scrutiny derived from the politics of the Women's Liberation Movement. Like Sheila Rowbotham, she draws on psychoanalytic concepts in order to understand 'the relationship between our experience in fantasy, dream and ecstasy and the experience which is intelligible to us in terms of political strategy' (Rowbotham 1973: 44). Her female subject is contradictory but not absent, subject to the same identificatory structures of (mis)recognition as her male counterpart. This subject's fantasy is engaged, but it is engaged by representations produced elsewhere, by a patriarchal culture that for women is lived, as well as represented, in contradiction.

Winship's work on advertising draws on Judith Williamson's 1978 *Decoding Advertisements*. Williamson employs semiotics, Althusserian definitions of ideology, and Lacanian psychoanalysis in order to offer an analysis of how advertisements, as semiotic and ideological structures, *work*. Ideology, she argues, creates subjects, and ads work by creating us 'not only as subjects, but as particular kinds of subjects' (1978: 45). They assume 'an "alreadyness" of "facts" about ourselves as individuals: that we are consumers, that we have certain values, that we will freely buy things, consume, on the basis of those values, and so on' (1978: 42). On the basis of this they present us with signs (Catherine Deneuve/Chanel No. 5; the VW Polo/the independent woman) between which *we* make the connections, the meanings. We become, then, both the 'space' in which meaning is made and the active makers of that meaning. We 'step into' the subject position offered by the ad:

> You have to exchange yourself with the person 'spoken to', the spectator the ad creates for itself. Every ad necessarily assumes a particular spectator: it projects into the space in front of it an imaginary person composed in terms of the relationship between the elements within the ad. You move into this space as you look at the ad, and in doing so 'become' the spectator . . . (1978: 50–1)

Above all, she argues, the ad offers us, as object of desire, ourselves as coherent and unified subject. It thus acts, like Lacan's mirror image, as ideal ego, offering to bind our 'fragmented' selves into unity via the product – and Williamson notes the sheer number of magazine ads which offer their female spectator an image which is presented precisely as her mirrored self.

Williamson's account is based on a Marxist analysis. Ads, she writes, 'obscure and avoid the real issues of society, those relating to work: to jobs and wages and who works for whom. They create systems of social differentiation which are a veneer on the basic class structure of our society' (1978: 47). Although she draws on Lacanian concepts, and though a majority of the ads she analyses – inevitably – foreground issues of sexuality and sexual difference, hers is neither an explicitly feminist account nor an argument based on the concept of an inherently split subjectivity. For her, ads are engaged in creating ideological structures based on '*false* differences' which it is the business of the cultural critic to unmask. The implication is that we can be restored to 'reality and real emotions' (1978: 47), once what she calls the 'culpable depth' of the 'discourse of the unconscious' (1978: 61) can be brought to light and so countered.

Although Janice Winship draws on and explicitly acknowledges Williamson's analytical techniques, therefore, her own definition of the 'alreadyness' on which ads depend is rather different. It is, first, ideologies of *femininity* with which she is concerned. Second, these ideologies are not only a matter of lived experience, but of lived experience as contradiction. 'Within the ads are inscribed the images and subject positions of "mother", "housewife", "sexually attractive woman" and so on, which, as we work to understand the ad, embroil us in the process of signification that we complete', she writes, drawing on Williamson. 'Yet', she adds, 'we do not come "naked" to the ads or to any ideological representation and simply take on those representations. We already have both a knowledge of images of women from other discourses and an acquaintance with "real" women in our everyday lives. The signification of an ad only has meaning in relation to this "outside" knowledge of the ideology of femininity' (1980: 218).

Ideologies of femininity are not only contradictory, and hence a 'terrain for women's struggle'; they are *lived* as such. Discussing women's magazines, Winship argues that 'femininity is not merely a passive acceptance by women of patriarchal domination'; it ' "manoeuvres" within and against masculine hegemony', representing what she calls 'an *active subordination*' (1978: 134–5). Her term implies both subjection *and* resistance, and returns us to Jacqueline Rose's argument that femininity is a position that is never fully achieved. As women, argues Winship, our pleasures in cultural forms such as the women's magazine are constructed always within the terms of masculine fantasy and desire. We have only to look at the magazine's cover image – the coy, smiling, anonymous female face – to see that 'what appears to be *central*' to the magazine and its appeal, the relation of women to women, 'is simultaneously defined in relation to absent men/masculinity'. This woman, in her perfection, 'is a *man's* woman' (1978: 133–4). Nevertheless, within these boundaries the magazines also offer fantasies for women. We are offered sexual fantasies – 'like dream fantasies', argues Winship, the magazine stories about male stars are 'emotionally and sexually charged' – and (sexually charged) fantasies of resistance and escape. Although in both the magazine's fiction and its 'star features' female sexuality is finally returned to its 'proper' place within the family, 'this final containment of sexuality within the family form allows the fantasized extramarital sexual relation to be "experienced" but to remain at the level of fantasy, reconciled with [the readers'] affirmed position as wives and mothers' (1978: 148).

A similar argument is made by Rosalind Coward in her 1984 collection of essays on popular culture for women, *Female Desire*. Feminine positions, she argues, 'are neither distant roles imposed on us from outside which it would be easy to kick off, nor are they the essential attributes of femininity'. They are 'produced as responses to the pleasures offered to us; our subjectivity and identity are formed in the definitions of desire which encircle us. These are the experiences which make change such a difficult and daunting task, for female desire is constantly lured by discourses which sustain male privilege' (Coward 1984: 16). Women's magazines, advertising, romance fiction, pop songs: all create and 'stage-manage' pleasure in this way, offering '[p]ublicly sanctioned fantasies [which] confirm men's power, women's subordination' (1984: 203). In romance fiction, for example, women 'do acquire power . . . Men are injured, or rendered the helpless slaves of passion. The great heart-breakers are brought into line and the proud and arrogant are apparently humbled by their sexual desire for the good heroine'. This 'power', however, works in the service of the patriarchal nuclear family, playing on the Oedipal myths which sustain it: the 'potent father, the abolition of the rival mother, and taking the mother's place are the classic structures of childhood fantasy in a nuclear patriarchal family' (1984: 196). Nevertheless, writes Coward, fantasy itself can never quite be contained. It is a realm where the private fantasies of the individual unconscious, in which 'the positions of masculine and feminine are much less clearly fixed' (1984: 204), threaten the precarious structures of patriarchal representations. Pleasures 'escape, slip out between the cracks and perhaps spell the ruin of existing definitions of female desire' (1984: 16).

In Dreams . . .

Winship, Williamson and Coward all make use of psychoanalytic work on dreams and fantasy. For Winship and Williamson, advertising and romance fiction 'employ a means of representation analogous to the dream work of dreams which Freud describes, giving the illusion of describing a "reality" but only alluding to that reality: condensation, displacement, representability and secondary revision. They are fantasy . . .' (Winship 1978: 148). Since this aspect of psychoanalytic theory plays such an important role in feminism's appropriation of psychoanalysis for cultural studies, it is worth elaborating in more detail here.

For Freud, dreams offer a disguised fulfilment of normally repressed unconscious desires. With the 'psychic censor' relaxed in sleep, unconscious wishes can achieve disguised expression by attaching themselves to recent images/perceptions. The disguise is the result of the 'dream-work', which, in Madan Sarup's words, 'transforms the "latent" content of the dream, the forbidden dream-thoughts, into the "manifest" dream-stories – what the dreamer remembers' (1992: 6). This 'dream-work' has four aspects. The first is condensation, in which two or more ideas are compressed, to become a composite image that carries a number of repressed desires. The second is displacement. Here the unconscious wish is disguised by being displaced on to a figure or image with which it is associated in some way, but which does not itself attract repression. The third aspect of the dream-work is what Freud calls 'considerations of representability'. Dreams, that is, must rely on visual material, and must therefore transform the desires that they express into visual form. Finally, there is 'secondary revision'. In this process, the dream is reorganized so as to become a relatively coherent and comprehensible narrative; when we recount our dreams, we are engaged in this process, smoothing out gaps and contradictions to produce a recognizable story.

Adapting Freud's account, with Lacan's crucial addition that the processes of the dream are also those of language itself – like the dream, language operates through condensation (metaphor) and displacement (metonymy) beneath a surface of narrative coherence – clearly provides one way of conceptualizing the play of female desire within a narrative whose structures are imposed from without. It is in this way that Janice Winship analyses the stories of women's magazines. They are, she writes, '*symbols* onto which the emotions of relationships are displaced, . . . punctuated by "magical" moments which allow a resolution (wish fulfilment) to be achieved' (1978: 148). The problem with this concept of fantasy, however, is that it seems to fix female desire forever within a repressed unconscious – a 'latent' content manifest only in 'disguised' form. Fantasy, then, becomes *mere* fantasy, and from the concept of an inherently split subjectivity through which politics and analysis must always operate offered by Jacqueline Rose or Cora Kaplan, we seem to be returned to an either/or choice: fantasy *or* reality, pleasure *or* analysis, femininity *or* feminism, the psychic *or* the social.

Tania Modleski's study of soap opera text (1979, 1984)[6] offers a more complex view of the operations of fantasy. Contrasting the narrative structure of the soap opera, with its multiple characters and absence of narrative resolution, with Laura Mulvey's account of the functioning of the 'classic (male) narrative film', Modleski argues that it not only offers specifically feminine fantasy and pleasures, but that these pleasures have also a feminist potential. Unlike the 'ideal ego' offered to the male spectator via the central male protagonist of mainstream film, the soap opera offers its female spectator a 'multiple identification' which, in a patriarchal symbolic order, 'results in the spectator being divested of power' (1979: 14). She is constituted within the terms of a Freudian femininity, as 'a sort of ideal mother' whose own desire is repressed in favour of sympathy with 'the conflicting claims of her family (she identifies with them all), and who has no demands or claims of her own' (1979: 14). Soap opera, however, offers also, in the person of the 'villainess', the 'negative image of the spectator's ideal self' (1979: 15). This figure, who deploys the *strategy* of 'feminine weaknesses' for her own manipulative ends, seeks to resist and control her 'feminine passivity', and so 'act[s] out the spectator's fantasies of power' (1979: 16–17). As spectators, then, we simultaneously repudiate and identify with the figure of the villainess. Her (always shortlived) power is simultaneously desired and disclaimed, the anger which fuels it both expressed and disavowed.

For Modleski, then, the fantasies which underpin the soap opera are complex structures through which female desire is both affirmed and disavowed. Soap operas' pleasures, of deferral and absence of resolution, of multiple identification and a recognition of the fractured nature of subjectivity, are the reverse of those offered to the male spectator of the conventional narrative. As de-centred narratives, soap operas lie outside the patriarchal structures of pleasure that Laura Mulvey identified as central to the male-centred text. This fact, argues Modleski, may give them a subversive potential. They 'may not be an entirely negative influence on the viewer; they may also have the force of a *negation*, a negation of the typical (and masculine) modes of pleasure in our society' (1984: 105). And she likens their structure to Luce Irigaray's conception of an alternative *female* symbolic, one that would be no longer centred on the primacy of the phallus.

Structuring Desire

Modleski's account is tentative in its conclusions. The 1984 essay attributes to the soap opera a rather more certain subversive potential than its earlier version, but even here there is a tendency to argue that soap opera fantasies, whilst they 'satisf[y] *real* needs and desires', do so – like dreams – in a 'distorted' form (1984: 108). Female fantasy and the popular culture for women which it informs, is here once again seen as equivalent to the hallu-cinatory wish-fulfilment of the dream. In the 1980s, however, a more complex interpretation of the psychoanalytic concept of fantasy emerged, which drew on feminist readings of the 1964 essay, 'Fantasy and the Origins of Sexuality' by Jean Laplanche and Jean-Bertrand Pontalis.[7] Laplanche and Pontalis' focus is on the *structure* of fantasy. Fantasy, they argue, offers 'a scenario with multiple entries' for the fantasizing subject (1986: 22–3). Our identification, that is, is not fixed: in fantasy we cross boundaries of sexual difference and we shift position within and across the poles of the fantasized scenario. Fantasy, they write, is inseparable from desire and from sexuality. Sexuality *begins* for the individual at the moment when, 'disengaged from any natural object, [it] moves into the field of fantasy and by that very fact becomes sexuality' (1986: 25). But fantasy is 'not the object of desire, but its setting. In fantasy the subject does not pursue the object or its sign: he appears caught up himself in the sequence of images'. It is the *staging* of desire, its *mise-en-scène*, in which the subject, whilst always present, 'cannot be assigned any fixed place' (1986: 26).

Finally, what Laplanche and Pontalis' account emphasizes is the 'mixed nature' of fantasy. Fantasy crosses the boundaries between conscious and unconscious, and there is continuity between the consciously indulged daydream and the repressed unconscious fantasy. The structure of fantasy, they argue, is formed on the basis of three 'primary' fantasies: fantasies of 'the primal scene' which picture 'the origin of the individual; fantasies of seduction, [which picture] the origin and upsurge of sexuality; fantasies of castration, [which picture] the origin of the difference between the sexes' (1986: 19). 'Secondary' fantasies, however, – unconscious or conscious, dream, daydream or narrative fiction – rework these original fantasies, using the 'kaleidoscopic material' of the present. As Elizabeth Cowie explains, the fantasy 'hovers between three times: the present provides a context, the material elements of the fantasy; the past provides the wish, deriving from the earliest experiences; the dreamer then imagines a new situation, in the future, which represents a fufilment of the wish'. Fantasy, then, is a 'privileged terrain' on which social reality and the unconscious meet and are 'entwined' (Cowie 1984: 84). In this account any simple opposition between 'fantasy' and 'reality' disappears. First, fantasy is fundamental in the structuring of sexuality and desire. Second, fantasies engage with and structure our perceptions of social reality as well as with 'primary' (unconscious) material, in their reworking of the 'kaleidoscopic' elements of the subject's social existence.

It is this account which underpins Rosalind Coward's arguments for the *fluidity* of the positioning of desire in fantasy, in which 'the positions of masculine and feminine are much less clearly fixed' than 'existing definitions of female desire' assume. It is the work of Valerie Walkerdine, however, which goes furthest in seeking to develop the implications of this more mobile conceptualization of fantasy for a feminist cultural studies. The focus of Walkerdine's work is, she writes, on 'the production of subjectivity in everyday practices and how to understand the place of the popular within this' (1997: 57). It constitutes an engagement with 'the complex and painful intersection of the psychic and the social' (1997: 14) through an exploration of the forms of fantasy which, in contemporary (patriarchal) culture, structure the subjectivity and lived experience of girls.

Walkerdine's 1984 essay, 'Some Day my Prince will Come', deals with the ways in which girls' comics function to prepare the cultural ground for the girl's 'insertion . . . into romantic heterosexuality' (1984: 163). Popular culture, she argues, *produces* 'forms of thought and positions for women':

In this sense then, we can say that texts do not simply distort or bias a reality that exists only outside the pages of books – in the 'real world' – but rather that those practices *are* real, and in their construction of meanings create places for identification, construct subject-positions in the text itself. So we need not point to some untainted reality outside the text, but to examine instead how those practices within the text itself have relational effects that define who and where we are. They are not just images which are distasteful, to be tossed away and replaced by more politically acceptable ones. I suggest that we have to engage with the production of ourselves as subjects in and through our insertion into such cultural practices . . . (1984: 164–5)

Walkerdine here combines a psychoanalytically informed understanding of how texts position us with an account of the *productivity* of cultural practices drawn from the work of Michel Foucault. Power, argues Foucault, does not simply operate through processes of repression, censorship and denial. It works positively to construct the positions which, as subjects, we inhabit. According to Foucault:

What gives power its hold, what makes it accepted, is quite simply the fact that it does not simply weigh like a force which says no, but that it runs through, and it produces, things, it induces pleasure, it forms knowledge [*savoir*], it produces discourse; it must be considered as a productive network which runs through the entire social body much more than as a negative instance whose function is repression. (Foucault 1979b: 36)

As Lois McNay (1992) has argued, Foucault's conceptualization of power, like Lacan's rereading of Freud, is attractive to feminism because it serves to position female subjectivity *within* culture and history rather than as always the 'Other' of male-centred culture. In particular, Foucault argues that *sexuality* is the effect of historically specific power relations. The relationship between power and sexuality is not a negative one, in which power seeks to control an 'unruly sexuality', he argues. Rather, the production of sexualized subjects is itself a form of regulation: ' "Sexuality" is far more a positive product of power than power was ever repression of sexuality' (Foucault 1979b: 37).

Like other forms of popular culture for women, then, girls' comics, in Walkerdine's view, operate to produce and regulate female subjectivity within a patriarchal culture. For Walkerdine, however, the crucial mechanism through which the reader is 'inserted' into the text is that of fantasy. What girls' comics, like classic fairy tales, offer their reader is a constant reworking of the Oedipal narrative through which the girl enters femininity. Walkerdine, however, makes two central points about the operation of these fantasies. The first is that these fictions, to engage their readers, must 'play upon wishes already present in the lives of young children', with 'the resolutions offered [relating] to their own wishes or desires' (1984: 168–9). Like Modleski's reading of soap opera, Walkerdine's comic story is a complex fantasy structure that produces both the resolution and regulation of desire. It becomes, then, an arena of struggle. Following Jacqueline Rose, Walkerdine argues that femininity is an identity which is *not* 'fitted easily onto girls', but is instead 'struggled over' (1984: 181). Walkerdine's second point is that such fantasy structures are not separable from the social. The reader who engages in this fiction, she argues, 'lives a "real" life which is at the same time organised in relation to fantasy' (1984: 169).

In her later work, Walkerdine both develops this concept and explores the ways in which female fantasy is constructed in relation both to male (patriarchal) fantasy and to class. In 'Video Replay: Families, Film and Fantasy' (1986), she gives an analysis of the viewing of the video of *Rocky II* (1979) by a working-class family, the Coles, focusing particularly on two family members, Mr Cole and his six-year-old daughter, Joanne. In the case of Mr Cole, her focus is on discourses of 'fighting', discourses which are 'fictions, set and worked out in the film itself' but which are also 'lived out in the practices in which Mr Cole is inserted' (1989: 183), since he sees himself *as* a fighter. For Mr Cole, *Rocky II* offers fantasies of 'omnipotence, heroism and salvation', but whilst such fantasies are the result of a very specific male working-class experience of 'oppression and powerlessness' (1989: 172), they are not *separate* from Mr Cole's lived existence. They also structure his lived social and domestic experience: 'There is no "real" of these practices which stands outside fantasy, no split between fantasy as a psychic space and a reality which can be known' (1989: 183). The fantasy of masculinity as 'fighting/being a fighter' structures Mr Cole's conscious self-identification and regulates his domestic relations, but it also reaches back into his unconscious, as 'a defence against powerlessness, a defence against femininity' (1989: 182). Like all fantasies, it is structured partly in the unconscious.

Walkerdine's account of Mr Cole's daughter Joanne ('Dodo') draws also on her own childhood experiences. Mr Cole's infantilization of his daughter as 'Dodo' confirms his identification as a 'fighter' on her behalf, but it also creates a fantasy identification for *her*. It is an identity, however, which is 'fractured', since Joanne is seen by Mr Cole as *both* the fragile and feminine 'Dodo' *and* a working-class 'fighter' like her father. Joanne, like Walkerdine before her, must somehow inhabit this fractured identity. Thus the 'fantasy-structure' of *Rocky II* not only intersects with the domestic dynamics of the Cole family in complex ways; it is also a part of the power relations within the family. Fantasy, 'is invested in domestic relations just as much as it is in films', and to understand this we need not only to examine the 'regimes of meaning' constructed within discursive practices but also to 'go beyond the present use of psychoanalysis', to understand the ways in which fantasies structure not only texts but also lived experience and lived relations (1989: 192, 189).

For Walkerdine, then, 'lived experience' cannot be separated from an analysis of subjectivity. In *Daddy's Girl* (1997), which continues her work on young girls and popular culture, she makes explicit the challenge she is making to a male-centred cultural studies. Against Raymond Williams' view of working-class life and culture, she is 'posing fictions and fantasies, processes of subjectification and modes of conscious and unconscious subjectivity, which define, though differently, subjects of all classes' (1997: 16). Against the concept of 'working-class experiences' in E.P. Thompson's work, she insists that we 'cannot . . . separate something called "working-class experiences" . . . from the fictions and fantasies in which those lives are produced and read' (1997: 35). At the same time, however, her use of the work of Michel Foucault, with its emphasis on 'histories' and 'archaeologies' of cultural practices and 'regimes of truth', seeks to counter the a-historical tendency of psychoanalysis. Discussing her use of the work of Laplanche and Pontalis on fantasy, she argues that these fantasies have to be 'understood in terms of the complex intertwining of parental histories and the regimes of truth, the cultural fantasies which circulate in the social' (1997: 180). What psychoanalysis adds to this, in addition to its detailing of how fantasy *works*, is its insistence on the *failure* at the heart of identity, and particularly – following Jacqueline Rose – at the heart of feminine identity.

Walkerdine's challenge is posed at the level of research method as well as of theoretical concept. The researcher, too, she argues is caught up in 'regimes of truth', occupying a 'fantasy space in which certain fictions are produced', fictions of 'knowledge' and 'truth' (1989: 194). Walkerdine refuses any position of 'objectivity', therefore, and instead uses her own subjectivity as a resource. The cultural fantasies which structure the subjectivities of the little girls she studies also structure her own, so that she explains the interaction of cultural and individual fantasy, and of the way in which a dominant male fantasy can in turn structure the fantasies of the female child, by reference to her own experience. 'My father did not *invent* Tinkerbell or the bluebell fairy', she writes. 'Rather he used what were available cultural fantasies to name something about his deep and complex feelings for his daughter. In return, I, his daughter, took those fantasies to my heart and my unconscious, making them my own' (1997: 181). This technique has the effect of refusing to assign the status of object to the little girls in the study: their subjectivity is uninvaded. One might object, however, that it also has the effect of constantly displacing the object of analysis, away from the little girls being studied, about whose responses to the video texts we learn very little,[8] and on to the subjectivity of the researcher herself. For Walkerdine, however, that is precisely the point.

Telling a Different Story

'I am well aware that I want to tell a different story from the ones already told', writes Valerie Walkerdine (1997: 25). She reminds us that cultural studies, like culture itself, has been a matter of stories: those told, often about themselves, by Raymond Williams and Richard Hoggart, and more recently by Stuart Hall. Psychoanalysis, too, is a teller of stories, stories about infant subjectivity recounted in the form of the case-history. Finally in this chapter, then, I want to return to another autobiographical narrative which seeks to challenge the dominant narratives of cultural studies by 'telling a different story', and which both uses and critiques psychoanalysis to do so.

Carolyn Steedman's *Landscape for a Good Woman* (1986) presents itself as adopting the structure of psychoanalytic case study, 'the narrative form that Freud is described as inventing'. The written case-study, writes Steedman, 'allows the writer to enter the present into the past, allows the dream, the wish or the fantasy of the past to shape current time, and treats them as evidence in their own right. . . . Case-study presents the ebb and flow of memory, the structure of dreams, the stories that people tell to explain themselves to others' (1986: 20–1). Steedman's text is more complex than this however, interweaving the narratives of her own and her working-class mother's lives, of fairy tales and of two written case studies: Freud's story of 'Dora' and the story of the little watercress girl recounted by Henry Mayhew in *London Labour and the London Poor* (1851). Through this interweaving, both the class-based narratives of cultural studies and the psychoanalytic narratives of sexual difference are challenged.

Recounting her own childhood, Steedman, as Elizabeth Abel points out (1990: 192), presents us with two 'primal scenes' which function as a critique of the Freudian 'primal scene'. In the first, the child watches as her father is accosted by the 'solid and powerful' 'forest-keeper' because he has picked bluebells in the woods. The bluebells, 'snatched . . . from my father's hand', lie with 'their white roots glimmering, unprotected', and her father is 'the loser, feminized, undone' (Steedman 1986: 50). Here then is a story which repeats both the psychoanalytic account of the rupturing of the 'dyad' of infant and child through the intervention of the powerful 'third term',[9] and, with its forests and 'forest keeper', the mythical version of that story, the fairy tale. It is a story, however, which functions on the axis of class rather than sexuality. It is the father who is 'feminized' by his class position. The child's subjectivity is structured along lines of class as much as/more than along lines of gender.

The second 'primal scene' which the child observes also functions along the axis of class, but positions the child this time with the mother, when another disciplinary figure, a (female) health visitor, accuses Steedman's mother of having a house unfit for a baby. As Elizabeth Abel (1990: 193) observes, this is not only 'a class encounter between two same-sex adults', it is also an encounter which creates rather than breaks the girl's identification with the mother, an identification which is formed primarily on the basis of a shared *class* identity. As the health visitor leaves, we return to the present for the adult narrator's vow of class solidarity: 'And I? I will do everything and anything until the end of my days to stop anyone ever talking to me like that woman talked to my mother' (Steedman 1986: 2).

These stories, then, serve to critique the psychoanalytic focus on sexual difference in the construction of subjectivity. Freud's story of Dora misses its economic implications, and Steedman endorses the little watercress girl's definition of herself in terms of labour rather than sexuality. Nevertheless, it is the marginalized story of working-class *femininity* that is Steedman's concern, and in the stories above narratives of sexual difference structure as well as being subverted by those of class. When Steedman writes that a 'little girl's body, its neat containment, seems much more like that of a man than it does that of a woman, especially if she does not really know what lies between his legs' (1986: 94), she both describes her childhood identification with her father across the boundary of sexual difference, and signals the impossibility of that identification. Like Walkerdine, too, Steedman presents her childhood subjectivity as structured through the narratives and metaphors of the fairy tale. Finally, too, this *is* a psychoanalytic case study, 'as full as Dora's of gaps, contradictions, repetitions, and revisions that interrupt and interlard the exposition' (Abel 1990: 197). Since psychoanalysis, in Jacqueline Rose's words, is 'one of the few places in our culture where it is recognised as more than a fact of individual pathology that most women do not painlessly slip into their roles as women, if indeed they do at all' (1986: 91), Steedman cannot do without it in presenting her story of a subjectivity constructed on the boundaries of class and sexual difference.

Linda Williams (1990: 270) has described psychoanalysis as 'an unavoidable partial explanation' in feminist cultural analysis. For theorists like Jacqueline Rose, its importance is much more central than that. Because it *starts* from the question of sexual difference and insists on the intractability of the unconscious, it cannot be dispensed with by a feminist politics and cultural analysis. Its problem – and perhaps its strength – for a feminist cultural studies, as Rose acknowledges, is its incompatibility with a fully social and historical account of the subject in culture. In the chapters to follow, psychoanalysis – or at least 'the feminist rereading of Lacan's rereading of Freud' (Donald 1991: 2) will constantly recur as an 'unavoidable partial explanation', even when, as in the 'ethnographic' studies which I shall consider in the next chapter, the focus is most firmly on social experience and 'lived cultural forms'.

Notes

1. See the discussion by Ella Shohat and Robert Stam of Freud's appropriation of colonial discourse to describe his investigations of female sexuality, in *Unthinking Eurocentrism* (1994: 148–51). The quotation is from Freud's *Studies on Hysteria*. See also Mary Ann Doane's discussion of the trope of the dark continent in 'Dark Continents: Epistemologies of Racial and Sexual Difference in Psychoanalysis and the Cinema' in her *Femmes Fatales* (1991: 209–48).

2. See also Cora Kaplan's comments in her discussion of Kate Millett's *Sexual Politics*. Mitchell, she argues, 'poses the contradiction between patriarchy and capitalism as a loophole through which feminism can view the creation of the feminine unconscious, but like big Alice with her eye to the keyhole there's not much she can do about it'. If, as Mitchell argues, patriarchal psychic structures 'are not the thin voile of false consciousness, but rather the very flesh and blood of female subjectivity', then it becomes impossible to see how they can be thrown off in the way Mitchell envisages (Kaplan 1986a: 23).

3. See Gallop (1982: 7–13). As Gallop points out, Mitchell apologizes for her omission of the discussion of language, arguing rather oddly that the issue of language 'really amounts to the whole framework and thrust' of Lacan's theory, but that her 'inexcusable' omission can be excused only 'by the inexhaustible number of other omissions' (Mitchell 1975: 397).

4. See for example Freud's discussion in his (1931) essay 'Female Sexuality', where he writes that the effect of the castration complex in the female is that she 'acknowledges the fact of her castration, and with it, too, the superiority of the male and her own inferiority; but she rebels against this unwelcome state of affairs'. This can result in a 'masculinity complex'. He adds in a note that it is 'quite natural' that feminists should reject this explanation, since they will 'refuse to accept a view which appears to contradict their eagerly coveted equality with men' (1977: 376–7). The implication is that feminism is itself a manifestation of the masculinity complex.

5. A very similar argument is made by Cora Kaplan, who argues that to work from a position which accepts the instability of female subjectivity, rather than from one which claims 'a feminist psyche in control of femininity', leads in her view to 'a more optimistic political scenario', one which 'can and ought to lead to a politics that will no longer overvalue control, rationality and individual power, and which, instead, tries to understand human desire, struggle and agency as they are mobilized through a more complicated, less finished and less heroic psychic schema' (Kaplan 1986c: 227).

6. Modleski's article 'The Search for Tomorrow in Today's Soap Operas', first published in 1979, was reworked for her 1984 book, *Loving with a Vengeance*. Since there are differences between the two versions, however, I shall quote from both.

7. Elizabeth Lyon's article, 'The Cinema of Lol V. Stein, which drew on this essay, appeared in *Camera Obscura* in 1980. Elizabeth Cowie's 'Fantasia', which sought to bring together 'fantasy as a political problem, psychoanalysis' specific conceptualisation of fantasy, and the film as a particular site of the representation of fantasy' (1984: 71), was published in 1984, having first been presented as a paper in 1982, at one of a series of workshops in London called 'Re-opening the Case: Feminism and Psychoanalysis'.

8. In Walkerdine's account of the six-year-old Eliana Porta's 'watching' of the video of *Annie*, we learn that Eliana and her friend continue to play throughout the screening of the film, apparently ignoring it apart from one comment made by Eliana (1997: 114–19).

9. See Sarup (1992: 122) on Lacan's view of the Oedipus complex: 'The child submits to the Law of the Father. The paternal figure serves to separate the child from an all-encompassing relation with the mother. The father intervenes into this imaginary dyad and represents the Law. The Father embodies the power of the phallus and the threat of castration. ... The phallus is the pivotal term around which the social production of both sexes is oriented.'

|5|

Ethnographic Turns

In recent accounts of the 'ethnographic turn' in post-1970 cultural and media studies,[1] an agreed history emerges. It begins with Stuart Hall's development of the 'encoding/decoding' model, presented initially in his 1973 stencilled paper, 'Encoding and Decoding in the Television Discourse' and then, in edited form, in the 1980 CCCS collection, *Culture, Media, Language*. The model is then tested out, principally by David Morley in his 1980 study of *The 'Nationwide' Audience*. It is a model that is concerned to contest and partially incorporate a number of competing paradigms for the understanding of the reading/reception process. In the 1973 paper, Hall's model is clearly pitched against traditional 'mass communication' research paradigms based on empirical, quantitative methods such as content analysis or audience effects surveys. This opposition is picked up in the first and most influential of such histories, David Morley's introduction to *The 'Nationwide' Audience* (1980a). Broadly speaking, argues Morley, 'mass communication' research can be characterized as a series of oscillations between, on the one hand, 'message-based studies, which moved from an analysis of the content of messages to their "effects" on audiences; and, on the other, audience-based studies, which focused on the social characteristics, environment and, subsequently, "needs" which audiences derived from, or brought to, the "message" ' (1980a: 2). Both types of study assume a 'transmission' model of the communication process: the 'sender' originates the message, which is then transmitted and 'received' by the audience member. Both conceive of 'effects' as *behavioural* effects on *individuals*. Neither has a concept of the media *text* as itself a complex structuring of meaning.

What the Hall–Morley model proposes instead is that:

1) The production of a meaningful message in the TV discourse is always problematic 'work'. The same event can be encoded in more than one way. . . . 2) The message in social communication is always

complex in structure and form. It always contains more than one potential 'reading'. Messages propose and prefer certain readings over others, but they can never become wholly closed around one reading. They remain polysemic. 3) The activity of 'getting meaning' from the message is also a problematic practice, however transparent and 'natural' it may seem. Messages encoded one way can always be read in a different way. (Morley 1980a: 10)

Texts, then, are multi-layered and multi-referential, but their meanings are 'structured in dominance', with 'preferred' readings inscribed within the text. The model, as Stuart Hall later said, 'reflects the beginnings of structuralism and semiotics and their impact on cultural studies' (1994: 254). The text is seen as a complex structure of meanings, containing a multiplicity of codes or discourses. But the model is also concerned to reject the dominant context within which those theoretical approaches had been developed in Britain. That context was film theory, in which structuralist and semiotic approaches had been combined with psychoanalytic theories of the subject.

Thus whilst *The 'Nationwide' Audience*, like Hall's 'Encoding/Decoding' paper, begins by positioning itself against 'mainstream mass communications research', Morley's chapter 'Texts, Readers, Subjects', also published in 1980, opens with an attack on film theory. The 'dominant theoretical position' advanced by the film studies journal *Screen* is, argues Morley, too universalist and determinist. In focusing on the ways in which texts position us as subjects and construct our subjectivities, it forgets that when we encounter texts we are *already* positioned socially and historically. Our readings are made from those social/historical positions, and they will vary accordingly (1980b: 163). Morley's own standpoint insists on 'the centrality of the question of structural determination' – on the way in which texts position us ideologically – but at the same time asserts the range of readings which can be made by audience sections placed differently within the social formation. The relation between text and audience, he argues, is one which can only be studied empirically (1980a: 161–2).

It is a matter, then, of balancing structure with agency. In a 1994 interview, Stuart Hall referred the issue back to arguments with and within Marxism. It is Marx's '1857 Introduction', argues Hall, which, 'carefully read', provides the basis for a model of 'what I call "articulation," an understanding of the circuits of capital as an articulation of the moments of production, with the moments of consumption, with the moments of realization, with the moments of reproduction' (1994: 255). It is a matter too of bringing together the 'two paradigms' of cultural studies outlined by Hall in 1980: culturalism and structuralism (Hall 1986). Raymond Williams' focus on experience and on culture as a whole way of life was to be combined with Louis Althusser's structuralist interpretation of ideology. The solution to the difficulty of this enterprise lay in the appropriation of

Antonio Gramsci's concept of hegemony. Hegemony – Gramsci's term for the process by which dominant social groups exert leadership not by force but through ideological struggle and mastery – is, argues Hall, 'never a permanent state of affairs and never uncontested'. Unlike Althusser's 'dominant ideology' with its emphasis on the determining power of ideological *structures*, hegemony suggests rather 'the (temporary) mastery of a particular theatre of struggle'. As a matter of 'the dispositions of contending forces in a field of struggle', it is always open to contestation from below (Hall 1980a: 36).

The problems inherent in this coupling of structuralism and culturalism are freely acknowledged by Hall. The two concepts are, he admits, fundamentally antagonistic, the one asserting the determining power of ideological structures in the shaping of our sense of 'lived' experience, the other insisting that experience itself provides the grounds for cultural expression and social change. Nevertheless, argues Hall, although the two concepts 'hold out no promise of an easy synthesis', it is the space – and the relationship – between them that defines the field of cultural studies. And it is Gramsci's concept of hegemony which offers the greatest promise in holding the two together in an 'articulated unity', and which thus 'comes closest to meeting the requirements of the field of study' (1986: 48).

It is this rather uneasy formulation which David Morley incorporates as his research model in *The 'Nationwide' Audience*. One consequence is that, despite the insistence by both Hall and Morley on a number of determinate 'moments' in the communicative process, each with its own form of hegemonic struggle over meaning, the 'struggle' we actually find described is that between text and audience. The text, as in the film studies model, takes on the function of (ideologically/psychoanalytically) determining *structure*, whilst the audience – potentially resistant, bringing to the text specific histories and experiences – carries the weight of the emphasis on community and 'everyday life' found within culturalism. For Virginia Nightingale, surveying what she calls the 'cultural studies audience experiment', this means that the research remains in essence textually focused. Whilst it might explore structured *inequalities* in audience positioning, it is never able to account for a *diversity* of audience readings (Nightingale 1996: 49).

For Nightingale this limitation is a result of Hall's failure, in his writings of 1980, fully to engage with the explanatory opportunities offered by the work of Michel Foucault. For Foucault, as we have seen (Chapter 4), power does not operate simply through the imposition of repressive structures. It *produces* discourse within and across a range of power networks, and in so doing produces also a range of (potentially contradictory) subject positions that we inhabit. Such a framework would offer a way of theorising diversity and difference in reading positions,[2] but for Stuart Hall in 1980, Foucault's refusal to engage with issues of structural determination and state power makes his work finally less than useful for a politically engaged cultural studies. Despite David Morley's own moves in the direction of discourse theory as a way of understanding the range of often contradictory readings made by his research subjects, his work of 1980 follows Hall in aligning these discursive positionings with class structures.[3] Although in his later study, *Family Television* (1986), Morley was to move away from this emphasis on class towards gender as the principal differentiating factor in patterns of television viewing, interestingly this also marked a shift away from a focus on the text as a structuring principle in the construction of meanings. It did not, as it might have done, signal a greater engagement with those approaches, developed primarily within film studies and influenced by psychoanalytic theory, which placed the *gendered* subject at their centre. Morley's concern in this later study is no longer with 'the pattern of differential audience "readings" of particular programme materials', but focuses instead on 'the analysis of the domestic viewing context itself' (1986: 14). It thus – and despite Morley's own acknowledgement of feminist research – permits an emphasis on gender as a structuring principle of power within the *family* whilst leaving class as the overall structuring principle within *society*. Morley was, he says, 'aiming to lay the groundwork for the development of a set of culturally differentiated "appreciation indexes", that would accommodate the varied patterns of taste and response as between different sub-sectors of the audience' (1986: 50). Once engagement with the text is removed/bracketed out as a relationship through which meanings and pleasures are constructed, we are no longer talking about the construction of gendered subjectivities – simply about the ways in which, as already gendered audience members, our viewing preferences might differ.[4] Gender becomes a 'sub-sector' of the experiential *context* of viewing, rather than a central structuring principle of the viewing relationship. It is, as Elspeth Probyn comments, an aspect of 'the realm to be studied', from which the researcher can properly distance himself.[5]

Feminist 'Ethnography'

Culturalism, as we have seen (Chapter 3), offered a very inadequate theorizing of women's history and experience. The work on subcultures at the Birmingham CCCS which grew out of this approach, as Angela McRobbie and Jenny Garber noted (1976: 209), was equally marked by the absence of girls and women from its central concerns. When we turn, then, to the paragraph outlining feminist interest in 'ethnographic' research methods in the Introduction to the 'Ethnography' section of the 1980 collection, *Culture, Media, Language*, we find a rather different account from that of Morley and others outlined above. What is emphasized here is the importance of women's experience as the mainspring for theory, in a research project in which women are both object and subject of research. Whereas 'the available Marxist theories', it argues, 'could not account for the specificity of female experience – its oppressed form often first recorded in an ethnographic moment – it was necessary to return to experience and the subjective plane both to record and to substantiate this reality as a firm critique of available theory and to find materials towards the preliminary construction of alternative and more adequate theories' (Grimshaw *et al.* 1980: 75). The process is aligned with the 'consciousness-raising' undertaken by Women's Liberation groups of the 1970s.

The 1980 'Introduction' is careful to differentiate the cultural studies use of the term 'ethnography' to describe 'qualitative' research into ' "lived" cultural forms' from the definition of ethnography to be found within anthropology. The latter, according to Marcus and Fischer, sees ethnography as:

A research process in which the anthropologist closely observes, records, and engages in the daily life of another culture – an experience labelled as the fieldwork method – and then writes accounts of this culture, emphasising descriptive detail. These accounts are the primary form in which fieldwork procedures, the other culture, and the ethnographer's personal and theoretical reflections are accessible to professionals and other readerships. (1986: 18)

Nevertheless, ethnographic techniques, as Beverley Skeggs points out, pose quite specific problems for a feminist analysis. Writing about the production of categories of class and gender within nineteenth-century social science, she argues that it was through the development of research techniques such as ethnography that such 'scientific' discourses were established. The ethnographic observations upon which they were based, which were concerned to mark the rationality of the middle-class researcher through the classification of his 'others', focused predominantly on women. It was working-class women and people of other races whose 'degeneracy', observed and classified, could best indicate the distance travelled by the rational man along the path of progress. Thus '[o]bservation *and* interpretation of the sexual behaviour of working-class women on the basis of their appearance was central to the production of middle-class conceptualizations' (1997: 4–5). For Skeggs, then, the researcher is *always* implicated in the ethnographic research process. Like Valerie Walkerdine (see Chapter 4), she argues that, whatever the claims to objectivity of the resulting categorizations, they are inevitably imbued – whether admitted or not – with the fantasies and projections of the (middle-class) researcher.

It is this recognition which has marked feminist 'ethnographic' research. Experience, as the 1980 'Introduction to Ethnography at the Centre' noted, has been central in the development of feminist theory – experience not as observed but as both productive of theory and, as Teresa de Lauretis writes, as marker of the 'subjective limits' and 'discursive boundaries' of that theory (1986: 5). This is an argument also made by Annette Kuhn. Writing of the difficulties that the category of experience poses for the film and cultural theorist, she argues:

Emotion and memory bring into play a category with which film theory – and cultural theory more generally – are ill equipped to deal: experience. Indeed they have been wary of making any attempt to tackle it, and quite rightly so. For experience is not infrequently played as the trump card of authenticity, the last word of personal truth, forestalling all further discussion, let alone analysis. Nevertheless, experience is undeniably a key category of everyday knowledge, structuring people's lives in important ways. So, just as I know perfectly well that the whole idea is a fiction and a lure, part of me also 'knows' that my experience – my memories, my feelings – are important because these things make me what I am, make me different from everyone else. Must they be consigned to a compartment separate from the part of me that thinks and analyses? Can the idea of experience not be taken on board – if with a degree of caution – by cultural theory, rather than simply being evaded or, worse, consigned to the domain of sentimentality and nostalgia? (1995a: 28)

Kuhn is writing here in the context of producing her own 'memory texts'. Such 'memory work', she argues, gives us a way of understanding not only how texts work but also 'how we use films and other images and representations to make our selves, how we construct our own histories through memory, even how we position ourselves within wider, more public histories' (1995a: 39).[6] Such exploration is also the work of the feminist 'ethnographer', for whom the value of ethnography lies not in the categorization of 'others' but in the construction of a 'rhetorical space' in which the experiences and discourses of women can be both legitimated and explored (Skeggs 1997: 38).

Angela McRobbie's 'The Politics of Feminist Research: Between Talk, Text and Action' (1982) outlines the terms and the issues for such research. The meeting of feminism and ethnography, she writes, has been by no means unproblematic. She describes the way in which in her own early research she sought to fit her findings into the class framework dominant within cultural studies: 'I felt that somehow my "data" was refusing to do what I thought it should do. Being working-class meant little or nothing to these girls – but being a *girl* over-determined their every moment.' It is only, she feels, within an understanding of how 'relations of power and powerlessness permeated the girls' lives – in the context of school, authority, language, job opportunities, the family, the community and sexuality' that issues of class might begin to be rethought. No such account can be objective: *representations* of the lives and understandings of others are always *interpretations*, partial truths. But feminism 'forces us to locate our own autobiographies and our experience inside the questions we might want to ask', so that on the one hand we must recognize the 'resources and capacities of "ordinary" women and girls who occupy a different cultural and political space from us – by virtue of *age, class, race* and *culture* – to participate in their own struggles as women but quite autonomously'; on the other hand, we can empower their voices by articulating and translating them, using feminist research 'as a weapon of political struggle' (1991c: 61–79).

Feminist Audience Research

Feminist 'ethnographic' audience research had from its beginnings, therefore, rather different preoccupations from those outlined by David Morley. Dorothy Hobson's (1982) *'Crossroads': The Drama of a Soap Opera* was the first of such studies. Hobson's study of the Midlands-based soap opera began as part of a research project developed within the conceptual framework of the 'encoding/decoding' model. It was concerned to link 'the understanding of the production process of specific episodes or programmes with the audience reception and understanding of those same episodes or programmes' (1982: 107). Hobson interviewed production staff and watched with viewers, following such observation with a (transcribed) unstructured interview. Thus she writes of her experience of viewing with a young mother: 'I became part of the shared experience of viewing in that situation and I struggled to concentrate against the same odds. . . . The three year old invited me to help her eat her tea, the five year old to look at drawings from play school and talk about new shoes . . .' (1982: 112–3). As a result, her view of the text–viewer relationship underwent a considerable shift. She found that her subjects watched the programme in a 'distracted' fashion whilst simultaneously completing household tasks, often relying on the dialogue alone for information since they were not free to watch the screen. She also found that the women refused in their discussions to isolate the individual episode as an object of analysis, but instead ranged backwards and forwards over the serial as a whole, drawing on knowledge and experience both of the serial itself and of their social positioning as women in order to produce their interpretations. Their 'readings' were made through reference to their own experiences and understandings as women. For this female audience, then, soap opera viewing became a space within which to negotiate their own subjectivities and positioning as women. For the mainly male directors and producers of *Crossroads*, however, the programme was 'appalling', 'abysmal', 'tacky', an insult to their professionalism for which they felt only contempt (1982: 156–71). Hobson sees these opposing views as a 'clash of cultures' (1982: 169), in which a dominant, elitist, 'rational' and masculine set of cultural values is pitched against the subordinate values of women's experience and pleasure. As a result, Hobson takes Hall's 'determinate moments' and splits them apart. Like Hall she argues that a television programme 'is a three part development – the production process, the programme, and the understanding of that programme by the audience or consumer'. But for her it is the moment of viewing that is the point at which meaning is constructed.

There is no question of a 'dominant' or 'preferred meaning': the audience transforms and so *produces* the text. Thus to 'try to say what *Crossroads* means to its audience is impossible for there is no single *Crossroads*, there are as many different *Crossroads* as there are viewers' (1982: 136).

Such a position privileges the moment of viewing with its grounding in experience, but in subordinating the voice of the researcher to that of her subjects it avoids two important issues. The first is the ideological effectivity of the text. As Charlotte Brunsdon objects, '[t]he fact that the text is only and always realized in historically and contextually situated practices of reading does not demand that we collapse these categories into each other' (1989: 126). The text remains a text and thus an object for analysis. The second concerns the precise relationship of the researcher and her theoretical/analytical discourse to the women whose readings and context of reading she explores. Simply to celebrate these readings is not to 'return to experience and the subjective plane' in order to 'find materials towards the preliminary construction of alternative and more adequate theories', as the 'Introduction to Ethnography at the Centre' proposed. It is, whatever its status as a *political* act, to evade the issue of the differences between the discourse and interpretations of the researcher and those of the 'ordinary women' whose voices she transcribes and interprets.

Janice Radway's (1984) study of romantic fiction and its readers in the US, *Reading the Romance*, tackles this issue rather differently. Radway studied a 'community' of women romance readers in a Midwestern town which she called Smithton, using a combination of questionnaires, observation, and group and individual interviews to obtain her material. The group was loosely organized around Radway's contact, Dot, who worked in a bookstore selling romantic fiction and who, through her production of a regular review newsletter, had become the focal point for a group of women who relied on her judgement in choosing their romance reading material. Taking as her starting point the women's characterization of the 'ideal romance', Radway also analysed the genre's structural and ideological features, and the 'unconscious needs that underpin and reinforce the more conscious motives . . . that prompt [the readers] to seek out the romantic fantasy' (1987: 120).

Radway's analysis splits the meaning of the romance text, and therefore its meaning for its readers, from the meaning of the act of reading itself. Her analysis of the 'ideal romance' sees it as representing women's felt needs for nurturing and relationship in a patriarchal culture which systematically represses men's capacity to nurture, whilst at the same time it offers the promise that these needs can in fact be fulfilled within the heterosexual relationship. From an initial state of isolation and loss (the loss of her relationship with her mother), the romance heroine journeys towards 'the promise of a mature, fulfilled, female identity' through her relationship with the hero (1987: 135). Initially 'a man incapable of expressing emotions or of admitting dependence', the hero must be transformed via 'the combination

of her womanly sensuality and mothering capacities' into a figure possessing both 'masculine power' and a quasi-maternal sensitivity to the heroine's
emotional needs (1987: 127). For Radway, the romance's initial scenario of
unfulfilled heroine and emotionally repressed hero signals women's dissatisfaction with gendered relationships as constructed within patriarchy. 'All
popular romantic fiction', she writes, 'originates in the failure of patriarchal
culture to satisfy its female members' (1987: 151). But its 'magical solution'
produces a reaffirmation of patriarchy:

> Because the romance finally leaves unchallenged the male right to the
> public spheres of work, politics, and power, because it refurbishes the
> institution of marriage by suggesting how it might be viewed contin-
> uously as a courtship, because it represents real female needs within
> the story and then depicts their satisfaction by traditional hetero-
> sexual relations, the romance avoids questioning the institutionalized
> basis of patriarchal control over women even as it serves as a locus of
> protest against some of its emotional consequences. (1987: 217)

The 'act of reading' is given a rather different significance, however.
Radway's readers saw romance reading as a 'declaration of independence'
(1987: 7), a carving out of 'a solitary space within an arena where their self-
interest is usually identified with the interests of others and where they are
defined as a public resource to be mined at will by the family' (1987: 211).
In indulging their own 'private pleasure', they refused the demands of
husband and children and claimed, at least vicariously, the right to the
nurturance which the story's heroine discovers in heterosexual romance.
They also insisted on the independence and assertiveness of the romance
heroine, arguing that they themselves were strengthened by identification
with such qualities. The distance between Radway's own textual analysis
and the women's readings leads her to conclude that the meaning of the
event of reading should be analytically separated from the meaning
produced within the reading relationship. Whilst the first might constitute
an 'oppositional act', the second disarms that impulse since it 'supplies
vicariously those very needs and requirements that might otherwise be
formulated as demands in the real world and lead to the potential restruc-
turing of sexual relations' (1987: 213).

Although Radway's 1987 Introduction to the British edition of *Reading
the Romance* seeks to align its conclusions with those of Dorothy Hobson,
in fact they have a very different emphasis, as her 1986 essay, 'Identifying
Ideological Seams' makes even clearer. Whereas Hobson's use of ethnography to align the voice of the researcher in defence of those of her subjects
leads her to argue that meaning is not intrinsic to the text but is produced
by viewers, Radway frames her understanding of the 'oppositional impulse'
of reading within an overall emphasis on the ideological power of the text.
'Although in restoring a woman's depleted sense of self romance reading
may constitute tacit recognition that the current arrangement of the sexes is

not ideal for her emotional well-being,' she argues, 'it does nothing to alter a woman's social situation' (1987: 212). The task of the feminist researcher is to understand 'how romance readers understand their reading and the context that gives it meaning' in order to 'show how that view of the activity structures and orders a situation which we think those readers might benefit from seeing differently' (1986: 106). Although the preface to her 1986 essay suggests that the 'patriarchal surface' of the romance may conceal a 'womanly subtext' visible to its readers, so that the women become sophisticated readers rather than dupes of the texts, and although she argues that such readings can constitute 'a common ground between ideological positions where feminist critics and female audiences may come together to transform the social and material relations that affect women's lives' (1986: 93), such a meeting, it seems, can be achieved only through a transformation of the understandings of romance readers. They, it is clear, remain positioned within the 'false consciousness' of patriarchal ideology; the feminist researcher 'can stand elsewhere' (1986: 106–7).

For Radway, then, experience is a suspect category.[7] When in the 1987 Introduction to the British edition of *Reading the Romance* she seeks to position herself and her own history *within* the research process, she is, as she confesses, uncomfortable with the 'personal' tone of this writing. Nevertheless, she confronts – at times uneasily – two issues central within any feminist cultural studies. The first is that of the construction of female subjectivity within patriarchal culture. Using the 'object relations' theory of Nancy Chodorow,[8] she argues that as a result of a family structure which assigns the nurturing role to women, male subjectivity is constructed through separation and difference, whilst female subjectivity is constructed always as a 'self-in-relation'. This construction, however, must be challenged and changed. We must be able, she argues, 'to identify the seams, as it were, those points of intersection between the discourse and practices that together constitute individual subjects (including ourselves) in particular ways and address the needs produced as a consequence of that constitution' (1987: 110). Despite her attempt to 'stand elsewhere', therefore, here and elsewhere Radway does identify herself as woman – if not as theorist – with the women whose readings she researches. 'If I have demonstrated anything in *Reading the Romance*', she writes, 'I hope it is that women everywhere do indeed use the myth of the romance to think through their condition' (1987: 117).

The second and related issue is the place of fantasy in the construction of subjectivity and material social relations. Radway cites Valerie Walkerdine in arguing that a 'rewritten romance' must 'imagine new ways to construct female subjectivity . . . but it must also address the question of how such fantasies are used to address and then repress conflict within real social relations' (1987: 117). For Walkerdine, the complex fantasy structures of popular culture are an 'arena of struggle' over subjectivity, but they do not constitute an arena that is separable from the social. Nor do they constitute an arena from which the researcher can remain aloof. We have, she argues, 'to engage with the production of ourselves as subjects in and through our insertion into such cultural practices' (1984: 165). For Radway, however, 'real social relations' *are* separable from fantasy structures, whose function is to accommodate their readers to the 'hierarchy of control' within patriarchy. As woman, the researcher may find herself implicated in their myth-making, but as feminist ethnographer whose aim is to 'understand better the connection between world views, ideology, and relationships of power' (1986: 105), she must stand outside them.

Unlike Hobson, then, Radway does not align the position of 'feminist theorist' with that of 'female reader'. Instead the latter, despite the oppositional impulse which prompts her reading, is aligned with the textually inscribed reader/spectator. The feminist theorist reads and interprets both discourses. For Ien Ang, reviewing *Reading the Romance*, the 'recruitist' drive of Radway's feminist politics is summed up as: 'Radway, the researcher, is a feminist and *not* a romance fan, the Smithton women, the researched, are romance readers and *not* feminists' (1988: 183). The implicit point of contrast in the review is Ang's own 'ethnographic' study of Dutch viewers of the American prime-time soap opera, *Dallas*,[9] first published in 1982, and in its English edition in 1985. Unlike Radway's study, *Watching 'Dallas'* draws its material not from interviews, but from letters written in response to an advertisement placed in a women's magazine asking why readers liked or disliked the serial. But like Radway, she treats the responses as texts which should be read 'symptomatically', as themselves discourses which call upon 'socially available ideologies and images' in order to explain readers' experiences of pleasure and its contradictions. Like Radway, Ang seeks to theorize the difficult relationship between feminism, women and the text directed at a female audience.

For Virginia Nightingale 'the most important shift in Ang's research was from the focus on the "meaning" of the programme as popular culture to a focus on the "pleasures" experienced in viewing the programme – particularly feminine pleasures' (1996: 77). It is the absence of a discussion of 'the *pleasurableness* of the pleasure of romance reading' in Radway's book that Ang finds its most notable absence (1988: 185). Her own concern, she writes, is to present 'a framework within which *Dallas* could be taken seriously', by focusing on 'issues concerning pleasure and its vicissitudes, its relations with ideology and cultural politics' (1985: vii–viii). She is concerned to locate herself within the cultural studies framework outlined by Hall and Morley – indeed she sees her book as performing a 'pedagogic' function in introducing Dutch readers to such approaches. But at the same time her focus on the 'feminine pleasures' of *Dallas* necessarily places her analysis in a difficult, at times contradictory, position in relation to them.

Citing Morley, Ang argues that a text 'functions only if it is "read". . . . And this reading does not occur just anyhow. . . . A reader has to know specific codes and conventions in order to be able to have any grasp of what a text is about' (1985: 27). But in the case of *Dallas* fans, she argues, this shared reading position is not a matter of 'knowledge of the world, but a subjective experience of the world: a "structure of feeling"' (1985: 45). Ang, then, borrows the terminology of culturalism and Raymond Williams rather than the encoding/decoding model of Hall/Morley in order to account for the pleasures of the female viewers of *Dallas*. For Williams, as we saw (Chapter 3), an era's 'structure of feeling' represented the expression of its 'lived experience rather than its officially articulated beliefs' (1977: 131), an experience often felt as 'a certain kind of disturbance or unease, a particular type of tension' (1979: 168) because of its distance from official ideologies. Ang's use of the term, however, identifies it with a particular constituency of viewers, women, and a particular kind of 'structure of feeling', the tragic. The division 'knowledge of the world'/official ideology versus 'subjective experience'/(tragic) structure of feeling is thus one constructed along gender lines.

For the Hall/Morley class-based distinction between dominant, negotiated or oppositional reading positions, Ang substitutes an opposition between reading positions grounded in the 'ideology of mass culture' – the denigration of popular cultural forms found within 'official' discourses – and its opposite, 'the popular aesthetic'. The first is seen as equivalent to Hall's 'dominant ideology': viewers can 'negotiate' within its discursive space. The second is by implication, then, an 'oppositional' position. Ang draws for her definitions here upon the work of French sociologist Pierre Bourdieu. Bourdieu's *Distinction* (1979) is concerned to identify patterns of cultural 'taste' with class positioning. He argues that 'nothing more rigorously distinguishes' the dominant class from the working class than the former's 'disposition' towards 'the legitimate consumption of legitimate works, the aptitude for taking a specifically aesthetic point of view on objects already constituted aesthetically' (1986: 182). Such 'high culture' taste is clearly invested with social value: Bourdieu notes 'the very close relationship linking cultural practices (or the corresponding opinions) to educational capital (measured by qualifications) and, secondarily, to social origin' (1986: 165). Bourdieu therefore argues that we can speak of a 'cultural economy' as well as a financial economy. Both are fields of struggle organized hierarchically. In both the individual begins with certain endowments (financial or cultural capital) and competences, and proceeds to invest within these limits in the hope of profit. They are not simply separate, however. Cultural capital is convertible into economic capital via educational qualifications, and the 'legitimate' cultural judgements and tastes which thus mark out the educated middle classes 'fulfil a social function in legitimating social differences' (1984: 7) and thus preserving economic inequalities.

In opposition to 'the aesthetic disposition' of the dominant classes is 'the popular "aesthetic"'. In place of the disinterested and educated appreciation of form to be found in the appreciation of 'legitimate' culture, we find here the 'more direct, more immediate satisfactions' of popular culture with its emphasis on collective gatherings and spectacular delights – 'fabulous decors, glittering costumes, exciting music, lively action, enthusiastic actors' (1986: 178). Such 'vulgar' pleasure is of course the province of the working class, and as such low in cultural capital. When, by contrast, popular culture is appreciated by middle-class intellectuals, such appreciation is marked by a critical distance and emphasis on form which clearly signals its difference from the emotional responses of the 'vulgar'.

As forms of such popular entertainment, Bourdieu lists circus, melodrama, sporting spectacles, music hall and cinema. He identifies them, as we have seen, with a particular class fraction; his only reference to distinctions of *gender* is to note that since 'men are, *ex officio*, on the side of culture whereas women (like the working class) are cast on the side of nature', women are less likely to possess the 'aesthetic disposition' required for 'the legitimate consumption of legitimate works' (1986: 182). Ang, however, appropriates Bourdieu's categories for a gendered opposition. Those respondents who dislike *Dallas*, she writes, take their discursive stance from the dominant 'ideology of mass culture' in which ' "female" forms of "mass culture" such as soap opera and popular romances are the lowest of the low' (1985: 119). Like Bourdieu's 'aesthetic disposition', this is the assured discourse of 'legitimate' culture, characterized by intellectual distance, an affirmation of 'high-principled cultural values', and 'a consistent and elaborated "theory" on American television series' which sees them as undermining such values (1985: 93). Even viewers who like the programme often affirm this from a position within the 'ideology of mass culture', either by ironicizing their own responses or by seeking to find arguments for the programme's worth as 'serious' drama.

Viewers who counter the 'ideology of mass culture' with an emphasis on the *pleasures* of *Dallas* are positioned, argues Ang, within Bourdieu's 'popular aesthetic'. This, she writes, 'is based on an affirmation of the continuity of cultural forms and daily life, and on a deep-rooted desire for participation, and on emotional involvement. In other words, what matters for the popular aesthetic is the recognition of pleasure' (1985: 116). Pleasure 'eludes our rational consciousness'; it is a matter of emotion, of a 'structure of feeling'. Like Tania Modleski and Andreas Huyssen,[10] Ang argues that definitions of 'mass culture' have persistently identified it as a 'feminized' culture, whilst 'real', 'authentic', 'high' culture, with its accompanying aesthetic, moral and social judgements, is seen as the province of men.

It is women, then, who possess the 'cultural competence' to 'understand and evaluate *Dallas* in a melodramatic way' and thus obtain pleasure from the text (1985: 79). For Ang, here, the *structure* in this 'structure of feeling' is provided by the text. The 'tragic structure of feeling' is, she writes, 'inscribed in the meaning-system of *Dallas*', in its combination of melodramatic scenario – with its focus on intensity and excess – and the lack of narrative resolution, the endless deferral and delay, of soap opera. But this tragic structure of feeling 'will only make sense if one can and will project oneself into, i.e. recognize, a *melodramatic imagination*', and 'it is mainly women who are susceptible to the melodramatic imagination, a type of imagination which appears to express mainly a rather passive, fatalistic and individualistic reaction to a vague feeling of powerlessness and unease' (1985: 79–82). Women's pleasure is the pleasure of *recognition*, recognition of an emotional structure which 'is felt as "real" and which makes sense for these viewers' (1985: 87). Unlike the romance fiction which was the object of Radway's study, soap opera has no utopian 'happy ending': 'the problems in *Dallas* can never be solved and are essentially cyclical: the patriarchal status quo is non-viable but remains intact' (1985: 123). The pleasures it offers, therefore, are masochistic scenarios indulging feelings of fatalism and passivity.

Ang draws for her characterization of *Dallas* as 'melodramatic soap opera' on the accounts of melodrama produced within feminist film theory.[11] Like film melodrama, she argues, *Dallas* represents 'the eternal contradiction, the insolubility of inner conflicts, the unbridgeability as it were of the antithesis between pleasure principle and reality principle' (1985: 72). But the continuous narrative of *Dallas* imprisons its characters in a world of irresolvable contradictions, 'in which the area of the personal is all-prevailing, but in which at the same time all personal lives are perverted. For not a single individual in a soap opera is free to construct his or her own life history' (1985: 76). Like Janice Radway, then, Ang identifies women's pleasures in popular texts with specific textual structures and sees these structures as essentially masochistic. Unlike Radway, however, she is concerned *not* to see these pleasures as bound up in ideology. Whereas her account of dominant frameworks of understanding is of an *ideological* position (the ideology of mass culture), her analysis of the readings made by *Dallas* fans sidesteps the issue of ideology through its use of the terminology of 'structures of feeling' and their identification with Bourdieu's rather romanticized vision of 'the popular aesthetic'. Such terminology, as we have seen, implicitly locates popular pleasures on the side of the oppositional.

Ang is acutely aware of the contradictions which this poses for a feminist analysis. 'How', she asks, 'must the fact that so many women obviously get pleasure from watching soap opera be judged politically from a feminist perspective?' (1985: 118). Her concern to bridge the gap between the feminist researcher and the 'ordinary' woman by siting herself within the contradictions produced by being both, leads her to reject not only the political critiques of the ideological conservatism of soap opera made by some feminist critics, but also any feminist critiques of *Dallas* made by her respondents. Both, she argues, in refusing to engage with the issue of pleasure, succumb to the 'ideology of mass culture'. Nevertheless, she is unconvinced by arguments for the *ideological* progressiveness of soap opera; judged in these terms, she feels, its melodramatic structure can only be seen as reinforcing the patriarchal status quo. Her solution is to turn to theories of fantasy. Fantasy, she writes, is 'a dimension of subjectivity which is a source of pleasure *because* it puts "reality" in parentheses, because it constructs imaginary solutions for real contradictions which in their fictional simplicity and their simple fictionality step outside the tedious complexity of the existing social relations of dominance and subordination' (1985: 135). It is 'the place of excess, where the unimaginable can be imagined' (1988: 187). For feminists, as for other women, it can function 'by making life in the present pleasurable, or at least livable', but this does not preclude participation in radical political activity or a radical political consciousness (1985: 135).

Ang's solution is a way of retaining the concept of the text as structuring agent whilst refusing its effectivity in constructing the subjectivities of its viewers. The first of these positions aligns her both with Hall and Morley and with feminist film theorists writing about melodrama; the second argues for a greater complexity in the construction of subjectivity. It is nevertheless an uneasy solution. Ang recognizes that fantasy can not be divorced from the social. Feminism itself, she argues, is 'sustained by collective fantasies of a social future in which the oppression of women will have ceased to exist' (1985: 121). Within the sphere of cultural *production*, such fantasies and the fictions they inform are a site of feminist struggle, an intervention into the politics of representation. In arguing for the value of the 'pessimistic, sentimental or despairing' fantasies offered by *Dallas*, however, Ang finds herself insisting on fantasy's divorce from social and political reality at the level of cultural *consumption*. It is, she argues, 'the act of fantasizing itself' not the fantasy-content that is liberatory for the viewers of *Dallas*. 'In terms of *content*', she concludes, 'the fantasy positions and solutions brought about by the tragic structure of feeling and the melodramatic imagination' can only be judged as 'inclined to conservatism' (1985: 134–5). Despite her criticism of the 'recruitist' feminism of Janice Radway, therefore, Ang's conclusion is not as different as she suggests. Since the feminist researcher is engaged in cultural *production* and her subjects (and herself *as* subject) in cultural *consumption*, the distinction she makes serves to reinstate the hierarchical division between researcher and researched which is so problematic for the feminist ethnographer – and which Ang herself has been so concerned to refuse.

Discourse and Everyday Life

If Ang accuses Radway of a 'recruitist' conception of the politics of feminist research, her own analysis moves towards what Charlotte Brunsdon has called a 'redemptive reading' of popular culture. Such readings, argues Brunsdon, seek to counter 'both the left-pessimist despair over and the high-cultural dismissal of mass and popular cultures'. The 'redemptive reading' seeks to identify the 'progressive' potential of the popular text, although it is not simply celebratory of popular culture since it 'starts with an acceptance of the uncongenial politics of whatever cultural text' and 'then finds, at the least, incoherences and contradiction, and at the most fully articulated subtexts of revolt' (1989: 121). In the case of feminist research, such readings result from the attempt to bridge the gap between the feminist theorist and the 'ordinary' woman of the audience. But, argues Brunsdon, this move from the 'bad' text to the 'good' audience carries its own dangers. However motivated by a desire to defend women's pleasures, such readings can in effect 'eliminate the text as a meaningful category' (1989: 125). If it is the *act* of fantasizing rather than its content that carries resistive potential, as Ang suggests, then we risk abandoning the political pressure for a *different* content. As Brunsdon argues, '[t]he problem of working always with what people are, of necessity, watching, is that we don't really ever address that something else – what people might like to watch'. If feminism ceases to be, in Ang's term, 'recruitist', it may end by simply endorsing the range of texts currently on offer to women, thus 'reproduc[ing] and elaborat[ing] the dominant paradigm' (1989: 126). As Ellen Seiter *et al.* point out, 'there is nothing *inherently* progressive about pleasure' (1989: 5, my emphasis).

Mary Ellen Brown's study of *Soap Opera and Women's Talk* (1994) moves still further in the constituting of what Brunsdon calls 'the "good" audience'. Brown begins by locating her work within both the tradition of cultural studies audience research and a feminist cultural politics. Using the work of Hall and Morley, she argues that soap operas are hegemonic texts, designed to reinforce 'dominant conceptualizations of women', but caught up nevertheless in ideological struggle, as their female audiences appropriate them 'to critique these same values' (1994: 5). This critique she sees as effected by 'feminine discourse'. Much of women's pleasure in soap opera comes, she argues, through 'feminine discourse' or 'gossip':

> Their position in culture as a silenced majority has created for women individually and as a group an awareness of the pleasures of talk with other women. Some of their active pleasure comes simply from the freedom women have in all-women groups to say what they please without censure. The contrast between the freedom of all-women groups and the experience of not being heard or accepted can also bring up, for some women, reactive pleasures ['pleasures that come from an understanding that one's ideological positioning is problematic']. Likewise, the difficulties that women often have with expressing their ideas and feelings in 'man-made' language can mean that there is pleasure in simply seeing and hearing other women express their feelings. (1994: 18)

'Gossip', then, may be pleasurable as freedom from restraint on women's speech, as expression of feelings, and as a politicized consciousness-raising about women's oppression. There are parallels, writes Brown, between 'women's gossip networks that sometimes form around soap operas' and the small group consciousness-raising that took place in the 1970s Women's Movement (1994: 173). Soap operas actively encourage such gossip: they draw on women's discourses and are designed to be talked about, creating gaps 'where audiences fill in and mediate with pieces from their lives'. And, like gossip itself, they 'defy boundaries' since they are 'open-ended' texts which challenge 'the cultural dominance of systems that close off, limit, and contain meaning for women such as language or the classical Hollywood narrative with its definitive endings' (1994: 19).

Brown, however, focuses her discussion of the 'progressive' potential of the soap opera not on the soap opera text but on the text of the audience. The key concept in this shift is that of the 'tertiary text', a term taken from John Fiske (1987). The 'tertiary text' for Brown is 'the spoken text' produced when 'people talk about their lived experience in relation to what they have seen and heard on television' (1994: 13). It is through the production of *this* text that the female audience of the soap opera is able to activate the 'resistive' meanings available within the soap opera text itself. For Brown, then, the female audience of the soap opera is active in the production not only of pleasure or fantasy but, via communal discursive networks, of texts – texts which are both expressive and creative of a specific 'women's culture'. To explain this she draws, like Ang, on Bourdieu's concept of 'cultural capital'. The soap opera's position in discourse, she writes, 'marks its audience as having low social status' (1994: 114). Like romance fiction, it is regarded as *trash* by the dominant value system. Its fans, however, choose it – in defiance of these values – as their cultural capital, and in so doing constitute themselves as a site of opposition to dominant or official culture, operating a 'symbolic inversion' between high and low culture (1994: 150).

This inversion is a site of pleasure and of play for women, argues Brown, offering 'carnivalesque' laughter and parodic pleasure.[12] In offering a challenge from a marginalized group to 'the hierarchy of sites of discourse' (1994: 151), it also constitutes a potential site of political transformation. The women within such oral networks experience 'sociocultural empowerment' through the valuing of 'illegitimate' knowledge: 'Part of the pleasure women experience in groups of other women who share a knowledge of mutual subordination is in having clear boundaries – in having a cultural space from which to speak' (1994: 95). Paradoxically, then, 'the very devaluation of soap opera in dominant culture can protect the boundaries of women's culture' and provide 'important points of contact for women and women's politics' (1994: 109, 176).

These are large claims, and ones that seem problematic in a number of ways. Brown both shifts the analytic focus away from the television text and simultaneously reclaims that text for 'feminine discourse', equating the soap opera's *narrative* openness (in which the story is 'never-ending') with *ideological* challenge. Even more problematically, she elides the distance between feminist researcher and soap opera fan by appealing to an all-inclusive 'women's culture', a 'social infrastructure of exchange offering an alternative construction of reality' to that of dominant patriarchal culture (1994: 38–9). Thus 'women's culture' and 'feminist culture', 'feminine discourse' and feminist politics become the same thing, since 'gossip networks can be thought of as not only political but perhaps even subversive' (1994: 171). Such a formulation not only elides the difference between feminine and feminist but also ignores other sources of difference between women, differences such as class, ethnicity, age and cultural location. For Brown, then, the feminist researcher can be 'a member of the group, a fan, and also the researcher' (1994: xi) without any sense of contradiction. At the beginning of her study she cites Charlotte Brunsdon's (1993) categorization of the shifting conceptions within feminist television criticism of the relationship between the feminist critic and 'other women'. These categories, suggests Brunsdon, are: first, the 'transparent', in which the critic speaks *as* 'woman'; second, the hegemonic or 'recruitist' in which the feminist seeks to transform 'women' into feminists; and, third, the 'fragmented', in which the very concept of 'woman' becomes problematic, fractured as it is by so many differences (of class, ethnicity, culture), and the feminist's position correspondingly partial. For Brown, however, Brunsdon's third position is an unproblematic one. This feminist researcher is flexible, 'wandering on both sides of the boundary that separates fan from critic' and crossing 'boundaries between the separation of herself from other women and the alliance of herself with other women' (1994: 15–16). She is in fact, argues Brown, very like the soap opera fan herself: constantly moving between involvement and analysis; 1970s consciousness-raising is thus assimilated to 1990s soap opera viewing, as 'the content, style, flow, and narrative conventions of soap operas, by holding one in a complex relationship to the discourses of femininity, feminism and dominant culture', produce 'emancipation' for their female spectators (1994: 182).

Gendered Play

Ann Gray's *Video Playtime* (1992), by contrast, takes as its reference point not only the research methods established by feminist researchers within the Birmingham CCCS Women's Studies group of the late 1970s, but also the political and methodological issues raised within this work. Taking as its starting point the rapid take-up of the VCR as home entertainment across the social spectrum in the 1980s, her study is of how women use, and what they think about, this new piece of entertainment technology. Like the work of Dorothy Hobson, its emphasis is on the domestic context of viewing rather than on the texts that are viewed or the subject positions that these texts construct for their 'ideal' audience. But it is concerned also to insist that this context is a diverse one, constituted both by the different house-hold members who may be present and by the differing texts viewed. Each context, she argues, 'offers specific and distinct viewing experiences for the women in the study' (1992: 12). Her study, of 30 largely working-class women from Dewsbury, West Yorkshire, therefore 'straddles several previously separate areas of social and cultural research: the study of home-based leisure, television audience research, textual analysis and work on domestic technology' (1992: 3). Finally it is an exploration of the construction of gendered subjectivities within and across this complex matrix of constitutive elements.

Gray's method lies within the 'ethnographic' tradition of cultural studies research. It has, she writes – wary of the implications of the term – 'ethno-graphic intentions' (1992: 32). It is also positioned firmly within the tradition of feminist research, with all the complexities that this implies. Unlike Brown, Gray is acutely aware of the problems inherent in assuming too easy an identification with the women in her study. The researcher, she writes, 'has access to quite powerful institutions and intellectual capital' which distance her from the women she studies (1992: 34). At the same time, however, she is, like Brunsdon, critical of a 'fragmented' feminist (or post-feminist) position, which would assert that no commonalities between women can be assumed. The duality male/female may be a division constructed socially and culturally, she argues, but it has very real material consequences for the experiences and subjectivities of women: 'I would want to hold on to a category which enables not just differences to be revealed but also those profound and persistent commonalities which would seem to exist between women and which can form the basis of social critique' (1992: 31). Like Annette Kuhn, she writes 'as a woman who is an academic researcher and teacher' but whose own subjectivity 'bears the traces of past "investments" through which I became firmly positioned as a feminine subject'. There are both acute differences and shared positions, then, between herself as researcher and the women in her study. In her 'ethnography' of female subject positions, with their contradictions and coherences, Gray the researcher is firmly – if contradictorily – positioned as a woman (1992: 34).

Gray draws on both Janice Radway's use of the theoretical framework offered by Nancy Chodorow and Ien Ang's use of Pierre Bourdieu's analyti-cal categories to construct her own theoretical framework. She finds useful Chodorow's focus on the difference in 'relational capacities' of men and women, produced as a result of growing up in families where the nurturing role is assigned to women. The result, argues Chodorow, is that girls see their identity as bound up in relationships whilst boys have firmer ego-bound-aries: 'The basic feminine sense of self is connected to the world, the basic masculine sense of self is separate' (Chodorow 1978: 169). Chodorow, however, assumes a universalism for the family structures she describes, and thus comes close to an essentialist account of gendered differences. She also, argues Gray, assumes that 'the family' functions identically across social and cultural boundaries, and that its influence can be studied in isolation from that of other social and cultural institutions.

The work of Pierre Bourdieu, in contrast, examines the unequal distribution of 'cultural capital' across class differences, and the role which family and education play in this, but it does not, as we have seen, focus on gender as a primary determinant in the formation of cultural tastes and preferences. Gray's model combines the two in the following mapping:

middle class   *masculine*
bourgeois distance (Bourdieu)  separate self (Chodorow)

self-in-relation (Chodorow)   popular aesthetic (Bourdieu)
feminine   *working class*

Such a mapping, she argues, allows us to 'conceive of the constitution of the subject in terms of both class and gender'. Bourdieu's 'aesthetic disposition', she suggests, might be more readily attained by Chodorow's masculine 'separate self', whilst the 'popular aesthetic' appears more closely aligned to the feminine 'self-in-relation' (1992: 25). Most significantly, perhaps, this framework offers a way of thinking about the class/gender matrix in both social and psychic terms, as both social positioning and subjectivity in process.

Gray's subjects, then, followed the patterns of earlier studies (Hobson 1982, Morley 1986) in having less leisure time in the home than their male partners, in feeling guilty about 'taking time off' from domestic labour to read or watch television, in having less access to the 'mastery' of entertainment and information technology, in bowing to their male partner's viewing preferences in the context of shared viewing, and in accepting the culturally dominant valuation of 'male' genres above 'female' ones. In gendered terms, this produced the following set of oppositions in the women's descriptions of film and television genres (1992: 161):

'Male' genres	*'Female' genres*
Hard	Soft
Tough	Soppy
Real	Fantasy
Serious	Silly
Factual	Fictional

Evaluated in terms of hierarchies of cultural taste, however, the table of oppositions becomes:

Positive evaluation	*Negative evaluation*
Classics	popular
Quality	trash
Important	trivial
British	American

Gray found that women with less formal education used the first set of oppositions to distinguish their own from their partners' tastes, whereas women with higher education tended to use the second set of terms in order to align themselves with their male partners and distance themselves from a feminized 'low culture'. Despite this attempt at distancing and fear of becoming 'enmeshed' in the world of the 'female' text, however, for all the women in the sample, including those with higher education and in paid employment, '[b]eing able to relate to characters and identify with the emotions and situations in which they found themselves was crucial to enjoyment' (1992: 162). What Gray suggests is that both aspects of the Bourdieu/Chodorow matrix are operating here. Women with greater educational and cultural 'capital' seek to distance themselves from textual involvement by entering the 'space' created by public critical discourse with its emphasis on 'quality' programmes and films. Nevertheless, the 'relational' quality of women's textual identifications and sense of self was still expressed for these women through their need for emotional identification with the text.

Like Charlotte Brunsdon (1981),[13] then, Gray argues that the existence of 'women's genres' is a matter not of essentialized psychic difference, as some psychoanalytic theory might suggest, but of differing cultural competences and access to cultural capital. She also argues, however, that despite their access to a critical discourse focused on issues of 'quality', 'educated' women share modes of pleasure and identification with working-class women. For all women this produces contradictory subject positions, since all – including the working-class women – share the dominant cultural evaluation of 'women's genres' as being of a lower order than male-preferred genres. Such arguments link Gray's conclusions with those reached from within rather different research traditions by both Annette Kuhn and Charlotte Brunsdon. For Gray's description of the 'educated' female subject caught in the contradictions produced by her cultural and discursive positioning is also, of course, a description of the feminist 'ethnographic' researcher. She, too, is like Kuhn's 'scholarship girl', distanced but engaged, 'living on both sides of the us/them divide' (Kuhn 1995a: 100). Like Kuhn, then, Gray offers her own 'memory text' (Kuhn 1995a) as a way of indicating both the distance and the closeness of the 'very particular level of identification which I had with the women in my study' (1992: 34). Like Charlotte Brunsdon, too, she recognizes the pull towards a 'fragmented' position for the feminist researcher that is exerted by the recognition of such contradictions, but seeks to move beyond it. Her study reveals, she argues, that whilst gender 'rarely reveals itself in pure form, but . . . intersect[s] with other determinations' (1992: 31), it remains a central duality, not only in dominant discursive categorizations but also in the lived experience of women (and men).

Rethinking Class and Gender

In 1982 Angela McRobbie described her unease at having to fit her 'data' on the experiences of teenage girls into the class-based framework dominant within cultural studies. Her conclusion that '[b]eing working-class meant little or nothing to these girls – but being a *girl* over-determined their every moment' marked the direction of future feminist 'ethnographic' research. Later researchers like Ann Gray, as we have seen, have sought to return to issues of class as a determinant of subjectivity which intersects with that of gender. It is the work of Beverley Skeggs, however, which, in seeking to 'reinstate class in feminist (and) cultural theory' (1997: 2), most thoroughly picks up the challenge articulated by McRobbie in 1982: that it is only within an understanding of how 'relations of power and powerlessness permeate [women's] lives – in the context of school, authority, language, job opportunities, the family, the community and sexuality' that issues of class might begin to be rethought (McRobbie 1991c: 65).[14]

Skeggs' *Formations of Class and Gender* (1997) is based on her 11-year study of a group of (initially 11, later 83) working-class white women from the north-west of England, begun when all the women were taking courses in Community Care, Pre-Health Care or Pre-Social Care at a local further education college. Like the other studies examined in this chapter, therefore, it is 'ethnographic' research which seeks to explore 'the processes by which "real" women negotiate and understand them "selves"' (1997: 1). Skeggs describes it as, in part, a contribution to 'modernist ethnography' (Marcus 1992), defined as ethnography which concentrates not on communities but on 'the complex formation of identity across a range of sites in relation to wider global issues' (Skeggs 1995b: 192–3). Thus it analyses the attempts, over time, of 'a specific group of women to negotiate class, gender, hetero/sexuality, femininity, caring and feminism' (1997: 2). But it is also a critique of existing methodologies and theoretical frameworks, and a significant and self-reflexive contribution to feminist cultural theory.

Skeggs is critical of the assumptions underpinning traditional ethnographic research methods. Ethnographic studies of (working-class) women, like those of other culturally defined 'others', she argues, generated categorizations of these 'others' which affirmed the power and identity as rational subjects of those doing the categorizing. The 'objective' ethnographic investigative gaze is thus a middle-class gaze which, like other classificatory technologies, contributes to the production of discursive frameworks which 'enable, legitimate and map onto material inequalities' (1997: 5). Cultural studies ethnography, however, has a very different aim. It is, argues Skeggs, less a method than a methodology – that is, it combines particular methods in certain ways in order to serve purposes which are both theoretical and political. Its aim is to 'provide a space for the articulations and experiences of the marginalized' (1997: 23). Finally feminist theory, developed through the interaction of experience and interpretation, both shifts the focus of research by placing the experience of *women* at its centre, and radically questions both the concept of 'experience' and that of 'woman'. 'Experience' can no longer be thought of as either the possession of the unique individual or as the locus of 'truth' or 'authenticity' if we are to understand it, as feminism does, as a struggle over both material conditions and the meaning of those conditions. 'Woman', as Skeggs, like Gray, argues, is both a discursive and a lived category, but it is one which is 'classed and raced and produced through power relations and through struggle across different sites in space and time' (1997: 27).

Like other writers examined in this chapter, Skeggs draws in part for her theoretical framework on the work of Pierre Bourdieu. From being born into relations of gender, race and class, she argues, 'we occupy the associated social positions such as "woman", "Black", "working-class"' and the meanings associated with those positions (1997: 9). The interrelationship of these positions brings access to and/or limitations on the range of 'capitals' available to us. For the working-class women in Skeggs' study, femininity operates as a form of cultural capital, but in a society in which masculinity and whiteness are the valued (and normalized) forms of cultural capital, femininity brings little social, political or economic worth. It cannot be traded for reward in the labour market; it can merely be traded tactically, within the institutions of marriage and heterosexuality. For working-class women, its value rests in offering routes into respectability: to be respectable is to be feminine rather than sexual, and hence to 'avoid being positioned by the vulgar, pathological, tasteless and sexual' (1997: 100). Thus the women in Skeggs' study seek to convert their caring practices into educational capital via qualifications in order partly to increase their worth in the labour market, but more importantly to generate *some* value for themselves through respectable femininity.

If Skeggs' analysis draws on the work of Bourdieu, however, it also has roots in feminist cultural theorists from Charlotte Perkins Gilman onwards, as the account above indicates. Moreover, a Bourdieuian perspective, as Toril Moi argues (1991: 1036), offers theoretical flexibility, with its argument that 'gender is always a socially *variable* entity, one that carries different amounts of symbolic capital in different contexts', but it is a classificatory theory rooted in the social and material, in which the field of representation and discourse is merely 'the play of opposing images' (Bourdieu 1986: 165), with no explanatory or transformative power of its own (Butler 1999). For Skeggs, however, both class and femininity are bound up in representation, a matter not only of social positioning but of subjectivities which are produced and reproduced in relation to representational systems. Class, she writes, 'is a discursive, historically specific construction, a product of middle-class political consolidation, which includes elements of fantasy and projection' (1997: 5). Categories of class and gender limit and control our access to social and symbolic capital, but they are categories produced within discourse out of the fantasies and projections of the categorizors, and reproduced through representational systems. For those categorized, they operate as a 'structure of feeling' in which, for working-class women, 'doubt, anxiety and fear inform the production of subjectivity'. Skeggs, then, uses Raymond Williams' terminology as a way of characterizing the structured nature of working-class women's affective experience, but it is a use filtered through the work of Carolyn Steedman, Valerie Walkerdine and Annette Kuhn. Like Annette Kuhn, she argues that to be a working-class woman is to inhabit the constant fear of never having 'got it right' (1997: 6).

Skeggs' recentring of the issue of class within feminist cultural theory also owes much to the work of black feminist and post-colonial theorists. In the same way as Homi Bhabha (1983) argues that colonial stereotypes are products of 'colonial fantasy' which are nevertheless internalized by the colonized, and Patricia Hill Collins that representations of black women as 'stereotypical mammies, matriarchs, welfare recipients, and hot mommas' have acted as 'controlling images' in the regulation of black women's sense of identity (1990: 67), so Skeggs argues that textually mediated femininity acts as a regulatory device for the women in her study. Femininity, she argues, is an uninhabitable position: it signifies powerlessness and lack of agency. To seek fully to inhabit it would incur incalculable costs to subjectivity. But its *performance* signals respectability; to 'pass' as feminine – like 'passing' as white – is to refuse a classification ('working class') which would position the women as outside the norms of respectability – as 'vulgar, tarty, pathological and without value' (1997: 115).

Like other theorists of femininity, then (Doane 1982, 1991; Butler 1990), Skeggs sees it as masquerade, as an imitation without an original. But it is not a masquerade that allows the women in her study to 'play' ironically with identity and identification, as those theorists have suggested. This 'passing' 'wants to be taken seriously . . . because it speaks from a position of powerlessness and insecurity. In this sense their attempts to pass are not a form of insubordination; rather they are dissimulations, performances of a desire not to be, a desire not to be shamed but to be legitimated' (1997: 87). It is a position which is *not* inhabited as an identity – Skeggs' subjects 'did not recognize themselves addressed by the classed category of femininity' (1997: 116). It is also one whose performance is not felt to be necessary all the time, and one which brings pleasure – through shared practices of 'glamour' and dressing up – as well as anxiety, regulation and surveillance. But it is one that is lived, nevertheless. To 'pass' as feminine is to both appear and behave in certain ways, ways which involve not only the work of constructing one's appearance according to textually mediated ideals – ideals found in fashion images, magazines, advertising and other popular texts – but also bodily self-regulation. To the women in Skeggs' study, for whom femininity was at best a partially inhabited identity, disciplinary practices such as diet and exercise were viewed with some critical distance. Nevertheless, argues Skeggs, it is in the body that this sense of 'lack of fit' with ideals of femininity is experienced. Bodies, she writes, 'are the physical sites where the relations of class, gender, race, sexuality and age come together and are em-bodied and practised. . . . The texts of class, femininity, sexuality and race combine to produce a respectable body' (1997: 82, 84). For the working-class women in Skeggs' study, the body, like the image, is problematic. It must be invested in and regulated because 'letting oneself go' is a marker of non-respectability. But it remains 'the wrong size' for femininity, a source of constant anxiety about not quite 'getting it right'.

In the work of Skeggs, then, the 'ethnographic' research method is both rigorously applied and thoroughly interrogated. She describes her book as being 'about issues in feminist and cultural theory' (1997: 160), careful throughout to distinguish the two. If her reinstatement of class as a central issue for feminist ethnographers and theorists challenges earlier views of its marginality for female subjectivity, however, her conclusions also align her with feminist theorists writing from within very different research traditions. Like Denise Riley (see Chapter 2), she is acutely aware that the category 'woman' is an unstable and incoherent one, 'historically, discursively constructed, and always relative to other categories which themselves change' (Riley 1988: 1–2). Like the category 'working class', and intersecting with it, it is a category produced within the discourses of others and circulated within representational systems. Like Valerie Walkerdine, she argues that these representations include elements of fantasy and projection on the part of those constructing them, but that they nonetheless have structuring effects within the experiences and subjectivities of those positioned by them. The women in her research, she writes, 'are not the originators of their identities but are located in temporal processes of subjective construction. There are limitations on how they can *be*' (1997: 162). Their subjectivity, as Radway and Gray also argue, is not that of an autonomous subject but of a self-in-relation. Within the constraints of this 'structure of feeling', they deploy strategies in order to 'produce' themselves – as feminine, as respectable, as *not* working class – in ways which will maximize the cultural 'capital' available to them. For them, as for all of us, 'the category "woman" is lived and intimately experienced as a form of subjectivity inhabited through other categories' (1997: 166).

The Politics of Interpretation

Finally, then, Skeggs re-emphasizes the importance of the category of experience for feminist theory. But, like Probyn (1993), de Lauretis (1986) and Kuhn (1995a), she argues that the concept must be rethought. It is neither 'true' nor 'authentic', but productive of and produced by representation, discourse and subjectivity. This is, of course, as true of the feminist researcher as it is of the subjects of her research. Her understandings too correspond to the 'subjective limits' (de Lauretis 1986: 5) produced by her own specific history. Skeggs is acutely conscious of the twin temptations of the ethnographic researcher: either to produce her research subjects as objects of her (superior) knowledge, or to refuse to recognize the difference of her own experience and discursive positioning in seeking to claim 'rhetorical space' for them. Instead she insists that since experience 'is at once always already an interpretation and in need of interpretation' (1995a: 17), the researcher is inevitably also engaged in this process. She interprets the experiences and understandings of her subjects according to the (academic and political) frameworks of interpretation available to her. In so doing she, like other producers of 'legitimate' discourse, is engaged in a process of representation which is bound up in power relations. What differentiates her representations from those of the 'classing gaze' of traditional ethnography, however, is her own implication in the experiences and understandings she represents, and the self-reflexivity and sense of positionality which this generates. Like the other writers examined in this chapter, Skeggs offers her own 'memory text', in which she describes the sense of disjuncture she felt as she gained access to academic discourse: 'I felt caught in two worlds: one which theorized increased movement, access and playfulness and another which was regulated, circumscribed, denied and criminalized' (1997: 15). Feminist knowledge, the product of 'female-embodied, situated subjects who are part of a specific, emergent, conflictual history' (1995a: 7), must somehow bridge these worlds. Like all forms of knowledge, its representations are political, inserted into the network of power relations which positions all discourses. But representations, as feminist ethnography has shown, can 'play a key role in shifting the limits of our understandings' (1995b: 203), and the feminist theorist deploys hers strategically. As Ien Ang, writing about the politics of audience 'ethnography', argues:

> it is in the dialectic between the empirical and the theoretical, between experience and explanation, that forms of knowledge, that is interpretations, are constructed. Here then the thoroughly political nature of any research manifests itself. What is at stake is a *politics of interpretation*: "to advance an interpretation is to insert it into a network of power relations."[15] . . . audience ethnographies are undertaken because the relation between television and viewers is an empirical *question*. But the empirical is not the privileged domain of the *answers* . . . Answers (temporary ones, to be sure) are to be constructed, in the form of interpretations. (Ang 1989: 105–6)

Notes

1. The phrase is from Shaun Moores (1993). See also David Morley (1980a, 1989) and Graeme Turner (1990). This history also appears in feminist accounts of audience studies such as Gray (1992) and Brown (1994).

2. As we have seen in the work of Valerie Walkerdine (Chapter 4), it also permits an alignment of discourse theory and other theories of the subject such as those contributed by psychoanalysis. Nightingale argues that Hall's 'two paradigms' model of cultural studies also rendered 'out of bounds' the 'alternative rallying point' of 'Lacanian psychoanalysis (and its associated feminist and aesthetic developments)' (1996: 42).

3. In 'Texts, Readers, Subjects', David Morley's contribution to the 1980 CCCS collection, *Culture, Media, Language,* he offers the following comment: 'We deal here exclusively with the question of the reduction of discourses to classes. But it must be remembered that other structures and relations – for example, those of gender and patriarchal relations, which are not reducible to economic class – will also have a structuring effect on the distribution of discourses.' The comment is offered in parenthesis, however, and is not pursued.

4. Morley is careful to align the gendered viewing positions of his research subjects with differentiated positions of power within the family. In those families where the woman, by virtue of greater educational or earning power, was in a more dominant position, her viewing preferences matched more closely those of her male partner. See also Gray (1992) for an exploration of this issue.

5. See Elspeth Probyn's discussion of this issue in Chapter 1 of *Sexing the Self* (1993). In Morley's approach, she argues, ' "social differences" allow for an "experiential context" which is where "texts" are "read". This experiential context is then the result of "already constituted social differences" and as such it is an effect of the social. This sense of "experience" is, however, located in the realm to be studied, as the critic looks on' (1993: 26). Probyn argues for a more complex understanding of experience as always incorporated within theorising, since it is the 'enunciative position' from which the critic/theorist speaks.

6. As Kuhn points out, the 'culturalism' of Richard Hoggart and Raymond Williams also had its basis in 'memory texts', and Kuhn writes of her sense of recognition on first reading Hoggart's *Uses of Literacy*: 'I saw that it spoke in some way from inside its subject matter: Hoggart could name my experience not because his was the same as mine (it clearly was not) but because we shared a common stance in relation to it' (1995a: 99–100). It could be objected, however, that for Hoggart such experiences provide the basis for an assumed shared theoretical understanding – what he calls 'a wisdom derived from an inner, felt discrimination' (1958: 339) – rather than for an investigation of negotiated subjectivities.

7. She cites approvingly Terry Eagleton's (1978) criticism of Raymond Williams' use of the term, though she is concerned to add: 'Nonetheless, it seems equally true that particular people with particular consciousnesses inhabit the world'. Apparently dissatisfied with this formulation, she adds: 'What such an apparently simple-minded assertion means is that it is real, living individuals who make up communities, participate in social practices, and know them in specific ways.' Despite this concern to value the experience and understandings of these 'very real people', however, 'our' task is still seen to be one of convincing them 'to see how their situation intersects with our own and why it will be fruitful for them to see it as we do' (1986: 106–7).

8. Chodorow's (1978) *The Reproduction of Mothering* is an analysis of 'the reproduction of mothering as a central and constituting element in the social organization and reproduction of gender' (Chodorow 1978: 7). For Chodorow, the Oedipal journeys which Freud describes are indeed accurate descriptions, but they are not, as psychoanalysis assumes, the result of universal psychic processes. They are rather the result of a particular social organization which produces a division between the 'private, domestic world of women and the public, social world of men' (1978: 174). Because it is women who mother, the

first role identification for children of both genders is with their mothers. For girls, therefore, maturity means a continuity of identification. The girl's identification with her mother is established through the mother's *presence* and is unbroken, which means that 'women's sense of self is continuous with others' (1978: 207). A boy's identity, however, is established through separation and difference, and his identification with the father is based on the father's *absence*. None of this, however, is, according to Chodorow, immutable. It is rather the product of 'social structurally induced psychological processes' (1978: 7).

9. *Watching 'Dallas': Soap Opera and the Melodramatic Imagination* (1985).
10. See Modleski, 'Femininity as Mas(s)querade: a Feminist Approach to Mass Culture' (1986), and Huyssen, 'Mass Culture as Woman' (1988).
11. See particularly Laura Mulvey's 'Notes on Sirk and Melodrama' (1977). Ang, however, does not employ the psychoanalytic framework that underpins Mulvey's analysis. She therefore sees women's pleasure in melodrama as a matter of 'cultural competence' rather than of unconscious identification.
12. Brown is drawing here on Mikhail Bakhtin's concept of popular carnival as a space outside everyday power structures, in which social hierarchies are temporarily overturned in an atmosphere of laughter and play to produce 'a world inside out' (Bakhtin 1965: 11).
13. Writing about the soap opera *Crossroads,* Brunsdon argues that 'feminine' genres such as soap opera and the 'woman's film' are so designated because they both call on and practise 'the culturally constructed skills of femininity – sensitivity, perception, intuition and the necessary privileging of the concerns of the personal life' (1981: 36). Although these skills 'are not *natural* attributes of femininity', it is more likely 'under present cultural and political arrangements . . . that female viewers will possess this repertoire of both sexual and maternal femininities' (1981: 36).
14. In her 1995 chapter, 'Theorising, Ethics and Representation in Feminist Ethnography', Skeggs explicitly takes issue with McRobbie's 1982 rejection of class as a useful analytical category on the grounds that the concept was not used by the girls in her study. Researcher and researched, she argues, have access to different discursive resources so that the researcher can and must use concepts which the researched do not 'speak'. The subjects of her own research, she argues, also rarely spoke of class, but they articulated a knowledge of the limitations it imposes through their use of 'discourses of economic limitation and cultural choice' (1995b: 201).
15. Ang is quoting here from Mary Louise Pratt, 'Interpretive Strategies/Strategic Interpretations' (1986).

|6|

Identity Shopping: Women and Consumer Culture

[Woman is] the priestess of the temple of consumption . . . (Gilman 1998: 60)

Like a primitive culture which sacrificed little girls to its tribal gods, we sacrifice our girls to the feminine mystique, grooming them ever more efficiently through the sexual sell to become consumers of the things to whose profitable sale our nation is dedicated. (Friedan 1965: 203)

The society we know, our own culture, is based upon the exchange of women. . . . The economy – in both the narrow and the broad sense – that is in place in our societies thus requires that women lend themselves to alienation in consumption, and to exchanges in which they do not participate, and that men be exempt from being used and circulated like commodities. (Irigaray 1985: 170–2)

The connection between women and clothes surfaces often in these pages, . . . and it was with the image of a New Look coat that, in 1950, I made my first attempt to understand and symbolize the content of my mother's desire. (Steedman 1986: 24)

Women and Consumption

As the above quotations make clear, women's relationship to consumption and to consumer culture has been a central issue in feminist cultural theory. Women have so often been identified with consumption, and in particular with *mass* consumption, so often therefore positioned as that *against which* terms of positive value – 'production', 'authenticity', 'individuality', 'rationality' – can be defined, that understanding this relationship, and the way in which it has been defined by male theorists, has been crucial in understanding women's relationship to (Western capitalist) culture as a whole. But, as the quotations also make clear, the terms of this understanding are both complex and shifting. For Charlotte Perkins Gilman, writing in 1898, woman, excluded from the public sphere of production and culture ('true industry and true art'), and confined to the private sphere of domesticity and personal adornment, becomes not only truly a *consumer*[1] – a 'limitless demander of things to use up' – but also complicit in 'the creation and careful maintenance of this false market': its 'priestess' (1998: 60). For Betty Friedan in 1963, woman is more straightforwardly victim of the 'sexual sell', but she is also symptom of a society whose cultural values have become distorted, and in the use of 'we' ('we sacrifice our girls') Friedan betrays some unease: perhaps *women,* just as Gilman suggests, are participants in the sacrifice of *girls.* For both writers, the cultural power of consumption is signalled in the religious metaphor: it is a 'primitive' religion, outside rationality and with more than a hint of the unspeakable in its rites.

Luce Irigaray, writing in 1977, shifts the terms of the discussion. Quoting Lévi-Strauss and adapting Marx, she argues that the key to understanding woman's relationship to consumer culture is her status not as consumer but as commodity. For Gilman, too, 'He is the market, the demand. She is the supply' (1998: 43–4), but Irigaray goes further in arguing that women are given all the attributes of commodities in a capitalist/patriarchal order: 'the standardization of women according to proper names that determine their equivalences; a tendency to accumulate wealth, that is, a tendency for the representatives of the most "proper" names – the leaders – to capitalize more women than the others; a progression of the social work of the symbolic toward greater and greater abstraction; and so forth'. Women, then, become *fabrications,* 'disinvested of [the] body and reclothed in a form that makes [them] suitable for exchange among men', fetish-objects invested, like religious fetishes, with the fantasized characteristics of masculine desire, but without access to desire of their own (1985: 173, 180). But Irigaray also suggests a strategy of resistance to this process, a strategy located within the processes of consumption themselves. This is the strategy of *mimicry.* 'One must assume', she writes, 'the feminine role deliberately. Which means already to convert a form of subordination into an affirmation, and thus to begin to thwart it. . . . It also means "to unveil" the fact that, if women are such good mimics, it is because they are not simply resorbed in this function. *They also remain elsewhere*' (1985: 76, original emphasis).[2]

Finally, Carolyn Steedman's (1986) comment draws attention to some rather different aspects of women's relation to consumption, and to its ambiguities. Fashion's New Look, launched by Christian Dior in 1947, introduced, in Elizabeth Wilson's words (1985: 43), 'a full-blown romantic nostalgia into the austerity of the post-war world', with its 'nipped in' waist and full skirt that, in Steedman's words, 'took twenty yards of cloth' to make. For Steedman's working-class mother it represented her desire 'for things to be *really* fair, for a full skirt that took twenty yards of cloth, for a half-timbered cottage in the country, for the prince who did not come' (1986: 47). It was a desire which was outside any conventional political framework or understanding of class but was identified rather with the fantasy of the fairy tale, in which 'the cut and fall of a skirt and good leather shoes can take you across the river and to the other side' – to marry a prince (1986: 16). But this desire could be identified neither simply with consumption nor solely with fantasy: it was also a matter of work. A weaver's daughter, Steedman's mother always worked. Her 'coat and lipstick came from her own work' (1986: 37), but she also produced both the clothing and herself. The New Look skirt was to be made not bought. 'The post-war years were full of women longing for a full skirt and unable to make it', writes Steedman (1986: 32), surprising the reader with the final verb. Moreover, '[m]y mother did what the powerless, particularly powerless women, have done before, and do still; she worked on her body, the only bargaining power she ended up with, given the times and economic culture in which she grew' (1986: 141). For Steedman, then, women, particularly working-class women, are implicated in consumer culture in a range of contradictory ways: as commodified objects and signifiers in narratives of exchange; as consumers of both commodities and (masculine) fantasy; as objects of desire but also as desiring subjects; and as producers, both in the public sphere of work/employment, and through the privatized work whereby they produce themselves both as (fantasized) objects of another's desire and as subjects in a narrative of 'passing' and escape.[3]

As all of this makes clear, women have a different relationship to contemporary consumer culture from that of men, one which frequently places them outside the theoretical frameworks of male theorists. Women cannot be assumed to mobilize 'cultural capital' in the same way when, in Bourdieu's 'legitimate consumption of legitimate works' (1986: 182), they may themselves be that which is 'exchanged', 'invested in', 'fabricated', 'consumed'.[4] Moreover as *subjects* of exchange they have, as Celia Lury points out, been 'denied the opportunity to exchange their cultural capital as economic capital on the same terms as men' (1996: 154). If for women 'cultural capital', as Steedman suggests, often lies in the skills acquired in the 'work' of femininity, then these skills are little valued, even rendered invisible, since femininity is assumed to be 'natural'. Once visible, indeed, such skills become delegitimated, marking their possessor as 'vulgar, tarty, pathological and without value' (Skeggs 1997: 115). Equally, such 'investment' is not 'detachable', as 'investment' in career or 'work' identity is, from either a sense of sexed identity – identity *as female* – or from the body itself. Good girls, as every young woman knows, 'save themselves' within the markets of exchange; bad girls are 'cheap' (Ehrenreich *et al.* 1992: 94). Finally, then, if identity in consumer culture is increasingly envisaged as constructed through consumption, as style, for women such construction has both a longer history and a rather different meaning than for men. As

Carolyn Steedman argues, for women to 'step into the landscape and see ourselves' as *subjects,* we must also consider 'the *clothes* we wear there' (1986: 24), and this not only renders us image as well as subject but also positions us firmly *inside* the social and economic structures of exchange.

Style as Resistance

[S]tructuralism's main emphasis was on the specificity, the irreducibility, of the cultural. Culture no longer simply reflected other practices in the realm of ideas. It was itself a practice – a *signifying* practice – and had its own determinate product: meaning. (Hall 1980a: 30)

In Stuart Hall's 1980 account of the development of cultural studies at the Birmingham Centre for Contemporary Cultural Studies, the impact of the 'structuralisms' is seen as crucial in shifting the concept of culture nearer to that of ideology, envisaged as internally structured 'maps of meaning' whose codes and practices 'speak us' even as we speak and act (through) them. Roland Barthes' 'informal semiotics' of contemporary 'mass culture and its consumers' (Barthes 1985: 261), which included his 1967 study of 'the Fashion system', was a key influence, along with the structural anthropology of Lévi-Strauss. For Barthes, 'the Fashion system' could be analysed linguistically and semiotically, as structure and rhetoric, and as bearer of cultural stereotypes and myths[5] about women. Fashion, he writes, is both 'excessively serious' – having an educative function for young women – and 'excessively frivolous', and it is 'probable that the juxtaposition of the excessively serious and the excessively frivolous, which is the basis for the rhetoric of Fashion, merely reproduces, on the level of clothing, the mythic situation of Women in Western civilization, at once sublime and childlike' (1985: 242). Fashion's rhetoric works by substituting the signifier Woman for (real) women through the figure of the model or 'cover girl' whose 'body is no one's body, it is a pure form, which possesses no attribute . . ., and by a sort of tautology, it refers to the garment itself' (1985: 259). The garment, then, 'stands in for' the body of the model, which thus becomes for the woman reader of the fashion magazine 'simultaneously what the reader is' (wearer of the garment) 'and what she dreams of being' (the ideal represented by the model). This 'dreamed pleasure' has an ideological function: 'the woman's identity is . . . established, in the service of Man . . ., of Art, of Thought, but this submission is sublimated under the appearance of agreeable work and aestheticized' (1985: 252–3). The ideological positioning of woman can thus be analysed via the structures, codes and practices of 'the Fashion system'.

For Stuart Hall in 1980, however, the usefulness of structuralism for cultural studies was limited by the fact that 'it consistently down-played the notion of cultural contradiction and struggle' (1980a: 34). The cultural structures and practices that it analysed all served to support a *dominant* ideology, with which the lived experiences and value systems of the subordinate seemed irretrievably enmeshed and inevitably complicit. It was the work of Antonio Gramsci that for Hall, as we saw in Chapter 5, permitted a reconceptualization of the relationship of ideology to experience in which ideological domination is never fixed or given, but always contested, both at the level of the material (in class struggle), and at the level of the symbolic. Such struggle is always also, for Gramsci, *specific*, a matter of specific 'moments' and particular instances (1980a: 36). It was thus 'the complex relations between representations/ideological forms and the density or "creativity" of "lived" cultural forms' which the CCCS researchers set out to investigate (Grimshaw *et al.* 1980: 74).

For these researchers, then, 'mass' or 'consumer' culture was, as in Barthes' example of fashion, the *dominant* against which 'subcultural resistance' might be mobilized. The 1976 CCCS collection, *Resistance through Rituals*, edited by Hall and Tony Jefferson, articulates this view. Culture, write Clarke *et al.*, 'is the way the social relations of a group are structured and shaped: but it is also the way those shapes are experienced, understood and interpreted'. 'Dominant and subordinate classes', they continue, 'will each have distinct cultures. But when one culture gains ascendancy over the other, and when the subordinate culture *experiences* itself in terms prescribed by the dominant culture, then the dominant culture has also become the basis of a dominant ideology.' But this does not mean 'that there is only *one* set of ideas or cultural forms in a society. . . . Groups or classes which do not stand at the apex of power, nevertheless find ways of expressing or realizing in their culture their subordinate position and experiences' (1976: 11–12). The focus of the book is therefore on post-war youth subcultures as successive 'moments' in which such resistance is realized before being each in turn 'recuperated' by the dominant culture.

Youth subcultures are therefore specific; they are not simply manifestations of a generalized 'Youth Culture', the result of the post-war emergence of the 'teenage consumer'. Their 'deeper social, economic and cultural roots' (1976: 16) lie in class divisions. Youth subcultures, as Ken Gelder writes, were for the CCCS researchers 'always *working-class* youth subcultures' (Gelder and Thornton 1997: 84), their relationship to dominant culture mediated through the 'parent culture' of the urban working class, their 'resistance' not merely a matter of surface style and leisure consumption but an attempt to 'negotiate a meaningful intermediate space somewhere between the parent culture and the dominant ideology' (Hebdige 1979: 88) in the 'unsettled' class relations of post-war Britain. This 'space' was in one sense quite literal. Subcultures, write Clarke *et al.*, 'must be focussed around certain activities, values, certain uses of material artefacts, territorial spaces etc. which significantly differentiate them from the wider culture' (1976: 14). In this they manifest a continuity with older forms of working-class culture, though their appropriations of 'mass culture' styles also differentiate them from such forms. 'Much of working-class culture', writes John Clarke,

> has ... since the mid nineteenth century, taken shape around the sphere of leisure – football, the pub, working men's clubs, activities in the street, and so on. These are not simply institutions or even values expressed in particular activities, but forms of expression of the whole experience of the class. The rigours of work are not forgotten when the indulgences of leisure begin. But the 'relative freedom' of leisure has allowed a *displacement* of central class concerns and values, developed in work, to the symbolic activities of the leisure sphere. (1976: 176)

As this extract makes clear, both the working-class 'parent' culture and its subcultural offspring are seen as unremittingly masculine. The alternation of the 'rigours of work' with the 'indulgences of leisure' does not describe the rhythms of the working-class *woman's* existence, as Carolyn Steedman's account cited above demonstrates. Moreover, it is evident that the *real* site of 'class concerns and values' is 'work' or production, with leisure, or consumption, merely its displaced reflection. For the post-war youth subcultures to be seen as truly the heirs of this tradition of 'displaced' resistance, then, their activity too must be redefined as a form of displaced *work*. The subcultural stylist is therefore seen as a *bricoleur*, an active assembler and transformer ('re-*work*er') of objects/commodities appropriated ('stolen') from consumer culture so that they are resignified – made to carry oppositional and disruptive meanings. In this he is quite different from the 'ordinary' consumer of 'mass culture'.

It is not simply, then, that this early cultural studies account of resistance to 'mass' or 'consumer' culture has no space for female subcultural (or working-class) resistance. As Erica Carter writes, 'the analyses themselves are founded on a number of unspoken oppositions: conformity and resistance, harmony and rupture, passivity and activity, consumption and appropriation, femininity and masculinity' (1984: 186). Femininity, that is, is that against which resistance is defined. In this the CCCS researchers share some of the prejudices of the commentators on 'youth culture' whose views they attack. Clarke *et al.*, for example, criticize Paul Johnson's generalized condemnation of youth culture as characterized by '[h]uge faces, bloated with cheap confectionery and smeared with chain-store make-up, the open sagging mouths and glazed eyes, the hands mindlessly drumming in time to the music, the broken, stiletto heels, the shoddy, stereotyped, "with-it" clothes' (1976: 19), but without noting that this passive consumer is gendered *female*. Their own resistant subcultural *bricoleur* is by contrast male, defined in opposition to the feminized 'bustling commercial high streets, with their chain stores and supermarkets' (1976: 43) which mark the boundaries, and boundedness, of his territorial space. He is also contrasted with that other embodiment of 'youth culture', the member of the 1960s and 1970s 'counter-culture'. The counter-cultures that arose in 1960s America are, write Clarke *et al.*, quite different from working-class youth subcultures. Though *ideologically* oppositional, they arose *within* dominant middle-class culture and, with their emphasis on a 'swinging' lifestyle, should more properly be seen as *'profoundly adaptive'* to post-war capitalism with its need for 'a life increasingly focussed on consumption, pleasure and play' (1976: 64–5). Amongst these counter-cultures is to be counted the Women's Movement,[6] which Clarke *et al.* characterize as follows:

> As 'modern woman' undertook her 'long march' from *Woman's Own* to *Nova* and *Cosmopolitan* she passed from respectable homebody to bejewelled good-time-girl, swinger of the ad-trade, without pausing for so much as a nod at Mrs. Whitehouse on the way. Naturally, the older ethic was challenged, not in the name of a fuller liberation, but only in the name of those needs which could be satisfied by commodities. (1976: 64)

The subcultural appropriation of style as 're-working' is, then, contrasted with the 'inauthenticity' of the Women's Movement, whose 'opposition' remains within the feminized (and middle-class) sphere of consumption. Even in Dick Hebdige's (1979) *Subculture: the Meaning of Style*, which is far less inclined to measure subcultural style against notions of 'authenticity' and 'work', when issues of sexual identity are discussed it is via David Bowie's sexually ambiguous incarnations, and the conclusion reached is that although 'the Bowie-ites were certainly not grappling in any *direct* way with the familiar set of problems encountered on the shop floor and in the classroom', they were nevertheless 'attempting to negotiate a meaningful intermediate space somewhere between the parent culture and the dominant ideology: a space where an alternative identity could be discovered and expressed' (Hebdige 1979: 88). That is, gender stereotypes and sexual identity are 'really' to be understood in terms of class. Certainly, as Angela McRobbie and Jenny Garber note in their contribution to *Resistance through Rituals*, the 'feminising of the male image may in no way signal the complementary liberation of the female from the constraints of the female image' (1976: 215).

For McRobbie, the attempt to study the subcultural relationships of *girls* proved frustrating. Girls occupied no street 'territory' of their own, and although they could be seen as more active participants in some youth subcultures than in others,[7] their subcultural image, 'only a hair's breadth away from, on the one hand, the new sexuality of advertising and the modern fashion trade, on the other hand, the classic fetishism of the pornography trade', signalled renewed sexual subordination rather than liberation (McRobbie and Garber 1976: 216). The 'space' of *girls'* culture seemed to be located *within* both traditionally defined female spaces and the mass cultural forms against which masculine subcultures were seen to be constructed. These 'spaces', then, may be those of the bedroom or the school. Girls' 'resistance' occurs firstly via the performance of a sexualized femininity in opposition to the 'respectability' of school, and secondly through group solidarity in the construction of a fantasized world of romance in the face of the 'brutally sexist attitudes' (McRobbie 1978: 106) of their male peers. Thus the 'teeny-boppers' with whom Hebdige contrasts David Bowie's *subcultural* audience (Hebdige 1979: 60) *are* the girls studied by McRobbie.

It is clear, then, that not only do girls, in the words of McRobbie and Garber, negotiate 'a different space, offering a different type of resistance to what can at least in part be viewed as their sexual subordination' (1976: 221); their 'resistance' is also much more ambiguous. As McRobbie comments, the very strategies which serve as opposition to the middle-class ideology of 'respectable' femininity found within the school, also serve to lock working-class girls more firmly within a sexualized 'feminine culture' (1978: 108). As Erica Carter writes in her study of women and consumerism in 1950s West Germany, there is no 'authentic' female experience to be found beneath the 'façade' of femininity. Girls tend to 'live out the contradiction of their lives ... *within* a teenage consumer culture' (1984: 213).

Enemies of Glamour

For the male researchers of the CCCS, then, as for the critics of a generalized and untheorised 'Youth Culture' whom they attack, 'mass' or 'consumer' culture is a feminized culture of consumption and the only 'authentic' resistance is to be found in working-class male subcultures. For them, the Women's Movement, which began as part of a middle-class counter-culture marked by negation rather than resistance, becomes politicized only when it moves forwards into the (implicitly masculine) 'harder, sharper, more intense and prolonged politics of protest, activism, community action, libertarian struggle and, finally, convergence with working-class politics' (Clarke *et al.* 1976: 68).[8] For the feminists of the Women's Liberation Movement of the 1970s, by contrast, the feminine 'fashion and beauty' system of consumer culture was seen as the product of patriarchal ideology, an ideological and physical trap for women. Simone de Beauvoir had argued that '[t]he purpose of the fashions to which [woman] is enslaved is not to reveal her as an independent individual, but rather to offer her as prey to male desires; thus society is not seeking to further her projects but to thwart them' (1988: 543). 'Second wave' feminism, as we have seen, organized political demonstrations against beauty contests and attacked 'the cultural image of femininity' (Friedan 1965: 318). Adrienne Rich, for example, listed as one of eight characteristics of male power the power to 'confine [women] physically and prevent their movement' by means such as rape, sexual harassment, economic dependence, purdah, foot binding and 'high heels and "feminine" dress codes in fashion' (Rich 1986: 37). As Sandra Bartky argued in her critique of the 'fashion–beauty complex', 'Feminists are widely regarded as enemies of the family; we are seen as enemies of the stiletto heel and the beauty parlour, in a word, as enemies of glamour. Hostility on the part of some women to feminism may have its origin here' (1982: 137–8). Women's positioning within an ideology of consumption, like their confinement to domesticity and 'full-time mothering', was seen as part of their political oppression in the sphere of the personal.

For the feminist researchers of the CCCS, writing in *Women Take Issue* in 1978, the relationship of women to consumer culture was a difficult issue to tackle. Women's identification with consumption positioned them outside – even, as we have seen, in opposition to – the 'relations of production' which were central to the class analysis of the CCCS, yet such an exclusion renders women's oppression doubly invisible. First, it renders invisible the extent to which women have in fact worked outside the home and have suffered oppression in the workplace. Second, it offers no framework for the analysis of consumption as itself a site of women's ideological and material oppression and/or resistance. Much of the analysis of *Women Take Issue* is concerned, then, to emphasize women's *work*. 'Women "Inside and Outside" the Relations of Production' analyses women's socio-economic position in terms of 'the articulation between patriarchal relations and capitalist development' (Women's Studies Group 1978b: 48). Women's domestic labour, argue the authors, has to be understood in terms of 'the benefit to *capital* of the family as an *economic* unit. . . . Under capitalism, labour power is replenished and replaced in the sphere of private consumption, primarily within the family.' But the benefits to capital of woman's role as mother and wife are secured through the operations of *patriarchy*, through the functioning of a 'masculine hegemony' (1978b: 46–7). Woman is not only a buyer and a *consumer* of commodities in the domestic sphere, however; she is a *worker* there, transforming commodities into services and into items of consumption (meals or clothes, for example) for her family. Increasingly, she is also a wage earner. In the workplace as well as the home, however, women 'live within their femininity' (1978b: 65): in service occupations; using 'feminine' skills such as sewing or cooking; and in part-time and low-status work which is seen as supplementary to their domestic role. Finally, women work in occupations where 'female sexuality on display' is a part of the work itself. For secretaries, receptionists and 'boutique assistants' the commodification of their own sexuality is part of the job (1978b: 66). For these women, who are at once consumer, producer and commodity, their 'labour power' cannot be valued, 'owned' or 'sold' in any way that will separate it either from consumption or from their sense of self.

This understanding of the inseparability of consumption and work for women is developed further in Janice Winship's chapter on woman's magazines, 'A Woman's World: "Woman" – an Ideology of Femininity'. We need to explore, she argues, 'the processes by which femininity "manoevres" with and against masculine hegemony in its capitalist forms'. Femininity, continues Winship, 'is not merely a passive acceptance by women of patriarchal domination'; it represents what she calls, in a very ambiguous phrase, 'an *active subordination*' (1978: 134–5, original emphasis). The 'split' within capitalist society between production/consumption; work/leisure; work/personal life; work/everyday life is one which operates, she argues, only for men. It depends on a concept of the labourer who is a 'free' individual able to sell his labour – separable from himself – 'freely'. Women, however, live out the relations of capitalism 'through their femininity'. Consumption and work are interwoven; moreover, the 'individuality' which *women* are urged to acquire is one constructed through the consumption of commodities. Like housework, this 'work' is 'repetitious and invisible. . . . Unlike housework, however, you work at constructing *yourself* into the commodity men will "consume" '. Thus the 'achievement of individuality, through the narcissistic construction of *you*, the *particular* loved object, relies not on work at the point of production but on work at the point of consumption' (1978: 145–6). It is work, however, which is represented as pleasure/leisure, and the contradictions inherent in its aim – the construction of individuality *as dependence* – are masked through its setting within a framework of fantasy and romance.

'Work', then, is redefined in *Women Take Issue* to include 'work at the point of consumption'. The aim is to produce a more complex analysis of 'patriarchal and capitalist relations' (1978: 137), in which women are rendered visible and reconceptualized as active. Yet as Winship's uneasy phrase ('an *active subordination*') indicates, this activity has an ambiguous value, serving often to confirm women's subordination. For Jane Gaines, however, Angela McRobbie's contribution to *Women Take Issue*, 'Working Class Girls and the Culture of Femininity', points in a rather different direction. Quoting McRobbie's account of the ways in which teenage girls subvert the middle-class culture of school through a 'vulgar' assertion of sexuality, Gaines argues:

> What is significant here for feminist theory (and different from male subculture theory) is that the counter-ideology is produced with the most despised signs of 'femaleness' and the accoutrements of 'femininity.' Sexual maturation – the functioning of the body which most nearly escapes culture – is deployed to turn the body into an instrument of disruption. What better site for disruption of the social order than the seeming scene of the origin of women's oppression? (1990: 8–9)

Suggestive though this argument is, and however important this formulation for the development of feminist theories of cultural consumption and a feminist 'body politics' (see Chapter 7), its tone is rather different from the note on which McRobbie, in 1978, concludes her chapter. Working-class girls, she argues, are pushed by the attitudes of adolescent boys even 'further into compliance with the traditional female role [with] marriage [forced] upon them as the only legitimate channel for the exercise of their sexuality'. Thus the 'culture of adolescent girls can be seen as a response to the material limitations imposed on them as a result of their class position, but also as an index of, and response to their sexual oppression as women.' Working-class girls, she concludes, are 'both saved by and locked within the culture of femininity' (1978: 107–8).

Consumer Culture and Modernity

Janice Winship's description, quoted above, of the 'split' which has developed under capitalism between production/consumption; work/leisure; work/personal life; work/everyday life, draws attention to another reason why understanding the relationship of women to consumption has been so important. Theorizing consumption, and the development of consumer culture, has been central in the theorization of modernity as a whole.[9] 'Modernity', as Elizabeth Wilson notes (1985: 63), is an imprecise term, but one which remains useful in seeking to encapsulate both the social, cultural and economic changes identified with the process of industrialization in Western capitalist societies, and the subjective experience of those changes. It is a term identified particularly with the accelerated sense of change in the major cities of the Western world towards the end of the nineteenth and in the early decades of the twentieth century, changes producing a new sense of 'the complexity and danger, as well as the richness and excitement, of everyday life in the modern city' (Nava 1997: 56). Celia Lury cites four factors crucial in producing the focus on *consumption* that is such a central feature of this modern urban experience:

1. The importance of the circulation of *commodities*, that is, things appropriated or produced for exchange on the market within a capitalist division of labour.
2. *Changes in the interrelationship of different systems of production and consumption or regimes of value*, and the multiplication of relatively independent sites for the use of things. These changes are seen to have created a situation in which the activities of the users of commodities and other things are linked through a whole set of inter-related cycles of production and consumption, associated with, but not determined by, the industrial division of labour and economic exchange on the market.
3. The relative *independence of practices of consumption from those of production*, and the growing power and authority that this gives (at least some) consumers.

4. *The special importance given to the consumption or use of cultural objects or goods* in contemporary societies by specific social groups or cultural intermediaries. (Lury 1996: 4)

The growth in practices of consumption and their separation from processes of production are crucial, then, in the development of modernity. The precise place of *women* in this development is, however, less clear – as we can see if we examine recent debates about the figure of the *flâneur/flâneuse*, that archetypal occupant of the nineteenth-century city. The *flâneur* was the ironic, detached observer of the modern city, strolling through its crowded public spaces, watching and browsing but not inter-acting – in the words of Walter Benjamin, 'botanizing on the asphalt' (Benjamin 1973: 36). For Janet Wolff this figure is wholly masculine, his access to the pleasures of the street symbolizing the gendered divide of public/private space. The *flâneur*'s gaze, described by Benjamin as 'the gaze of modernity which is both covetous and exotic' (1970: 67), thus antici-pates the 'male gaze' identified by feminist film theorists as characteristic of cinema – itself a source of visual pleasure developed in the new leisure spaces of the city. It is not so much, argues Wolff, that women were debarred from the city streets. Working-class women, she points out, 'always, and necessarily, traversed the public sphere of work and the street', but 'the *ideology* of separate spheres and of women's proper place . . . operat[ed] to render invisible (or unrespectable) women who were in the street' (1995: 95). As the city developed, its public spaces of spectacle, leisure and consumption – the international exhibitions, galleries, museums and leisure gardens – constituted an urban experience gendered masculine. The *female* equivalent of the *flâneur* becomes, then, the prostitute, but she is a street-walker whose gaze, whatever irony and detachment it might possess, marks her as commodity as well as (worker and) consumer.

For Elizabeth Wilson the prostitute might indeed be seen as the '*flâneuse*' of the nineteenth-century city. Prostitution, she argues, 'became, in any case, a metaphor for the whole new regime of nineteenth-century urbanism . . . Prostitution comes to symbolize commodification, mass production and the rise of the masses, all of which phenomena are linked' (1992: 105). Yet, as Rachel Bowlby points out, when Walter Benjamin also uses the image of the prostitute, 'saleswoman and wares in one', as emblematic of the city, it is as a figure *available* to the *flâneur* – for consumption or contemplation – not as his like (Bowlby 1985: 10). The detached, ironic *flâneur* was an artist; he might view the pleasures of mass culture but he could never be absorbed by them (Lury 1993: 184–7). For women, however, the appeal of the new urban culture was more ambiguous. As Bowlby argues, it was 'above all to women that the new commerce made its appeal, urging and inviting them to procure its luxurious benefits and purchase sexually attrac-tive images for themselves. They were to become in a sense like prostitutes in their active, commodified self-display, and also to take on the role almost never theirs in actual prostitution: that of consumer' (1985: 11). It is, then, the figure of the shopper, particularly the strolling window-shopper, who is the nearest female equivalent to the *flâneur*, but in becoming thus a 'public woman' (Wilson 1992: 93), the female shopper is – like the prostitute – uneasily positioned between the roles of consumer and commodity. That woman is present, indeed crucial in the constitution of modernity and the modern city is clear, then. In the narratives of modernity, however, her place is an ambiguous one, sliding constantly into that of the *other* of modernity's rational, detached, male subject.

The Rise of Shopping

That it is the shopper, with her opportunities to observe and admire, to both look and be looked at, who can most be considered a *flâneuse,* is an argument made by Mica Nava, in her account of the rise of the city department store.[10] As both Bowlby and Nava point out, the department store can be dated from virtually the same moment (the 1850s) as the great exhibitions, part of the same expansion of public space and spectacle. Built as 'fantasy palaces', with 'open staircases and galleries, ornate iron work, huge areas of glass in domed roofs and display windows, mirrored and marble walls', the department stores drew on the conventions of theatre and exhibitions and were visited as tourist attractions (Nava 1997: 66). They were also the first public places other than churches that were considered respectable for the bourgeois lady to visit unaccompanied. But they were an ambiguous space, 'neither wholly a public nor quite a private realm' (Wilson 1985: 144). If, as Elizabeth Wilson suggests, the presence of women in the urban street represented a threat, a fear that 'every woman in the new, disordered world of the city . . . [might be] a public woman and thus a prostitute' (1992: 93), this fear was countered by rendering the department store a 'home from home'. Not only were they provided with restrooms and tearooms so that women could spend the day there, they were also organized, as Bowlby notes, like 'a large, well-ordered domestic establishment' (1987: 191), with shop assistants trained to behave like well-mannered domestic servants. Women, then, entered this public arena as consumers of the spectacle it offered, but their window-shopping was carried out in a space that seemed constantly to return them to the domestic. The 'fantasy world of escape from dull domesticity' became, as Bowlby writes, 'a second home', and the real home could in turn be re-envisaged as a 'fantasy place' as commodities were bought to enhance and transform it. Yet such fantasies, like the fantasies of the perfect body offered by the fashion model, also constituted a form of regulation, for what the displays of the department store offered was always a vision of the *proper* household and the *correct* attire (Bowlby 1985: 4; Wilson 1985: 150).

If the department store resembled the nineteenth-century bourgeois domestic establishment, it can also be seen to have structural similarities with the woman's magazine. The magazine, Hilary Radner argues, 'has numbered pages, hence a certain order, but it is architectured rather than narrativized – a house that readers walk through at will rather than a movie in front of which viewers sit captive' (1995: 133). But if the magazine, in its representation of the 'woman's world', constitutes that world on the lines of the domestic,[11] it can also be seen to construct its ideal reader on the model of a particular kind of shopper. Her 'distractable attention', writes Bowlby, 'as she flips from one page to another, is of the same type as that of the impulse buyer drifting round the shop' (1987: 190). Bowlby points out, in fact, that the Paris *Bon Marché* department store produced its own appointments diaries from 1880 onwards, diaries which not only marked the dates of 'key events' like religious festivals and *Bon Marché* special sales, but also contained articles and editorials along the lines of the woman's magazine. Between the department store, the domestic establishment and the woman's magazine, then, there is a structural homology; all serve to position woman in a specific, though contradictory way. She is the responsible (middle-class) domestic manager and the active creator of system from the lack of narrative order with which she is presented; she is the observer of saints' days and religious festivals. But she is at the same time – as in Barthes' account of fashion's construction of woman as 'at once sublime and childlike' – the frivolous and distractable impulse buyer, the childlike seeker and willing consumer of the trivial and new. Finally, the very absence of narrative ordering which presents to the reader/shopper the space for activity and autonomy in the construction of her own preferred order, also serves to position her more firmly within a predetermined framework. She may not 'sit captive' in front of the film narrative, but neither is she invited to see herself as the narrative's hero. Instead, like the reader who is invited to construct herself in the image of the magazine's 'cover star' through careful application of a range of specified products, the woman who browses through the contents of the magazine or store is invited to construct herself through the work of consumption. The polarities of her identity are pre-given, and in working within them she creates herself as feminine.

If the department store was a place where *women* shopped, whether sensibly, for the home, or as a frivolous form of leisure activity, then it was *men* who were seen as doing the selling. As Rachel Bowlby writes, 'On both counts – women's purchasing responsibilities and the availability of some of them for extra excursions into luxury – it follows that the organized efforts of "producers" to sell to "consumers" would to a large measure take the form of a masculine appeal to women'. Such a conception, she argues, 'readily fitted into the available ideological paradigm of a seduction of women by men, in which women would be addressed as yielding objects to the powerful male subject forming, and informing them of, their desires' (1985: 19–20). Elsewhere Bowlby provides examples of this from instructional manuals for sellers from the early years of the twentieth century. One such, *The Mind of the Buyer* (1921) by Harry Dexter Kitson, provides four paradigms for the act of selling: the religious conversion, the courtroom scene, the military campaign and the seduction. The last two frequently overlap, as indeed they do in both literary accounts of seduction and popular accounts of 'falling in love' ('Cupid's arrow', being 'smitten' and so on). Kitson's account of the 'psychological moment' of the sale itself conflates the two, as he likens it to the moment when 'the seducer feels that he may, without fear of rebuff, press his victim to take the first drink' (Kitson in Bowlby 1993: 108).

The Rational Consumer

'The lure of mass culture', writes Andreas Huyssen, 'has traditionally been described as the threat of losing oneself in dreams and delusions and of merely consuming rather than producing' (1986: 55). It is a position that has been gendered feminine, as both Huyssen and Fredric Jameson point out. Jameson comments that 'the conception of the mindless consumer, the ultimate commodified "false consciousness" of shopping-centre capitalism, is a conception of "otherness." . . . degraded consumption is assigned to women, to what used to be called "Mrs. American Housewife"' (Jameson 1983: 4). If we turn to contemporary consumer culture, however, it is clear that we are all addressed as consumers, whether we are being shoppers, savers, voters, patients, parents, students or citizens in any other role. The consumer-citizen thus invoked is not, however, the consumer described by Charlotte Perkins Gilman in 1898 as a 'limitless demander of things to use up', or the eroticized victim of Kitson's account, but rather a rational being, though one prone to temptation. Readers of *Which? The Independent Consumer Guide*, for example, will find themselves addressed in the following terms:

> When new cars hit the showroom, it's hard to form a proper judgement of how good they are. You're likely to be seduced by the new-car smell and the shiny paintwork. And the first road tests that appear in newspapers and magazines can be unduly influenced by the latest gadgets the cars have, or some new technological innovation. (*Which?* March 2000: 28)

Which?, however, promises to counter this threat of seduction by 'bring[ing] some objectivity to the issue'. And for today's would-be *flâneur* it offers:

> *Britain's Most Famous Sights Assessed.*
> Before you set out for a tourist attraction, check out what it has to offer, what it's going to cost – and whether it's worth the effort of getting there.

The Which? Guide to Tourist Attractions offers you independent
assessments of hundreds of Britain's most popular sights – from theme
parks and palaces to gardens, nature reserves, caves and historic ships
. . . (promotional leaflet in *Which?* May 2000)

Rachel Bowlby (1993) discusses these two rather different consumers. One,
she writes, 'is the consumer as dupe or victim or hedonist . . ., infinitely
manipulable and manipulated by the onslaughts of advertising'. The other
is 'the consumer as rational subject, calculating and efficient and aware of
his aims and wants' (1993: 98–9). The first is Huyssen's 'feminized' inhab-
itant of 'mass culture' or 'consumer society'. The second is the 'citizen-
consumer' who is the implied reader of the *Which?* magazine reports
quoted above, an individual seeking to make independent judgements,
though susceptible to seduction by a 'shiny' surface. He is a figure anticipated in the third of Kitson's paradigms cited above: that of the courtroom
scene. Here, unlike in Kitson's other paradigms, the buyer is persuaded by
evidence and arguments: 'As each bit of evidence is submitted, the judge
(buyer) must test it' (Kitson in Bowlby 1993: 103). That this rational individual is gendered masculine is clear from *Which?* magazine itself: in the
May 2000 issue, for example, eight out of ten of the reader 'case-studies'
featured in the magazine picture successful male customers; the two women
pictured are unhappy (unsuccessful) mobile phone users.

This 'resistant' or 'rational' consumer occupies a very different relationship to the commodity from that of his 'feminized' counterpart. Like the
members of youth subcultures described by the CCCS in the 1970s, he is
active, a taker of commodities for his own purposes. Bowlby quotes from
Marx in *Capital*:

Commodities cannot themselves go to market and perform exchanges
in their own right. We must, therefore, have recourse to their
guardians, who are the possessors of commodities. Commodities are
things, and therefore lack the power to resist man. If they are unwill-
ing, he can use force; in other words, he can take possession of them.*

* In the twelfth century, so renowned for its piety, very delicate
things often appear among these commodities. Thus a French poet of
the period enumerates among the commodities to be found at the fair
of Lendit, alongside clothing, shoes, leather, implements of cultivation, skins etc., also *femmes folles de leur corps.***

** Wanton women. (Marx in Bowlby 1985: 27)

The aggressor here is not the seller but the buyer/possessor, the imagery
used is that of seduction or rape, and women are literally among the
commodities to be forcibly possessed. It is on this that Luce Irigaray draws
when she argues that the key to understanding woman's relationship to
consumer culture is her status not as consumer but as commodity. Yet this
poses – at least superficially – a problem for analysis when we consider that

it is women, as we have seen above, who have principally been viewed as occupying the role of consumer. What we are being offered, in fact, is two quite different models of the consumer, models that are mapped on to ideological assumptions about masculinity and femininity. One is the possessor of an individualized subjectivity and capacity for agency; he actively pursues and takes possessions, as he actively pursues rational arguments. He may use these possessions to signal his identity, but his identity is not submerged in them. The other is passive and manipulated, linked emotionally rather than rationally to consumption; there is no clear distinction between her identity as subject and her position as object; she is herself both commodified and exchanged. Her identity is constructed from and by the commodities with which she is identified.

The position of the rational or resistant consumer is, however, a precarious one. Like the members of youth subcultures who are to be distinguished from the feminized 'mainstream' of youth culture, or the 'subcultural' Bowie-ites who are to be distinguished from mere 'teenybopper' fans, he threatens constantly to slip into his feminized 'other'. Bowlby cites Jean Baudrillard's comments on today's 'citizen of consumer society':

> One must guard against interpreting this massive enterprise for the production of artefact, 'make-up,' pseudo-objects, pseudo-events which invades our daily existence as a de-naturing or falsification of an authentic 'content.' It is in the form that everything has changed: everywhere there is substitution, instead and in place of the real, of a 'neo-real' produced entirely out of the elements of the codes. (Baudrillard, in Bowlby 1985: 29)

For Baudrillard, as for other theorists of the postmodern, the 'rational consumer' has disappeared, since there is no 'real' to exercise his judgement. In Baudrillard's vision of contemporary society, argues Rachel Bowlby, the consumer cannot be '(just) an active appropriator of objects for sale. His or her identity, the constitution of the self as a social subject, a "citizen of consumer society," depends on the acquisition of appropriate objects . . . all the appurtenances of a "lifestyle" that can be recognized by other members of the society'. There is thus, writes Bowlby, a clear sense in which this 'consumer citizen is not so much possessor of as possessed by the commodities which one must have to be made or make oneself in the form objectively guaranteed as that of a social individual' (1985: 28). For some feminist writers, such a vision of contemporary consumer society produces opportunities to escape the gendered polarities outlined above. Mica Nava, for example, argues that consumerism 'is far more than just economic activity: it is also about dreams and consolation, communication and confrontation, image and identity' (1992: 167); within its fantasies oppositions between buyer and seller, active and passive, subject and object, break down. Since this 'discourse' of consumerism is one in which women are expert, she writes, in 'making themselves' within it they can contest and disrupt dominant gendered oppositions.

Others are less sanguine, pointing out that the contemporary mirroring and identification of the self and the commodity remains – not least for Baudrillard, for whom it is a 'privileged' position[12] – a specifically feminine characteristic. Hilary Radner draws attention to the way in which women are invited to locate their identity and value in the commodity: we can think, for example, of the television ads for L'Oréal hair products in which a series of famous women at once claim the position of subject (the one who speaks) and value themselves in terms of the commodity, as they turn to us and say, 'L'Oréal – because I'm worth it'. She suggests then that this 'new position of privilege is one of contradiction; it depends not on the generation of new models of femininity but on a rereading of old models. The old model, the pre-feminist model, is retained, in fact reinvented, replacing the feminist model of a woman-centred culture that rejected a femininity grounded in patriarchy and consumerism' (1995: 64). Indeed, as Rachel Bowlby points out, as the shop window replaces the mirror for the female shopper, the image reflected back is that of herself as commodity.

To return finally then to the strategies of resistance to this commodification proposed by Luce Irigaray: if women are commodities, asks Irigaray, and hence unable to step outside the order of exchange, '[h]ow can such objects of use and transaction claim the right to speak and to participate in exchange in general?' (1985: 84). Her answer, as we have seen, is the strategy of masquerade or mimicry. In *performing* a commodified femininity – perhaps to excess – women might create a critical distance from their image, and thus reclaim it for their own use. As Mary Ann Doane writes, [t]he effectivity of masquerade lies precisely in its potential to manufacture a distance from the image, to generate a problematic within which the image is manipulable, producible, and readable by the woman' (1982: 87). Judith Butler (1990) goes further, arguing that since gendered identity is itself a kind of performance, rendered 'natural' to us only through regulated (and regulatory) acts of repetition, then an 'excessive' or parodic masquerade can open up to question the very issue of gendered identity itself.

Yet to return briefly to the work of Beverley Skeggs discussed in the last chapter, studies of the 'performance' of femininity by actual women suggest that we should be wary of such claims. For the working-class women of Skeggs' study, such masquerade is desperately serious, the product of 'a desire not to be shamed but to be legitimated' (1997: 87). For them, to 'perform' an 'excessive' femininity would be to place themselves on the side of the vulgar, the tarty, the pathological and the valueless (1997: 115). Femininity may be a matter of commodification and performance, but for women without access to other modes of self-empowerment – other forms of 'cultural capital' – it also confers legitimacy. Hilary Radner, discussing the double-edged nature of the concept of femininity as 'masquerade', points out that the discourses of women's magazines have themselves appropriated such a concept. She quotes from a 1987 article in *Vogue* magazine that asks, 'Is femininity merely a costume? Playing dress-up? A put-on? A female role in the right time of day or place, that's assumed at will?' (Radner 1995: 175). The answer given suggests that it is, but that such performance is both pleasurable and, paradoxically, somehow aligned with the natural – women, that is, have to learn to be feminine, but such learning is the achievement of a mature identity. The article goes on, quoting designer Donna Karan, 'All women are female; not every woman is feminine. Femininity is an act a woman takes on, a gesture, a specific kind of sensuality' (1995: 175). Radner's own conclusion returns us to the ambiguity of Janice Winship's phrase, when she argues that for women femininity represents 'an *active subordination*'. The reader of the woman's magazine, argues Radner, operates a sort of double subjectivity. Like the women of Skeggs' ethnographic study, she is both inside and outside the system of consumerism, complicit with it but in constant negotiation:

> She is that subject who represents herself for herself, but she is also another subject who consciously creates, manipulates, and compensates for the figurability of an imaginary subject that projects cohesiveness as its founding assumption through a fictional body. This fictional body is created element by element as part of a narrative process grounded in product consumption. The woman as subject is invited to take control of the process whereby she represents herself. At the same time, she is constantly reminded that she must submit to a regime that externalizes figurability through product usage. (1995: 178)

Fashioning the Subject

Writing in 1979 about the processes by which the resistant forms of 'spectacular subcultures' are 'incorporated' into the mainstream, Dick Hebdige comments: 'Style in particular provokes a double response: it is alternately celebrated (in the fashion page) and ridiculed or reviled (in those articles which define subcultures as social problems)' (1979: 93). For Hebdige 'style', which is creative and resistant, is to be distinguished from 'fashion', which is the system through which the process of recuperation is effected. This process is made possible because both subcultural style and mainstream fashion are symbolic systems encoded through the commodity form. Capitalism, then, is seen to work here through the feminization of mass culture, for fashion, it is clear, is a feminine sphere, whilst subcultural style is a masculine affair. As Elizabeth Wilson comments:

> Women have been so wholly identified with mainstream fashion that it is hard for them even to have oppositional styles. Sartorial excess and deviance readily equates with rebellion for men. It *can* signify

revolt for young women – but even the bizarre can be fashionable, and attempts to outrage or . . . to be overtly sexual or sexual in some different ways, may also express submissiveness to a boyfriend even if rebellion at home. (1990: 32)

Fashion, like shopping then, is a feminist issue (McRobbie 1999: 41), but as with shopping, the precise nature of that issue is less clear:

Is fashionable dress part of the oppression of women, or is it a form of adult play? Is it part of the empty consumerism, or is it a site of struggle symbolized in dress codes? Does it muffle the self, or create it? (Wilson 1985: 231)

Feminist theorists of both the first and the second wave, as we have seen, viewed fashion as enslavement, one of the ways in which women are both physically oppressed (through the bodily constrictions of the fashionable garment) and confined to the sphere of the irrational and the objectified. Fashion is *work*, but work in the service of sexual subordination; it is also a system of representation in which woman is rendered as *passive* spectacle. Its links with other systems of visual representation, most notably cinema, can be articulated through the idea of the shop window as screen/mirror (Doane 1987) and through the development of fashion photography and the woman's magazine. These links, as Judith Mayne suggests, serve as a conceptual bridge between the everyday of women's lives and the spectacular screen image; both can be theorized in terms of the self-commodifying work of femininity:

Since women are spectacles in their everyday lives, there's something about coming to terms with film from the perspective of what it means to be an object of spectacle and what it means to be a spectator that is really a coming to terms with how that relationship exists both up on the screen and in everyday life. It is this phenomenon which speaks directly to women in their everyday lives. Women are *taught* to be objects of spectacle. (Citron *et al.* 1978: 83)

Fashion, as the site of that 'spectacle' in everyday life, has therefore received increasing attention from feminist cultural theorists. How, then, can we understand it?

One way is via its relationship to femininity and the female body. Dress, as Kaja Silverman argues, 'draws the body so that it can be seen' (1986: 149), bringing the body into discourse, mediating between nature and culture. Fashion, then, represents dress as artifice, transforming 'the "raw" of woman into the "cooked" of femininity' (Evans and Thornton 1989: 13–14). It not only displays the body, it mediates the body's physicality, ordering and regulating its sexual identity. Clothes, as Elizabeth Wilson points out, cannot really be envisaged apart from the body. They seem to be so much 'part of our living, moving selves' (1985: 1) that they not only construct gender, they naturalize it, rendering it 'self-evident'. In the case of women, then, fashion's ceaselessly changing display seems to render femininity *as* artifice and display. At the same time, however, it substitutes for the actual body, Wilson suggests, an ideal body – or rather an *idea* of the body – so that the 'very way in which fashion constantly changes actually serves to fix the idea of the body as unchanging and eternal' (1985: 58).

If fashion constructs the female body ideologically, as feminine, however, this construction is effected through *performance*. Femininity, as we have seen, has been viewed by some theorists in terms of *masquerade*, and fashion becomes a key element in this envisaging of a performance which is *excessive*, and which therefore opens up to question any notion of gendered identity as natural. But fashion has also been viewed as performance in two further respects. One returns us to the issue of women's presence on the streets of modernity. Fashion, as Wilson points out, can be a mask as well as a masquerade (1985: 156). It can confer an anonymity in the street which permits to today's teenage girl – as it did to the nineteenth-century bourgeois woman – the privacy of invisibility in a masculine space. By contrast, fashion can also be seen as a performative surface on which are acted out not so much – as in the theory of masquerade – an ironic distance from notions of femininity, but the contradictions of capitalism itself. Fashion, writes Wilson, '*speaks* capitalism' (1985: 14), that is, it displays on its surface, more literally than with other forms of popular culture, the contradictions and struggles which characterize contemporary society, and reveals through its shifts and reversals the instabilities of the gendered identities which it proclaims.

Finally, the concept of fashion as feminine performance has been used to return to the issue of subcultural style and the positioning of women within it. Angela McRobbie's early research on girls and subcultures, as we saw, concluded that the concept of subculture as it had been defined provided an inadequate framework for the analysis of *girls'* culture. In later work she returns to the issue through an analysis of 'second-hand style' and 'the opportunities [it] has offered young people, at a time of recession, for participating in fashion' (1989: 23–4). The second-hand ragmarket, she argues, blurs the distinction between production and consumption for its 'subcultural entrepreneurs'. Girls and young women have played a major part here, rediscovering past styles and items of clothing and imaginatively recreating them. Such recycling intervenes in the fashion system and allows a space for play, converting fashion into 'fancy dress'. Here, then, is a quite specific example of ironic masquerade, as the norms and expectations of femininity are disrupted through 'a knowingness, a wilful anarchy and an irrepressible optimism, as indicated by colour, humour and disavowal of the conventions of adult dress' (1989: 42). Viewed in these terms, such 'subcultural' display ceases to be, as it was for Hebdige, a *displaced* form of protest, always liable to recuperation because it is grounded in consumption rather than production. It becomes instead protest *on the site of* the construction of a restrictive femininity.

That fashion is also *work* is a fact also emphasized in McRobbie's analysis. This is so in conventional terms of paid employment: fashion is, as she points out, 'an almost wholly feminized industry' in terms of production as well as consumption (1999: 41). But sewing, as Carolyn Steedman described, is also a skill handed down from mother to daughter in white working-class as well as black and Asian families. As with Steedman's mother's dream of *making* her New Look dress, it becomes a way of *constructing* an identity, of 'passing' as (middle-class) feminine, but also increasingly of becoming a producer, of making and selling as well as buying, of inhabiting the space of the street in a new and more confident way, and of crossing the boundaries of class and ethnicity.

Finally, of course, fashion is pleasure as well as work. Hilary Radner (1995: 59) draws attention to the potential for auto-eroticism in a system that constitutes women as objects of their own gaze. Contrasting fashion with cinema, Evans and Thornton comment:

> Fashion, unlike cinema, generates images of women for women, a system of representations that one might suppose to be cut to the measure of a *female* desire. Might there be a specifically female gaze and, if so, how would it differ from the masculine gaze? Could it involve narcissistic identification, a desire to look which is reflexive, constructing identity through likeness and recognition? ... Can the fashion image be read as an index of women's visual pleasure as it negotiates, appropriates, encroaches on, and steals the gaze within a patriarchal symbolic order? (1989: 10)

To this we might add the fact that fashion is a matter of touch as well as vision, suggesting the potential for an auto-eroticism which is located elsewhere than in the (purely) visual. But the pleasures of fashion, like those of consumption more generally, are ambiguous. Evans and Thornton conclude that fashion is spectacle *and* surveillance (1989: 62), and that to think that the fashion image can satisfy desire or dress rewrite gender coding is a fantasy. But clearly, as Wilson suggests, fashion 'acts as a vehicle for fantasy' (1985: 246). Its performance of fantasy can be seen as restrictive – we often seem to be wearing the uniforms of a *patriarchal* fantasy – but also as the site of our own liberatory fantasies, a place where identity can be renegotiated.

Fans and Stars

If we return for a moment to the 'teeny-bopper' *others* of Dick Hebdige's resistant subcultures, we find that they are not only inscribed in 'mainstream' fashion systems, they are also *fans*. David Bowie's subcultural followers, for example, were 'those youngsters willing and brave enough to challenge the notoriously pedestrian stereotypes conventionally available to working-class men and women'. They were *not* 'the teeny-boppers who followed the mainstream glitter bands' (1979: 60, 62). The teeny-boppers, of course, were teenage *girls*, and if we look at the 1997 edited collection by Ken Gelder and Sarah Thornton, *The Subcultures Reader*, we find that one of the very few essays about *female* subcultures concerns 'Beatlemania' – girls as fans. If mainstream fashion is the feminized *other* of subcultural style, then, the passive female fan is the *other* of the active subcultural *bricoleur*. The two of course overlap, and they come together particularly around the fetishized image of the star.

The chapter by Angela McRobbie and Jenny Garber in the 1976 *Resistance through Rituals* begins to take up this argument. Intended, as McRobbie wrote later, 'both to complement and extend, and at the same time to be a critique of what later came to be known as subcultural theory' (McRobbie 1991b: xvii), the chapter shares in part the assumptions of Hebdige and others. Girls, write McRobbie and Garber, are marginal within working-class youth subcultures but 'strongly present' in 'the "complementary" but more passive sub-cultures of the fan and the fan-club' (1976: 211). But the essay also begins to frame the question in rather different ways, linking it to work on the importance of fantasy being developed within feminist thought at this time (see Chapter 4). Within the 'small, structured and highly manufactured area' available to the girls in McRobbie and Garber's study, a space whose limitations speak a future as well as a present 'general subordination', their 'Teeny Bopper culture' nevertheless offers 'a different space, . . . a different type of resistance', one bound up in structures of fantasy (1976: 221). For McRobbie and Garber in 1976, such a 'space' was on the whole viewed negatively: its fantasies, like those of the romance reader, signalled a broad acceptance of subordination, rather than the active resistance which characterized working-class male subcultures. Nevertheless, the suggestiveness of its notion of a negotiated space for resistance centring on the conjunction of fantasy, fashion, the fan and the star was subsequently taken up and developed in a range of different ways.

Ehrenreich *et al*.'s (1992) essay on 'Beatlemania' as a 'sexually defiant consumer subculture?', picks up some of the themes explored elsewhere in this chapter. 'Beatlemania', they argue, was 'the first and most dramatic uprising of *women's* sexual revolution', signalling a protest against the sexual repressiveness and 'rigid double standard' of teen culture, through its constituting of the Beatles as the (fantasized) *objects* of an active, pursuant female desire (1992: 85). For girls to 'abandon control – to scream, faint, dash about in mobs' was for them to actively embrace the category of 'bad girl' with its attributes 'vulgar, tarty, pathological and without value' (Skeggs 1997: 115), but to embrace it from *within* the consumer culture whose producers saw them as objects of manipulation. It was also, argue Ehrenreich *et al*., a refusal of the sexual structure of exchange, in which the 'cultural capital' of the young woman lies in her body as commodity, with its status as 'used', 'partly used' or 'intact'. A 1963 account of American teen culture quoted by Ehrenreich *et al.* illustrates only too clearly the way in which the operation of 'cultural capital' for *women* renders them always object as well as subject of exchange:

> A standard caution in teen-age advice literature is that, if the boy 'gets' his kiss on the first date, he may assume that many other boys have been just as easily compensated. In other words, the rule book advises mainly that the [girl's] popularity assets should be protected against deflation. (Hechinger and Hechinger, in Ehrenreich *et al.* 1992: 94)

The 'bad girls' of Beatlemania were in rebellion against such self-regulation, attempting to 'carve out subversive versions of heterosexuality' (1992: 100), but the fantasies which structured their desire were as much fantasies of *identification* as of possession. Ehrenreich *et al.* quote one former fan as saying, 'I didn't want to grow up and be a wife and it seemed to me that the Beatles had the kind of freedom I wanted ... I didn't want to sleep with Paul McCartney, I was too young. But I wanted to be like them, something larger than life' (1992: 103).

The links between fans, consumer culture and the *female* star have been traced by other writers, particularly in relation to cinema. Jane Gaines argues that the 'star style ... is a direct and intimate link to the body and consciousness of the female spectator', a key site of those 'muffled protests against oppression found in the very practices which seem to most graphically implement and spell out the patriarchal wish' (1990: 16, 23). This is an argument also taken up by Maria LaPlace, who argues that an analysis of the relationship between the female star and her fans can reveal 'elements of contradiction, discursive struggle and subversive signification' which undermine the overt message of the film itself (LaPlace 1987: 138). Her analysis of the marketing and consumption of the 1942 'woman's film' *Now, Voyager* and its star, Bette Davis, focuses on three 'discourses' within the film and its marketing: the discourses of consumerism, the female star and the romance narrative. The first, that of consumerism, is evident *within* the film in the transformation of its protagonist, Charlotte Vale, from passive object to active subject through the remaking of herself as glamorous and fashionable. For the consumer/fan, a parallel transformation was offered via the film's marketing which featured Davis as instructor in a 'how-to-be beautiful' guide, and advertisements for tie-in clothing, cosmetics and hairstyles. But if the fantasy is that of transformation *with* Charlotte Vale and *into* Bette Davis, such a fantasy transformation is empowering as well as regulatory. For 'Bette Davis' exceeds 'Charlotte Vale' in meaning, her image constructed across a range of films as well as through cinema-related texts (fan magazines, gossip columns, newspaper and magazine articles), in a way that could work to modify or subvert the film's narrative. The narrative outcome of *Now, Voyager*, in which Vale/Davis relinquishes sexuality in favour of a quasi-maternal role, argues LaPlace, is complicated by Davis' image as assertive, independent and powerful, with the result that Charlotte's final positioning outside marriage and domesticity could be seen as a (limited) assertion of female autonomy. Thus female desire may be regulated within the film's romance narrative, and harnessed to the creation of a female market through consumer culture, but it is also *produced* through the interaction of narrative, star and consumption. The fantasy desires and identifications offered by the narrative and the star may be acted out through consumption, activating 'wants and wishes, . . . (libidinal) pleasure, sexuality and the erotic, and a species of economic decision and choice' (1987: 145), even though they may be simultaneously contained within the structures that produce them. Through such processes of identification and desire, argues LaPlace, 'commodity consumption and the commodity aspect of the star system' can become 'a symbolic system in which women try to make sense of their lives and even create imaginative spaces for resistance' (1987: 165).

This argument is further developed in the work of Constance Penley, this time in relation to *cross-gender* identifications and desires. Her study of the fantasy narratives constructed around the *Star Trek* characters Kirk and Spock by 'a female fandom that is devoted to reading, writing and publishing sexually explicit poems, stories and novels depicting . . . Kirk and . . . Spock as passionate lovers' (1989: 258) is, like LaPlace's study, both textual and ethnographic. Like LaPlace, she argues that the fans' investment in this 'unique hybrid genre of romance, pornography, and utopian science fiction' (Penley 1992: 480) merges identification and desire, and like LaPlace too, she sees such 'female appropriations of a popular culture product' as demonstrating how women can 'resist, negotiate, and adapt to their own desires' a mainstream product offered for their consumption (1992: 484). The theoretical framework which she uses draws on psychoanalytic fantasy theory (see Chapter 4) to emphasize the fluid identifications of these 'slash' fantasies, identifications which are made across gender boundaries – or with 'the entire scene, or the narrative itself' (1992: 490). Such fantasies, she argues, in their representation of Kirk and Spock as lovers but as somehow *not* homosexual, permit the women fans to both '*be* Kirk or Spock (a possible phallic identification) and also still *have* (as sexual objects) either or both of them since, as heterosexuals, they are not *un*available to women' (1992: 488). But as Penley acknowledges, such cross-gender 'writing' of sexual and social fantasy is at the expense of a rejection of the female body as a 'terrain of fantasy or utopian thinking' (1992: 498). In a patriarchal culture in which the female body is a commodified object of exchange, it is simply not possible for these fans to 'imagine two women passionately in love with one another who go out and save the galaxy once a week' (1992: 490). Thus their 'politics of inner protest' is written on the *male* body. We might characterize the cross-gender identifications of 'slash' fantasy, then, as a sort of *masquerade* in the realm of fantasy, one which allows women a fantasized crossing of gender boundaries but which remains marked – in its rejection of the female body – by the gendered structures of exchange which it subverts.

Finally, I should like to turn to Jackie Stacey's (1994) study of female fans' memories of Hollywood stars in 1940s and 1950s Britain, *Star Gazing*. Stacey's study investigates 'how historical and national location affects the meanings of Hollywood stars for female spectators', but it also examines 'how the processes of cinematic spectatorship produce and re/form feminine identities', identities which are always 'in process', continually being transformed (1994: 73). Her argument begins from the idea of the 'impossibility of femininity' within a culture which defines it as 'an unattainable visual image of desirability' (1994: 65–6). Like other writers whose work we have examined in this chapter, she argues that the 'work of femininity' requires consumption – of both commodities and images – so that women are both subjects and objects of exchange, their sense of identity bound up with a sense of 'woman as image', forever unattainable, always invoking a sense of lack. She argues, however, that this 'work' also involves the 'active negotiation and transformation of identities which are not simply reducible to objectification' (1994: 208). Identities, she argues, are partial, provisional and constantly 'in process', but they are also fixed – however unsuccessfully, temporarily or contradictorily – by particular discourses. Like LaPlace, she argues that the idealized images of Hollywood female stars function as one such discourse, and her examination of spectators' memories of such stars suggests the way in which this relationship involves a 'complex negotiation of self and other, image and ideal, and subject and object' (1994: 227).

The material for Stacey's study comes from responses to an advertisement placed in two women's magazines and a follow-up questionnaire compiled according to the themes emerging from the letters. Her analysis of the results explores three 'discourses of spectatorship' (1994: 80) which emerge from the material she received: escapism, identification and consumption. All are analysed in terms of the specific historical construction and organization of femininity during the 1940s and 1950s, but all are also seen as means by which her respondents negotiate and construct a sense of feminine identity. Fantasies of 'escape', then, revolve around utopian ideals of 'abundance, community and transcendence' which are the product of wartime austerity, but they also involve a fantasized escape *into* a Hollywood ideal which both liberates and constrains. Similarly, discourses of consumption, though they serve to position women in the feminine role of consumer-consumed, also 'addressed women as subjects and encouraged their participation in the "public sphere" which could be seen to have offered new forms of feminine identity in contrast to their roles as wives and mothers' (1994: 223). In the context of wartime austerity the promise of self-transformation which such discourses could offer provided a means of negotiating the limitations of the present; in post-war Britain they could be used to contest the ideological push towards women's repositioning within the domestic sphere.

It is the theorization of *identification* that is central to *Star Gazing*, drawing together psychoanalytic and ethnographic analysis, the subjective processes of fantasy and the material practices of consumption. Like Valerie Walkerdine (Chapter 4), Stacey considers not only *'identificatory fantasies'* but also *'identificatory practices'* (1994: 171). The latter involve processes of both consumption and production, in the imitation of a star's hairstyle or clothing or the adoption of her manner of speech or behaviour. What is enacted is 'an intersection of self and other, subject and object' in the desired transformation of the spectator's own identity (1994: 167). 'Identification' is therefore seen as an active process of negotiation, operating across the poles of similarity and difference. Identification based on similarity ('the star is *like* me') is to be distinguished, argues Stacey, from identification based on difference ('the star is *unlike* me'). Such a concept opens a space for the recognition of differences *between* femininities, and prompts consideration of the idea that 'identification' is not, as it is so often considered in film theory, the polar opposite of 'desire', but rather may involve forms of homoerotic pleasure which take the spectator outside the regime of heterosexuality and the relations of heterosexual exchange (1994: 173). Equally, consumption – *of* the star and as *imitation of* the star – may also involve production, not only of a particular 'look' but also of an identity – however contingent, partial or fragmented.

Such a conclusion returns us to the figure of Carolyn Steedman's mother and the New Look coat that she dreamed of making if only she could afford the 20 yards of cloth. The 1950s New Look style, as Angela Partington (1992) demonstrates, may have been copied from the Hollywood star and the high fashion model, but it was appropriated by working-class women who reworked it to signify their own (perhaps 'illegitimate') pleasures and desires. For Partington, this complex process of negotiation constitutes, as it has for other theorists considered in this chapter, *masquerade*. 'Masquerade', she writes, 'implies an acting out of the images of femininity, for which is required an active gaze to decode, utilize and identify with those images, while at the same time constructing a self-image which is dependent on the gaze of the other' (1992: 156). It is thus both subversive of and complicit with the commodification of femininity in consumer culture. But the figure of Steedman's mother also reminds us of an issue that it is easy to forget in the analysis of consumer culture: that of exclusion. Her desire for the New Look skirt structured her identifications, but it also signalled her *exclusion* from consumer culture: she could *not* afford to make it. As Susan Willis argues in her attack on the notion of contemporary consumer culture to be found in the work of theorists like Jean Baudrillard and Guy Debord:

What typifies their writing is the image of a society in which consumers and commodities seem to circulate freely and endlessly in a fantastic democracy of consumption. Herein lies the great fallacy of late capitalism. Obviously, we do not all share equally in commodities nor do we even have equal opportunity to trade evenly in their signs – not racial minorities, not the unemployed, not women, children, teenagers, the elderly, not the populations of the Third World. (1991a: 59)

The strategy of mimicry or masquerade, Willis reminds us, is available, like the *flânerie* of the department store shopper of the late nineteenth century, only to *some* of us, and for women, who are always simultaneously subject *and* object of consumption practices, it is a precarious and ambivalent one.

Notes

1. Raymond Williams in *Keywords* (1983) gives the etymology of 'consumer' and 'consumption', noting that in almost all its early English uses, 'consume' had 'an unfavourable sense; it meant to destroy, to use up, to waste, to exhaust' (1983: 78). Whilst it acquired a more neutral sense in its descriptions of political economy as the pairing of 'production' and 'consumption', in its identification with 'mass consumption' and 'consumer society/culture' it has retained negative connotations – now firmly identified with the feminine. See also Lury (1996), Huyssen (1986).
2. Irigaray also proposes a more Utopian solution, which is that women should set up an alternative economy (of desire) based on '[e]xchanges without identifiable terms, without accounts, without end', and she suggests that such an economy has always existed as an undermining subtext to the patriarchal economy. 'But', she asks, 'what if these "commodities" refused to go to "market"? What if they maintained "another" kind of commerce, among themselves?' And she adds, 'Utopia? Perhaps. Unless this mode of exchange has undermined the order of commerce from the beginning . . .' (1985: 196–7). She identifies this alternative 'sociocultural economy' with 'female homosexuality', arguing that patriarchal culture is itself intrinsically 'homosexual', since it is a culture based exclusively on relations between men, in which women are merely the objects of exchange.
3. See Chapter 5 for a discussion of Beverley Skeggs' account of 'passing' in relation to class and femininity. In Skeggs' ethnographic study of a group of working-class women in the north-west of England she argues that the women's 'performance' of femininity, through which they seek to 'pass' as feminine, is in order to position them as 'respectable' and hence as *not* working class.
4. Bourdieu's list of objects that his subjects were asked to characterize as potentially constituting a beautiful, interesting, trivial or ugly photograph, is suggestive in this respect. The 'objects' are: a landscape, a car crash, a little girl playing with a cat, a pregnant woman, a still life, a woman suckling a child, a metal frame, tramps quarrelling, cabbages, a sunset over the sea, a weaver at his loom, a folk-dance, a rope, a butcher's stall, a famous monument, a scrap-yard, a first communion, a wounded man, a snake, an 'old master' (Bourdieu 1986: 180). Women, in Bourdieu's account, proved themselves less able to distance themselves via 'aesthetic neutralization' from the 'objects' photographed.
5. For Barthes' definition of myth see his 'Myth Today' in *Mythologies* (1973), first published in 1957.

6. Clarke *et al.* quote from Juliet Mitchell's (1971) *Woman's Estate* but qualify her argument as follows: 'Certainly, some of these groups aimed for a systematic inversion . . . but from the inside and *by a negation*' (1976: 62). This, they argue, made the groups particularly liable to re-incorporation within the dominant culture. It is notable that in the chronology they give of the counter-culture from 1965 to 1974, the only feminist book mentioned is Germaine Greer's *The Female Eunuch*.

7. McRobbie and Garber cite Mod culture as one in which, because of its greater preoccupation with 'style and consumption and looks' (1976: 217), girls could play a greater part. More recently, Caroline Evans and Minna Thornton have argued that it was Punk, with its mixing of 'the more familiar clichés of the prostitute look with the strictly private, "forbidden" gear of sado-masochism and fetishism' which permitted women to 'negotiate a social and ideological space for themselves through the deployment of oppositional dress' (1989: 20, 17).

8. This account makes an interesting contrast to those of writers like Juliet Mitchell and Sheila Rowbotham who describe their experience as precisely the reverse trajectory: from involvement in a Marxist politics which excluded women to a 'revolutionary' feminist politics (Rowbotham 1973: 36).

9. Stuart Hall (1992), for example, identifies the four defining features of the modern society as follows.

    1. The dominance of secular forms of political power and authority . . ., operating within defined territorial boundaries, which are characteristic of the large, complex structures of the modern nation-state.
    2. A monetarized exchange economy, based on the large-scale production and consumption of commodities for the market, extensive ownership of private property and the accumulation of capital on a systematic, long-term basis. . . .
    3. The decline of the traditional social order, with its fixed social hierarchies and overlapping allegiances, and the appearance of a dynamic social and sexual division of labour. In modern capitalist societies, this was characterized by new class formations, and distinctive patriarchal relations between men and women.
    4. The decline of the religious world view typical of traditional societies and the rise of a secular and materialist culture exhibiting . . . individualistic, rationalist and instrumental impulses . . . (Hall 1992b: 6)

10. Janet Wolff, however, argues that 'shopping and window-shopping do not constitute *flânerie*, because the desire for the object on display rules out the necessary distance which characterizes the *flâneur*'s relationship to the public sphere' (1995: 102).

11. See Ballaster *et al.* (1991) *Women's Worlds: Ideology, Femininity and the Woman's Magazine* for a discussion of this.

12. For Baudrillard, woman, like simulation, 'is but appearance . . . in the feminine the very distinction between authenticity and artifice is without foundation . . . there is no other femininity than that of appearances'. This, he argues is the 'privilege of the feminine . . . the privilege of never having acceded to truth or meaning, and of having remained absolute master of the realm of appearances'. Rather than seeking to speak as women and produce a women's discourse of 'truth', feminists should apply 'the capacity immanent to seduction to deny things their truth and turn it into a game, the pure play of appearances, and thereby foil all systems of power and meaning with a mere turn of the hand' (1990: 11, 8).

|7|

Technologies of the Body

In posing all those areas and sites in any social formation which need to be rethought from the perspective of the position and the oppression of women and the centrality of patriarchal relations, feminism has provoked a break with any residual attempt to give the term 'material conditions' an exclusively economistic or 'productivist' meaning. In raising the question of how to think of both the causes and the effects of the contradictions of gender, it has displaced forever any exclusive reference to class contradictions as the stable point of reference for cultural analysis. (Hall 1980a: 38)

The rediscovery of our early perception of ourselves and our own sexuality entered politics – not as a theoretical question but as a passionate and practical demand scrawled on a bog wall in a sit-in. 'Give me back my past, my childhood, my body, my life.' This helped us to connect a sense of femaleness to our sense of ourselves as political animals. Our bodies at least were female. (Rowbotham 1973: 23)

It is around the issue of the body that the relationship between feminism and cultural studies is at its most strained. Stuart Hall's 1980 account of the development of the impact of feminism on cultural studies, quoted above, speaks of the 'material conditions' of gendered oppression. A little later he writes of the need for cultural studies to consider 'the sexual division of labour, the construction of gender roles, identities and relations and the principle of sexual difference' (Hall 1980a: 39). But the central features of Sheila Rowbotham's account – patriarchy's control of women through their bodies, and the need for women to reclaim their bodies and to learn to speak *as women* – do not appear in Hall's description of feminism's impact on cultural studies. Instead, his account emphasizes the *structural* relations of patriarchy, which are seen as displacing class as the *exclusive* point of reference for cultural studies.

Discussing in 1991 the points of 'lack of overlap' between feminism and cultural studies, Sarah Franklin, Celia Lury and Jackie Stacey cite cultural studies' reliance in the 1970s and 1980s on the structuralist frameworks of Louis Althusser and Claude Lévi-Strauss as a key factor (Franklin *et al.* 1991: 8–14). Althusser's view of the social formation as composed of economic, political and ideological levels, each with its own 'relative autonomy', but determined 'in the last instance' by the economic, is clearly visible in Hall's account quoted above. The introduction of 'patriarchal structures of dominance and oppression' into the account, he argues, has forced a reconceptualizing of the social and cultural structures proposed by Althusser and Gramsci, and a rethinking of the importance of the economic as the ultimate determining principle in a social formation. Nevertheless, the terms remain the same: what are to be investigated are – now more complex – structural relationships and 'sites of contradiction'. What is missing is that which is most central to feminist analysis in the 1970s: its 'body politics'. It is this which produces the frequent sense of unease in the 1978 collection from the CCCS Women's Studies Group, *Women Take Issue* (see Chapter 3), the convolutions of its authors in trying to fit a feminist analysis to the structuralist analysis of class, and their recourse to feminist writers not specifically identified with cultural studies in the search for an adequate conceptual framework. It is in the contributions of Angela McRobbie to both this volume and the 1976 *Resistance through Rituals* that the sexualized female body most clearly emerges as a disruptive force, and one potentially uncontainable within the analytical framework of cultural studies. McRobbie writes in the language of Althusserianism – girls, she argues, experience 'material limitations . . . in and through the ideological apparatuses they inhabit' (1978: 107). But, as Jane Gaines has observed, what is being proposed in McRobbie's account is outside Althusser's structuralist framework. It is not only – as in the 'culturalist' strand of cultural studies – 'on the terrain of lived experience' (McRobbie 1991b: ix) that the girls' resistance to subordination is manifest: it is through the female body itself. In McRobbie's descriptions of teenage girls' use of their sexuality within the classroom, writes Gaines, '[s]exual maturation – the functioning of the body which most nearly escapes culture – is deployed to turn the body into an instrument of disruption. What better site for disruption of the social order', she adds, 'than the seeming scene of the origin of women's oppression?' (Gaines 1990: 8–9).

The second structuralist model of culture which Franklin *et al.* point to as a source of disjuncture between feminism and cultural studies is that found in the structuralist anthropology of Claude Lévi-Strauss and the semiotics of Roland Barthes, both of which have their origins in the structural linguistics of Ferdinand de Saussure. In his 1980 account of the development of cultural studies, Stuart Hall brackets together Barthes and Lévi-Strauss. Both, he writes, 'deployed the models of structural linguistics as a paradigm . . . for the scientific study of culture. . . . Lévi-Strauss employed this model to decipher the languages (myths, culinary practices and so on) of so-called "primitive" societies. Barthes offered a more informal "semiotics", studying the signs and representations in an array of languages, codes and everyday practices in contemporary societies' (1980a: 29–30). But for Lévi-Strauss, as Franklin *et al.* point out, it is the exchange of *women* that, as the distinguishing feature of human kinship structures, constitutes the founding cultural moment. In human society, writes Lévi-Strauss, 'a man must obtain a woman from another man, who gives him a daughter or a sister' (1972: 46). Hence for Lévi-Strauss, as for Freud, 'the universal presence of an incest taboo' underpins the symbolic order and makes possible the construction of cultural and representational systems. Thus the founding cultural moment is, in this structuralist analysis, also the originary moment of a universalized *patriarchy* – as Luce Irigaray points out when she argues that for Lévi-Strauss it is 'women's bodies – through their use, consumption and circulation – [which] provide for the condition making social life and culture possible' (1985: 171).

If we turn to Barthes' analysis of 'the Fashion system' which I discussed in Chapter 6, we find a similar analytical use of women's bodies. Fashion's rhetoric, argues Barthes, works by substituting the signifier Woman for the bodies of real women through the figure of the model or 'cover girl' whose 'body is no one's body, it is a pure form, which possesses no attribute' (1985: 259). Then, in a second process of substitution, the fashion garment itself 'stands in for' the body of the model as a pure sign within a symbolic system. Thus in Barthes' Fashion system, as in the structural anthropology of Lévi-Strauss, women's bodies, in Irigaray's words, 'provide for the condition making social life and culture possible' whilst being themselves simultaneously erased. Women, it is assumed, acquiesce in this erasure of the troubling specificity of their bodies. The 'woman's identity is . . . established, in the service of Man . . ., of Art, of Thought', writes Barthes (1985: 252–3).

Discussing the influence of structuralism on cultural studies of the 1970s and early 1980s, Maureen McNeil and Sarah Franklin draw attention to 'the aspiration to scientificity' (1991: 131) which underpinned structuralism, including the Marxist structuralism of Louis Althusser. Stuart Hall himself emphasizes this when he comments that the attraction of the structuralist model was that it held out the promise 'of a mode of analysis at one and the same time rigorous, scientific and non-reductionist, non-positivist' (1980a: 30). What this produces, argue McNeil and Franklin, is a tendency to reduce bodies (especially women's bodies) to texts, as in Barthes' analysis cited above, together with a failure to establish a critical perspective on the power relations and discursive structures to be found in science itself. One of the dominant metaphors in the development of early modern science was that of the exploration and domination of the female body of nature by means of the rational illumination of masculine science. Increasingly, however, science has taken the bodies of women as its literal object, so that, as Franklin *et al.* write, 'the female body becomes an object of scrutiny and investigation, devoid of subjectivity or personhood' (1991: 10). In its own 'aspiration to scientificity', write McNeil and Franklin, cultural studies has often been complicit with such objectification, indeed has borrowed its terminology for its own project.

That the discourse of science is caught up in gendered fantasies of power is an argument made also by Mary Jacobus, Evelyn Fox Keller and Sally Shuttleworth. In their introduction to *Body/Politics* (1990), they write:

> It is a truism that whereas nature, the body that scientific knowledge takes as its object, is traditionally constructed as feminine, the subject of science, i.e. the scientist, has usually been seen as masculine. The fantasies that attend such gendering of the production and reproduction of knowledge are at once sexualized and territorial (we speak not only of 'penetrating' or 'unveiling' nature's mysteries but of 'opening up new horizons' or 'pushing back the frontiers of knowledge'). In other words, hierarchies involving both gender and power . . . are intimately associated with the ideology and practice of science . . . (1990: 6)

These are metaphors which also leave their trace in cultural studies' accounts of its own development – as when Stuart Hall in 1980 describes the 'point where the Centre [for Contemporary Cultural Studies] began to desert its "handmaiden" role and chart a more independent, ambitious, properly integrated territorial space of its own' (1980a: 22). Interestingly, when Hall returns to such an account in 1992, the troublesome body of woman is seen to exact its revenge in a very dramatic way. Feminism, writes Hall, 'broke in; interrupted, made an unseemly noise, . . . crapped on the table of cultural studies' (1992a: 282). Bent on desecration and producing 'an unseemly noise', this body – aggressive, unclean, *abject*[1] – is a long way from that described in feminist accounts of attempts to reclaim the female body in the 1970s. We may compare, for instance, Susan Suleiman's account in *The Female Body in Western Culture*. 'Women', she writes,

> who for centuries had been the *objects* of male theorizing, male desires, male fears and male representations, had to discover and reappropriate themselves as *subjects*; the obvious place to begin was the silent place to which they had been assigned again and again, that dark continent which had ever provoked assault and puzzlement . . . The call went out to invent both a new poetics and a new politics, based on women's reclaiming what had always been theirs but had been usurped from them: control over their bodies and a voice with which to speak about it. (1986: 7)

This chapter, then, examines the question of the body and its emergence as a crucial point for analysis in the uneasy relationship of feminism and cultural studies.

(Re)Discovering the Body

> Armed with a gynaecological speculum, a mirror, a flashlight and –
> most of all – each other in a consciousness-raising group, women ritu-
> ally opened their bodies to their own literal view. (Haraway 1997: 41)

Donna Haraway's description of women's literal rediscovery of their bodies through the 1970s Women's Liberation Movement goes on to point out that 'in the context of the whole orthodox history of western philosophy and technology . . . visually self-possessed sexual and generative organs made potent tropes for the reclaimed feminist self' (1997: 42). But, as she argues elsewhere (Haraway 1990b), if the female body constituted a troubling disturbance for misogynist thought masquerading as 'neutral' science or philosophy – and hence became a 'potent trope' in the writings of second-wave feminists – it had equally been a problem for earlier feminist thinkers. In much of Western philosophical discourse, as well as in the discourses of nineteenth-century science, corporeality has been, in Elizabeth Grosz's phrase, 'coded feminine', so that '[p]atriarchal oppression . . . justifies itself, at least in part, by connecting women much more closely than men to the body and, through this identification, restricting women's social and economic roles to (pseudo) biological terms' (Grosz 1994: 14). For feminists like Mary Wollstonecraft, Charlotte Perkins Gilman and Simone de Beauvoir, therefore, the female body often seemed a trap, a limiting burden whose transcendence was a prerequisite for accession into the rational or public sphere. For Wollstonecraft, women had to be educated out of femininity and into rationality, and for Gilman too the threat of the feminine irrational was ever-present. To de Beauvoir, despite her devastating intellectual critique of the cultural myths of femininity produced by men, the female body appears as 'absorption, suction, humus, pitch and glue, a passive influx, insinuating and viscous'. This is, she argues, not only how men see the female body; it is how a woman 'vaguely feels herself to be'. Her body and its sexuality is for her 'a strange and disquieting burden' (de Beauvoir 1988: 407). Little wonder, then, that for these 'first wave' feminists the female body is seen as limiting women's capacity for both equality and transcendence – an obstacle to be overcome if women are to become fully social beings with access to cultural production and the public sphere.

For feminists of the 1970s, this view was to be contested and the female body both reclaimed and given a voice. If, as Adrienne Rich argued in 1977, '[t]he woman's body is the terrain on which patriarchy is erected' (Rich 1977: 55), then the demand for control over one's own body – control over whether, when and with whom one has children, control over how one's sexuality is expressed – becomes central to the feminist project because, in the words of Jacquelyn Dowd Hall, 'it is essential to a sense of being a person, with personal and bodily integrity, able to engage in conscious activity and to participate in social life' (1983: 341–2).[2] One visible expression of this aim was the publication in the early 1970s, initially in newsprint form, of the Boston Women's Health Book Collective's *Our Bodies, Ourselves*. For the women of the Boston collective, the book is a self-help manual that is both the result of and a contribution to the process of consciousness-raising. All the chapters are collectively written and include additional testimonies from unnamed women as well as numerous photographs of women together – making music, talking, exercising, engaged in DIY – together with diagrams of the female body and of sexual positions – though only, interestingly, in relation to heterosexual sex. The book emerges, then, from a process of consciousness-raising:

> From our beginning conversations with each other we discovered four cultural notions of femininity which we had in some sense shared: woman as inferior, woman as passive, woman as beautiful object, woman as exclusively wife and mother. In our first discussions we realized how severely those notions had constricted us, how humanly limited we felt at being passive, dependent creatures with no identities of our own. As time passed, with each other's support we began to rediscover ourselves. (1976: 18)

Such rediscovery is seen to be of women's *human* potential, but this is to be achieved not in spite of but *via* the embracing of a female-embodied identity. 'Our learned sense of inferiority', argues the collective, 'affected the way we thought about our bodies – our physical selves'. 'Experiences in the women's movement', however, 'have drastically changed our thinking and feelings about our bodies. . . . We have given each other support to begin learning about our bodies so that we could act to make some changes' (1976: 18, 24–5). This liberatory learning, as Donna Haraway indicates above, involves a quite literal seizing of the tools of a male-dominated medical science. As the Boston women describe it, upon realizing their unfamiliarity with their own sexual bodies, they began to engage in self-examination: 'To do this we use a mirror, flashlight and a clean plastic speculum'. Such self-examination, they add, 'is something we can choose to do alone or with others, once or often', and they encourage their readers to a similar self-exploration: 'The following description will mean much more if you look at yourself with a mirror while you read the text and look at the diagrams. It is written as if you were squatting and looking into a hand mirror' (1976: 26–7).

For these 1970s feminists, then, the body is to be wrested from the control of a male-dominated and misogynist medical practice so that, no longer object of the male medico-scientific gaze, the experiencing self and the knowing self may become one. 'We are our bodies', argue the Boston women. 'Our book celebrates this simple fact' (1976: 39). Thus menstruation, for example, is to be compared to 'a tree shedding its leaves in the fall', in stark contrast to a quoted description of the uterus by a male gynaecologist as 'a useless, bleeding, symptom-producing, potentially cancer-bearing

organ [which] therefore should be removed' (1976: 33, 148). This attempt
to reclaim 'an authentic delight in the body' (Bartky 1982: 138), in the face
of a medical objectification of the female body conceived as akin to territorial conquest, can be found throughout the activist writings of the 1970s. In
a contribution to the 1974 British anthology *Conditions of Illusion: Papers
from the Women's Movement*, for example, Angela Hamblin writes: 'Our
bodies are our territory, our sexuality and fertility, our raw materials. In our
male imperialist culture both are systematically exploited' (1974: 87).

The focus of such writings, then, is threefold. It is on the constraints on
the female body produced by what Sandra Lee Bartky calls 'the
fashion–beauty complex'; it is on the violation of female bodily integrity
represented by rape and other forms of sexual violence; and it is on the
medical control of the female sexual and reproductive body. The first of
these, according to Bartky, is, like 'the military-industrial complex', 'a
major articulation of capitalist patriarchy' (1982: 135). It functions both to
confine women *to* their objectified and passive bodies and to estrange them
from their bodies: 'On the one hand, I *am* it and am scarcely allowed to be
anything else; on the other hand, I must exist perpetually at a distance from
my physical self, fixed at this distance in a permanent posture of disap-
proval' (1982: 136). Liberation from this 'repressive narcissism' will be into
'authentic delight' in the body as active subject, nourished and supported
by the 'witness' of a revolutionary feminist community (1982: 140).

The second focus is one of the best-known areas of 'second wave' feminist activism. The technique of consciousness-raising, with its politicizing of
autobiography, produced from the naming and sharing of experience a
powerful analysis of rape as a political act designed to deny women subjectivity. As Susan Griffin argued in 1979, 'more than rape itself, the fear of
rape permeates our lives. . . . And the best defense against this is not to be,
to deny being in the body, as a self, to . . . avert your gaze, make yourself,
as a presence in the world, less felt' (cited in Hall 1983: 333). Out of this
analysis emerged both the self-help methods of the rape crisis centres and
attacks on patriarchal legal and medical systems which reinforced 'the
Blame (or Disbelieve) the Victim syndrome' (Morgan 1993b: 85). Robin
Morgan's 1974 essay, 'Theory and Practice: Pornography and Rape' is
perhaps the classic statement of the radical feminist position on rape in the
1970s. In it rape is defined as 'the perfected act of male sexuality in a patriarchal culture – it is the ultimate metaphor for domination, violence, subjugation, and possession'. It can be said to occur 'any time sexual intercourse
occurs when it has not been initiated by the woman, out of her own genuine
affection and desire' (Morgan 1993b: 82, 84). It is to be linked to pornography, as the title of Morgan's essay indicates, in the relationship of practice to theory. Pornography, she argues,

> is sexist propaganda, no more and no less. *Pornography is the
> theory, and rape the practice.* And what a practice. The violation of

an individual woman is the metaphor for man's forcing himself on whole nations (rape as the crux of war), on nonhuman creatures (rape as the lust behind hunting and related carnage), and on the planet itself (reflected even in our language – carving up 'virgin territory,' with strip mining often referred to as a 'rape of the land'). (1993b: 88)

The third focus emphasizes the need for liberation from medical control of the female body. The titles of chapters in *Our Bodies, Ourselves* are typical here in indicating the range and emphasis of this attack, moving as they do from 'Our Changing Sense of Self', through 'The Anatomy and Physiology of Sexuality and Reproduction' and 'Sexuality', to 'Taking Care of Ourselves', 'Rape', 'Self-Defense', 'Venereal Disease' and 'Abortion', to 'Pregnancy', 'Postpartum' and 'Menopause' and finally to 'Women and Health Care'. Throughout, the emphasis is on self-exploration and self-help, with an attack on 'medical mystifications'[3] and, typically, a listing of self-help and action groups. Again, Robin Morgan's argument is characteristic. 'Androcentric medical science,' she argues, 'like other professional industries in the service of the colonizer, has researched better and more efficient means of mining our natural resources, with (literally) bloody little concern for the true health, comfort, nurturance, or even survival of those resources. This should hardly surprise us; our ignorance about our own primary terrain – our bodies – is in the self-interest of the patriarchy' (1993c: 76).

What unites the three areas of focus is the desire to reclaim what is seen as a 'natural' female body, a body undistorted by patriarchal constraints or violence and possessing its own active sexuality. Yet even in its own terms this argument is uneasy. Despite their insistence that 'we are our bodies', for example, the women of the Boston Women's Health Book Collective revert constantly to the language of dualism. 'I watch my daughter', comments one woman. 'From morning to night her body is her home. She lives in it and with it' (1976: 40). For another, the dualism is even more pronounced:

> When I came back to Boston I decided that I really wanted to learn how to take care and be in control of a car myself. I learned about auto mechanics. It required a lot of work and discipline. In a way, I identify with the car. There is a connection between my feelings of wanting to take care and control of my life and the feelings of wanting to take care and control of my car. (1976: 22)

Home, car, territory, terrain: these are the metaphors employed. The question becomes one of control, with 'woman' remaining split between body and self, whilst man retains the single identity of would-be colonizer. The problem, as the Boston women are aware, is that to identify female subjectivity with the body is a dangerous move for women. The difficulty can be seen most clearly in 1970s arguments around 'the politics of the female orgasm'. For writers like Angela Hamblin in *Conditions of Illusion*[4] it is the distortion and mutilation of women's 'natural capacity for sexuality' which constitutes the primary marker of patriarchy. Women, as Masters and Johnson had discovered, 'have a natural capacity for sexuality far in excess of that of men . . . But thousands of years of patriarchal conditioning and exploitation has robbed us of our sexual potential and deceived us about the true nature of our sexuality' (1974: 87). The reclaiming of the orgasm represents therefore the reclaiming of an *active* – even, by patriarchal norms, an *excessive* – sexuality. In laying claim to the orgasm, woman thus also lays claim to the status of active, desiring subject, and – for that moment at least (since Masters and Johnston had established that there is only one kind of female orgasm, the clitoral orgasm) – to a non-alienated, unitary subjectivity.

It is a powerful argument but, as Donna Haraway has pointed out, one which is highly problematic in a number of ways. As the outline above makes clear, it relies on the same territorial metaphors and on the same symbolic structures as the argument for a unitary *male* subjectivity. If the self-identity of the phallus could be linked to the unitary nature of male subjectivity, then the self-identity of the clitoris could perform a similar function for women. Thus, as Haraway argues, 'orgasmic sexual pleasure became for (unmarked, i.e., white) women what it has been for (unmarked) men before, the sign of the "same," i.e., of the capacity to be (mis)repre-sented as the unmarked, self-identical subject – at least for a few intense seconds' (1990b: 147). That such a strategy could function only for 'unmarked' (white, middle-class) women is clear when we consider that the capacity of non-white women – and of prostitutes – to enjoy orgasm was never in doubt. It was indeed precisely this which in nineteenth-century scientific and medical discourses, as Sander Gilman (1985) has pointed out, marked their 'Otherness', as 'primitive', 'impaired', 'sick', 'diseased'. Such claims, as Haraway, Dowd Hall, hooks and other writers have argued, operate firstly to erase the cultural, historical and political differences *between* women's bodies – black, white, working-class, middle-class, young, ageing, ill, disabled, maternal or infertile. Secondly, in seeking to base claims to subjectivity on notions of the self-identity of the female sexual body, these arguments reinstate both the myth of unitary individual-ity and the absoluteness of sexual difference. Yet it is a concept of sexual difference in which the specificity of female sexuality is in fact lost. The female orgasm, like the male, now becomes the moment simultaneously of control and transcendence, affirming not the fluidity and amorphousness – the *non*-identity – of the body, but its oneness.

The strategy is dangerous – even for white women – in other ways too, as the tentativeness of the Boston women demonstrates. To reclaim a 'natural' sexualized female body as the self is to risk simply recoding 'female' once again *as* body, and hence uncontrollable, irrational, excessive, disruptive. Mary Jane Sherfey's work in the 1970s illustrates this. An American psychiatrist, Sherfey's work on the clitoral orgasm and on women's capacity for multiple orgasm was seen, along with the work of Masters and Johnson, as supplying scientific support for the feminist reclaiming of female sexuality. As such it appeared in early feminist anthologies like Robin Morgan's *Sisterhood is Powerful* (1970) and was quoted extensively in writings from the Women's Movement. Yet Sherfey's findings that women's capacity for orgasm vastly exceeds that of men actually lead her to conclusions very different from those of the feminist writers who use her work. She concludes, in fact, that 'the *forceful* suppression of women's inordinate sexual demands was a prerequisite to the dawn of every modern civilization and every living culture. . . . Not until these drives were gradually brought under control by rigidly enforced social codes could family life become the stabilizing and creative crucible from which modern civilized man could emerge' (Sherfey 1970: 224–5, original emphasis). Woman's corporeality is here once again *opposed* to reason, culture, civilization – all of which are, it seems, exclusively the work of men.

The Body in Representation

As the references above to pornography, to 'medical mystifications' and to 'the fashion–beauty complex' make clear, at the centre of 1970s discussions of the need to reclaim the female body was the body not simply as material presence but also as figure within representation. Indeed it is the relationship between the two that is at the centre of discussions of the body within feminist cultural studies. For the writers discussed above, that relationship is clear. Patriarchal ideology objectifies and distorts the female body and, to the extent that women too are caught up in this ideology, it estranges them from their bodies. The answer to Annette Kuhn's question (1995b: 6), 'Why are images of women so prevalent in our society?', for these writers, is that they are a form of symbolic violence designed to subjugate and coerce women. Women, however, have the power to retrieve an authentic female body that will in turn find self-expression – in action, sexuality, display and play (Bartky 1982: 139–40).

If we turn to American feminist film studies of the early 1970s, we find a similar emphasis. Behind Marjorie Rosen's (1973) analysis of 'the Cinema Woman [as] a Popcorn Venus, a delectable but insubstantial hybrid of cultural distortions' (Rosen 1974: 10), for example, lies the shadowy figure of the *real* woman, as yet unrepresented and unexpressed but now 'slowly awakening' (1974: 33). For British feminist film theory, however, as I have discussed more extensively elsewhere (Thornham 1997), the emphasis lay on the body of woman as *sign*, a textual figure readable only within the signifying system of film, her spectacular presence masking only an *absence* of reality.

For 1960s (male) film theorists, the fascination of cinema was precisely the contradiction between the spectacular 'fullness' of the cinematic image and the structure of cuts and absences from which it is constructed (Thornham 1997: 38). In 1970s feminist film theory, this becomes a preoccupation with the body of woman *as absence*. 'Within a sexist ideology and a male-dominated cinema', wrote Claire Johnston in 1973, 'woman is presented as what she represents for man'. Despite the 'enormous emphasis placed on woman as spectacle in the cinema', therefore, 'woman as woman is largely absent' (Johnston 1973: 26). Yet cinema, as Linda Williams (1991) reminds us, is a producer of somatic effects: from the erotic responses of the male spectator, which are the aim of pornography, to the tears produced by the 'woman's film' or 'weepie'. If feminist film theory was to move beyond a concept of patriarchal images of woman as simply repressive and coercive – with the implication that there exists somewhere a 'true' body of woman, undetermined by social constraints, which has yet to be expressed – it had, then, to theorize some connection between the 'woman on the screen' and the women in the audience. As Judith Mayne argued, 'there's something about coming to terms with film from the perspective of what it means to be an object of spectacle and what it means to be a spectator that is really a coming to terms with how that relationship exists both up on the screen and in everyday life' (Citron *et al.* 1978: 83).

It can be argued, then, that the turn towards psychoanalysis in feminist film theory – and in feminist cultural theory more generally – was an attempt to bridge exactly this gap. Psychoanalysis takes as its object precisely the point of intersection between the corporeal and the psychic – which it calls the unconscious. As Elizabeth Grosz reminds us, Freud's interest was 'in theorizing the interface between the soma and the psyche, between biology and psychology' (1994: 28). His concept of the ego is that of a mediator between the corporeal and instinctual (the id) and the cultural. Thus his work – whatever its problems for feminism (see Chapter 4) and however much it may have been caught up in a theorizing of the body *as text* – nevertheless holds out the promise of an understanding of an embodied subjectivity. Its sexed subjects, both men and women, are both fully corporeal and fully cultural.

In *Women Take Issue* this question of the 'body politics' of 1970s feminism is rarely raised explicitly (the topic does not, for example, appear in the index). The discussion of psychoanalysis by Burniston, Mort and Weedon is highly abstract and theoretical, and Janice Winship's analysis of what Bartky would call 'the fashion–beauty complex' in women's magazines focuses on the ideological contradictions in the text–reader relationship. Though Winship the researcher is seen to be inside not outside this relationship, it is 'lived experience' rather than the female body or sexuality that is posed against – or in relationship to – 'ideologies of femininity'. In Angela McRobbie's chapter on 'Working Class Girls and the Culture of Femininity', as we have seen, the sexualized body of the teenage girl appears as a disruptive force which cannot quite be contained by the theoretical structures within which McRobbie seeks to work. Only in Charlotte

Brunsdon's chapter, ' "It is well known that by nature women are inclined to be rather personal" ', is the question addressed directly, as Brunsdon charts the attempts by the Women's Movement to reclaim the female body, against the background of an ideological reduction of woman *to* her body, a body which is simultaneously *not* hers but 'defined in relation to men' (Brunsdon 1978: 21). Brunsdon argues, then, that 'arguments from nature have an ideological centrality in the subordination of women, precisely because their reference point is always biological and anatomical' (1978: 190), but, though she charts them, it is clear that she does not feel that attempts to reclaim an 'authentic' female body will provide an answer to such arguments. Her conclusion that '[w]e have somehow to hold the necessary articulation of female experience . . . with the struggle to understand the determinants on this experience' (1978: 31), is a move away from the terminology of the Women's Movement and a return to the conceptual framework – ideological structures versus 'lived experience' – of cultural studies.

The Disciplined Body

It seems as though 1980s culture exploded around a celebration of the body (-beautiful): the gym (or at least talk about it), body piercing, dance culture, and safe sex. . . . Just pick the body you want and it can be yours (for a price). Such a conception never questioned the body's status as an *object* (of reflection, intervention, training, or remaking), never even considered the possibility that the body could be understood as subject, agent, or activity. This pliable body is what Foucault . . . describes as 'docile,' though with an unforeseen twist: this docility no longer functions primarily by external regulation, supervision, and constraint, as Foucault claimed, but rather the consequence of endlessly more intensified self-regulation, self-management, and self-control. (Grosz 1995: 2)

It was feminist engagement with the work of Michel Foucault in the 1980s that promised a way of integrating the cultural studies focus on the dialectic between structure and agency with the 'body politics' of feminism. For Foucault, power does not operate through the repression of an 'authentic' body and its sexuality, as feminist writers of the 1970s maintained. It does not control the body through either ideology or force. Rather, it produces the body, in the words of Elizabeth Grosz, 'as a determinate type, with particular features, skills, and attributes' (Grosz 1994: 149) through its techniques of supervision, discipline and control. Foucault argues:

The body is moulded by a great many distinct regimes; it is broken down by the rhythms of work, rest and holidays; it is poisoned by food or values, through eating habits or moral laws; it constructs resistances. . . . Nothing in man – not even his body – is sufficiently stable to serve as a basis of self-recognition or for understanding other men. (Foucault 1979a: 153)

For Foucault, then, there is no 'authentic' body outside of history, for it is produced within and by history. Nor can it be 'reclaimed' from the field of politics or power, for it is always 'directly involved in a political field; power relations have an immediate hold on it; they invest it, mark it, train it, torture it, force it to carry out tasks, to perform ceremonies, to emit signs' (Foucault 1979a: 25). Equally, it cannot be separated from discourse, for discourses, in the words of Elizabeth Grosz, 'intermesh with bodies, with the lives and behavior of individuals, to constitute them as particular bodies' (1994: 150). Finally, if the body is always fully within history, it follows that sexuality, too,

> must not be thought of as a kind of natural given which power tries to hold in check, or as an obscure domain which knowledge tries gradually to uncover. It is the name that can be given to a historical construct: not a furtive reality that is difficult to grasp, but a great surface network in which the stimulation of bodies, the intensification of pleasures, the incitement to discourse, the formation of special knowledges, the strengthening of controls and resistances, are linked to one another, in accordance with a few major strategies of knowledge and power. (Foucault 1981: 105–6)

For feminism, Foucault's work poses a number of problems. First and most obviously, as the quotations above indicate, the body, in Foucault's thought, is always assumed to be male. This means that the specificity of the disciplinary and supervisory controls applied to women's bodies and pleasures by a patriarchal society are rendered invisible. Further, if the body is to be considered – as Foucault does consider it – as a source of resistance as well as control, the precise resistances which the sexually and historically specific bodies of women might present are equally invisible if the body is not considered in terms of sexual difference. In particular, Foucault's thought fails to deal with the complex relationship between complicity and resistance which can mark, for example, the silencing of women or the hystericization of women's bodies, in the context of a culture which reduces women to (the silence of) their sexually compliant bodies.[5]

Nevertheless, if Foucault ignores the question of sexual difference, sometimes it seems by omission, sometimes more deliberately, this does not mean that his work cannot be appropriated for feminism. As Lois McNay argues, 'Foucault's theory of power and the body indicates to feminists a way of placing a notion of the body at the centre of explanations of women's oppression that does not fall back into essentialism or biologism' (McNay 1992: 11); here lies its attractiveness for a feminist cultural studies. In the following section, then, I shall discuss the ways in which feminist cultural studies of the 1980s and 1990s has returned to key issues of the 1970s 'politics of the body' – the invasion and control of women's bodies through 'the fashion–beauty complex', violence and medical surveillance – via an appropriation of Foucault's theories.

Susan Bordo's work exemplifies this move. Bordo reminds us that 'neither Foucault nor any other poststructuralist thinker discovered the idea ... that the "definition and shaping" of the body is ... the focal point for struggles over the shape of power'. '*That*', she insists, 'was discovered by feminism' (1993a: 17), and she traces the discovery back to feminist thinkers like Mary Wollstonecraft (see Chapter 2 of this book). The feminism of the 1970s, she argues, went on to imagine the body as 'a politically inscribed entity, its physiology and morphology shaped by histories of containment and control – from foot-binding and corseting to rape and battering to compulsory heterosexuality, forced sterilization, unwanted pregnancy, and (in the case of the African American slave woman) explicit commodification' (1993a: 21–2). Yet, as we have seen, such imaginings are persistently drawn, first, to a dualism which tends to reinstate the equation 'body = female', and second to the utopian fantasy of an 'authentic' female body which might somehow be reclaimed. For Bordo, however, 'the body that we experience and conceptualize is always *mediated* by constructs, associations, images of a cultural nature' (1993a: 35). The 'material body' on which she insists is not a 'natural' or 'unmediated' body, but a body which is in the 'direct grip' of culture. That is, our bodies, she argues, are not (or not only) controlled via ideologies of femininity conveyed through images and representations; they are disciplined directly through 'the practices and bodily habits of everyday life' (1993a: 16). It is on these practices, particularly as they relate to 'the slender body' and its extreme manifestations in eating disorders among young women, that much of her work is focused.

For Bordo, then, there are clear parallels between the nineteenth-century 'hystericization of women's bodies', which Foucault identifies as a 'process whereby the feminine body was analyzed – qualified and disqualified – as being thoroughly saturated with sexuality' (Foucault 1981: 104), and the eating disorders of the late twentieth century. In both, culture *produces* the disorder in and upon the bodies of women. In both, there is a continuum between the normative and the disordered, at the same time as the distinction operates as a form of regulation and control. For the Victorian woman, *femininity itself* required the qualities seen in extreme form in the hysteric: 'the holding of breath, the loss of air, the relinquishing of voice, the denial of appetite, the constriction of body' (Bordo 1993b: 50). Whether we look at hysteria, agoraphobia or anorexia, then,

we find the body of the sufferer deeply inscribed with an ideological construction of femininity emblematic of the period in question. The construction, of course, is always homogenizing and normalizing, erasing racial, class, and other differences and insisting that all women aspire to a coercive, standardized ideal. Strikingly, in these disorders the construction of femininity is written in disturbingly concrete, hyperbolic terms: exaggerated, extremely literal, at times virtually caricatured presentations of the feminine mystique. (1989: 16)

Thus the body itself becomes the point of inscription of cultural norms, but it is not simply that it thereby becomes a 'docile body'. For the anorectic body is a point of contradiction and struggle: like the body of the hysteric, it does not merely embody a 'feminine' shame over bodily needs and appetites; it is also the embodiment of a quite '*un*feminine' desire for self-control and self-mastery. The anorexic refuses to be soft, compliant, passive; she insists on rigid self-control. Bordo cites a study of female anorectics which reports that 88 per cent of the subjects questioned responded that they lost weight because they 'liked the feeling of will power and self-control' (1993c: 323n). Anorexia is thus an embodied *protest* against the cultural conditions of femininity as much as it is an expression of those conditions. As a pathological protest, however, anorexia ultimately works to deliver the woman into the proprietorship of the medical scientist, just as hysteria delivered her into the hands of the scientist/analyst. In the 'political battle [which] is being waged over the energies and resources of the female body' (1993b: 66), argues Bordo, such 'pathologies of female protest function, paradoxically, as if in collusion with the cultural conditions that produce them, reproducing rather than transforming precisely that which is being protested' (1989: 22).

The medicalization of women's bodies is an issue to which Bordo also returns – as did the feminist activists of the 1970s – in relation to the issue of women's reproductive rights. In 'Are Mothers Persons?' she examines the ways in which conceptions of subjectivity and 'personhood' which originate in Enlightenment philosophy are played out in contemporary medical and legal practices. 'Although law and medicine claim to have a unified and coherent tradition concerning individual rights', she argues, 'in fact two different traditions have been established, one for embodied subjects, and the other for those who come to be treated as mere bodies despite an official rhetoric that vehemently forswears such treatment of human beings' (1993d: 72). The tradition regarding embodied subjects, then, is translated into medical and legal practice as the refusal to force individuals to submit without consent to medical treatment, even though their own or another's life may depend on it. Such coercion, it is maintained, constitutes a violation of the bodily integrity of the subject. Yet no such concept is seen to protect the reproductive rights of women – particularly when they are poor, non-Western or of non-European descent. Forced sterilization, the refusal of information about abortion, and enforced obstetrical intervention are all, writes Bordo, common in the United States. In particular, what has occurred in the 'Right to Life' and 'Fathers' Rights' debates, is the conferral of 'personhood' on the foetus, and with this a corresponding *loss* of subject-status for the woman. As men have fought the right to abortion of their pregnant partners, employing a rhetoric which figures not only the foetus as *child* but also themselves as *woman* ('That baby is a part of my body also'; the man feels 'raped of his reproductive rights'; quoted in Bordo 1993d: 91–2), so women are re-imagined as mere carriers of foetuses.[6] In this process what is lost, argues Bordo, is not only the concept of the woman as autonomous subject, but also the specificity of women's embodied subjectivity. As subjects whose embodiment is not fixed, but fluid, subject to change, able to house 'otherness' within the self, women's physical being challenges the modernist philosophical imagining of the subject as unitary, self-identical, its autonomy 'guaranteed' by the bodily integrity of the (male) body. Thus the backlash against women's reproductive rights is also a backlash against the feminist reconceptualization of subjectivity.

Bordo's work on women's reproductive rights is paralleled also by that of Paula Treichler and, in Britain, by that of Sarah Franklin and others at the Birmingham Department of Cultural Studies in the 1980s. Treichler's concern is with the construction, codification and mobilization of cultural definitions of childbirth. Like Bordo, she points to the ways in which these definitions operate to erase the subjectivity of women both discursively and within cultural practices. Medical textbooks, she points out, persistently describe childbirth as a process that concerns the foetus, the doctor and the uterus, but not, it seems, the woman. But definitions, as Foucault argues, are meanings 'that [have] become official' (Treichler 1990: 123); they are embodied in laws, policies and everyday practices. The erasure of the subjecthood of woman in medical and legal definitions of childbirth must therefore, she argues, be contested by feminists. Like Bordo, she is not arguing here for the return to a concept of an 'innocent', pre-cultural female body; childbirth and the maternal body are fully caught up in culture. Childbirth, she argues *'is* what it means' (1990: 115); the contest is over that meaning.

Franklin's concern, like Bordo's, is with the concept of 'foetal personhood' and its functioning within medical, legal and political discourses about abortion rights. Like Treichler, she cites the assertions of medical textbooks. 'The fetus is thought of nowadays not as an inert passenger in pregnancy', writes one, 'but, rather, as in command of it' (quoted in Franklin 1991: 193); it 'induces changes in maternal physiology which make her a suitable host'. In such accounts, writes Franklin, the relationship between foetus and 'host' is figured as an antagonistic one: the foetus – independent, active – must somehow mould the mother into a 'suitable host'. Such a construction of the foetus as autonomous being is aided, as Rosalind Pollack Petchesky has also argued, through the use of foetal imaging techniques that represent it not as situated within the mother's body but as somehow free-floating, suspended in space. Thus the foetus is made present to the mother not through her own bodily sensations but through the abstraction of the photographic image – the ultrasound image which becomes the first picture in the 'baby album'. Petchesky points to the voyeurism and fetishization present in such discourses, quoting one medical article on technological developments in 'foetal management' which describes them as 'render[ing] the once opaque womb transparent, stripping the veil of mystery from the dark inner sanctum, and letting the light of scientific observation fall on the shy and secretive foetus' (Petchesky 1987: 69).

In such an account, the foetus becomes a shy and mysterious 'little creature', to be tracked down by the clinician-photographer, with the mother no more than its habitat. In others, as Barbara Katz Rothman points out, the metaphor is of ' "man" in space, floating free, attached only by the umbilical cord to the spaceship'. In this description, she observes, the mother 'has become empty space' (1986: 114). For Franklin, the unifying factor in such discourses is what she calls *patriarchal individualism*, a concept which underpins the construction of foetal personhood in a number of respects, 'including how it is constructed through power/knowledge or discourse, how it is described through language and metaphor, how it is represented visually, how it is narrated and how it is positioned as a masculine subject' (1991: 201). The foetus is figured not only as male but also as a patriarchal citizen with rights and entitlements. Like Bordo, Franklin argues that this not only reasserts the identification of subject-hood with an autonomous male body (the foetus has individual rights because it is *separate from* the mother's body), but also effects, once again, the erasure of women's status as persons. The concept of foetal rights, argues Franklin, 'threatens the bodily integrity, the individual autonomy and the right to bodily sovereignty of women' (1991: 201). To endow foetuses with civil rights is to confer upon them a status in relation to the patriarchal social contract which women have never had. Women's bodies, which *can* be divided, have always placed them in a precarious relationship to a concept of individuality whose literal definition is 'that which cannot be divided'.

What all of these studies of the 'disciplining' of women's bodies have in common is a focus on the ways in which discursive practices intersect with social, economic, medical, legal and political structures to produce meanings about the female body which are embodied not only in representations but in cultural practices. The final area of such research which I shall consider here concerns a form of body-culture which seems, at least at first sight, to offer greater empowerment to women: exercise, body-building and 'working out'. Such practices, writes Susan Bordo, appear to have the opposite structure to anorexia: 'the body-builder is, after all, building the body *up*, not whittling it down. . . . We imagine the body-builder as someone who is proud, confident, and perhaps most of all, conscious of and accepting of her physicality' (1993c: 151). As the Boston Women's Health Book Collective insisted in the 1970s, exercise, the cultivation of physical strength and agility, can be a positive move against the cultural construction of femininity as learned passivity. But in fact, writes Bordo, 'a sense of joy in the body as active and alive is *not* the most prominent theme' amongst women body-builders interviewed by researchers (1993c: 151). Instead what they, like anorectics, emphasize is 'a quest for perfection' through absolute *control* of the body: 'the thrill of being in total charge of the shape of one's body' (1993c: 152). The body, indeed, is perceived as not-self, as alien; it must be relentlessly sculpted and shaped. 'You visualize what you want to look like', says one, 'and then create the form' (1993c: 152). As with the anorectic, however, this is not *only* a normalizing practice producing a self-monitoring 'docile' body. The muscled female body is a site of protest – against the 'soft', passive, commodified body of conventional femininity – as well as of control. Yet, as with the anorectic, the protest *against* cultural demands and norms is expressed through disciplinary practices that fix us more firmly within their grip.

In support of her argument, Bordo cites the shifts in body shape throughout the 1980s of that 'postmodern heroine', Madonna. Madonna's repeated reinvention of her own image, and subversion of conventional stereotypes of femininity, have been seen by some feminist writers as a deconstruction not only of ideologies of femininity but also of the very notion of a fixed or unitary identity. Whilst this might seem to be the case if we consider only *representations* of Madonna in images and videos, however, Bordo points to the strenuous regime of self-regulation which has produced this 'shifting' shape. Madonna's 'new' body, which appears to have no material history, in fact 'conceals its continual struggle to maintain itself, it does not reveal its pain' (1993e: 272). This does not mean, however, that Madonna's earlier, fleshy body should be considered a 'natural' body that is now subject to repression. *All* bodies, insists Bordo, are produced within culture, out of the cultural forms available to us.

Rebellious Bodies

> When I'm on stage I want my body to talk, I want it to almost sing with muscle. (Carol Mock, body-builder, quoted in Mansfield and McGinn 1993: 58)

Other writers, however, have given a rather different emphasis to their studies of exercise, body-building and 'the workout', stressing their ambiguities, their challenge to conceptions of 'the natural order', and their status as performance. Laurie Schulze, for example, reflecting in 1990 on her own earlier work, writes: 'Were I to reopen an inquiry into professional female bodybuilding today, I would attempt to begin the work of mapping female muscle culture as a terrain for resistance/refusal, rather than giving ground to the terrain of control. . . . I would investigate the meanings and pleasures made by the members of the bodybuilding subculture and its audiences from the experiences, performances, and texts they enjoy' (Schulze 1990: 67). She draws on feminist ethnography and on John Fiske's application to the world of professional wrestling of Mikhail Bakhtin's theories of the carnivalesque,[7] to argue that the 'unnaturalness' of female body-building, its emphasis on the spectacular, the excessive and the 'tasteless', all link it to 'resistant forms of 'low culture' rather than to forms of social control. 'A female body displaying "extreme" muscle mass, separation and definition', she comments, 'yet oiled up, clad in a bikini, marked with conventionally "feminine"-styled hair and carefully applied cosmetics juxtaposes heterogeneous elements in a way that frustrates ideological unity and confounds common sense' (1990: 68).

Annette Kuhn, in her analysis of the 1986 film, *Pumping Iron II – The Women*, makes a similar point. When women become body-builders, she argues,

> a twofold challenge to the natural order is posed. Not only is the naturalness of the body called into question by its inscription within a certain kind of performance: but when women have the muscles, the natural order of gender is under threat as well. Muscles are rather like drag, for female bodybuilders especially: while muscles can be assumed, like clothing, women's assumption of muscles implies a transgression of the proper boundaries of sexual difference. (1988: 17)

This argument that muscles function for women as a form of drag links Kuhn's analysis with the work of Judith Butler, who also uses the ideas of Michel Foucault to argue for the *performativity* of gender identity. There is no essence of heterosexual masculinity or femininity that precedes our performance of it, argues Butler. We construct the very notion of that essence – and hence of our stable and coherent identities as men or women – through the regulatory practices which structure our performances. Thus the individual whose gendered identity can *not* be read as stable or coherent within this framework, but who must nevertheless be recognized as a *person*, threatens the very notion of identity as 'self-identical, persisting through time as the same, unified and internally coherent' (Butler 1990: 16–17). Butler's discussion encompasses both the challenges to conventional understandings offered by anatomically ambiguous persons and the consciously transgressive performativity of parodic practices such as drag, cross-dressing and the sexual stylization of butch/femme identities (1990: 137). In the case of the female body-builder's muscular display, however, we can argue that such transgressive performativity is inscribed on the body itself, so that the body becomes, as Schulze suggests, a site of resistant play.

For Hilary Radner, Bordo's use of Foucault's work to emphasize the *disciplinary* function of the exercise workout underestimates the complexities and ambiguities of such practices. Bordo's argument that these practices should be understood in the context of a backlash against feminist agendas for women's empowerment leads us inevitably back, argues Radner, to the 1970s notion that there exists the possibility of an *un*mediated body which can be reclaimed for feminism. In fact, writes Radner, the 'discipline of the body is a given within any social formation' (Radner 1995: 145). What is marked by the 1980s 'aerobics craze' – which is the focus of Radner's essay – is a historical shift whereby the disciplinary practices which produce the feminine body in Western culture can be seen to move from the private to the public sphere. In a culture in which the feminine body is produced primarily through its function within the private sphere of the family, that body remains relatively unsubjected to the disciplinary practices of the public sphere, and hence a potential threat to a (masculine) public order produced by discourses of discipline and punishment. The late twentieth century, however, has seen the formulation of a new 'public body', in which the body of the citizen can now be designated as feminine. Such a shift necessitates new disciplinary procedures, but their meaning is both complex and ambiguous: they are produced by and productive of a move towards greater autonomy and self-mastery for women, even as they submit the female body to new technologies of social control.

Where Bordo chooses Madonna as her model, then, Radner cites the *Workout Book* of Jane Fonda as her 'exemplary moment'.[8] Fonda, whose metamorphosis from 'sex-kitten' to 'Citizen Jane' embodies the shift in women's position from the 1950s to the 1980s, offers herself in her *Workout Book* and videotapes as both producer and product of her exercise programme. She is a model of self-empowerment who has transformed both her body and her 'self', but the 'undocile' body that she produces through agency and activity is nevertheless constructed within a conventional heterosexual paradigm. 'I may dress for a man', Fonda is quoted as saying, 'but I exercise for myself' (1995: 150). 'By assuming control of her body, by making it over into an image that is her own', then, 'Fonda rejects a feminine heritage of passivity grounded in the helpless body . . . a body that is in excess of the self that controls it' (1995: 159). But she does this 'by submitting to a public discipline, or another technology or procedure of "domination" ' (1995: 146), one which permits her a degree of autonomy whilst still re-inscribing her within the (new) discourses and practices of a heterosexual femininity.

Sexing Foucault

Radner's reservations about Bordo's work concern the way in which Bordo appropriates Foucault's account of the production of the docile body in the eighteenth century to discuss the representation and production of a feminine body within contemporary culture. If the body is produced through the opposition between normalization and resistance, argues Radner, then a feminist politics which focuses on 'resistance' must always have as its implicit goal the *un-* normalized, *un*-disciplined body, whatever writers like Bordo may say about the body always being culturally constructed. To argue instead for a body produced always within a set of conflicting disciplines and procedures, however, leaves the feminist on uncertain ground, for the notion that women are *particularly* oppressed through the commodification and exploitation of their bodies becomes difficult to sustain. For some feminist writers, however, the problem lies not in specific appropriations of Foucault's work but within the Foucauldian framework itself, and they have sought alternative ways of conceptualizing the body which return to it its sexual specificity.

Elizabeth Grosz, for example, argues that throughout the majority of Foucault's writings 'the concept of the body that he utilized is a "neutral," sexually indifferent, and thus abstract body' (1994: 157). If for Foucault the body is 'the field on which the play of powers, knowledges and resistances is worked out', so that it is power which 'produces the body as a determinate type' (1994: 146–9), she writes, then we must ask questions about the ontological status of the sexed body. Is the sexually different body *produced* through the inscription of power on bodies, she asks, perhaps by carving out difference upon a continuum of (sexual) differences; or are we to assume that sexually different bodies require 'different inscriptive tools to etch their different surfaces' (1994: 156), in order to produce them as 'determinate types'? When Foucault writes that the 'rallying point for the counterattack against the deployment of sexuality ought not to be sex-desire, but bodies and pleasures' (1981: 157), he seems to assume a pre-sexed or sexually indifferent body. If we ask, however, *whose* bodies and which pleasures are to be such a 'rallying-point', Foucault's answer is not so sexually indifferent. Foucault's 'neutral' body, in fact, like that of earlier philosophers, is always implicitly male: it can only, comments Grosz, 'be unambiguously filled in by the male body and men's pleasures' (1994: 156).

For Grosz, then, the notion of the sexed body supplies the framework for her analysis. There is, she writes, 'an irreducible specificity of each sex relative to the other, and there must be at least, but not necessarily only two sexes' (1995: 77). This does not mean, she argues, that all women experience their bodies in the same way, nor does it imply that the *meanings* of those bodies and their bodily flows are pre-cultural or given. If women's bodies in Western culture have been persistently defined in terms of fluidity, indeterminacy, viscosity, seepage and flow, while men's bodies are seen in terms of solidity, self-containment and determinacy, this does not mean that men's bodies *are* somehow more solid and determinate than women's. Nevertheless, all women's bodies are marked as different from men's; there is 'an ineradicable rift' between the two. 'Each sex', she writes, 'has the capacity to (and frequently does) play with, become, a number of different sexualities; but not to take on the body and sex of the other' (1995: 77). Like Foucault, then, Grosz argues that 'the inscription, functioning, and practices of a body constitute what that body is', but she insists that, whatever their instabilities and whatever the capacities of bodies to exceed cultural boundaries, 'both sex and sexuality are marked, lived, and function according to whether it is a male or female body that is being discussed' (1995: 213).

A similar insistence marks the work of Rosi Braidotti. 'Sexual difference', she argues, 'is ontological, not accidental, peripheral, or contingent upon socioeconomic conditions; that one be socially constructed as female is evident, that the recognition of the fact may take place in language is clear, but that the process of construction of femininity fastens and builds upon anatomical realities is equally true' (Braidotti 1994: 186–7). Like Grosz, however, she insists that 'being-a-woman' is not 'the predication of a prescriptive essence, it is not a causal proposition capable of predetermining the outcome of the becoming of each individual identity' (1994: 186–7). The subject 'woman' is 'the site of multiple, complex, and potentially contradictory experience' (1994: 199), but subjectivity, argues Braidotti, is always embodied and always marked by sexual difference: one always *speaks as* a woman.

Braidotti's insistence on a 'female embodied self', then, represents a move to recover the idea of female embodiment as 'a positive, self-affirming political force' – a notion which, as we have seen, is difficult to maintain for a feminism which draws its conceptual framework from the work of Foucault. At the same time, however, it is a move which is not based on the notion of reclaiming an 'original' or 'natural' body; rather, the body which it envisages is one constructed through the act – the feminist project – of turning difference into a strength, of affirming its positivity. Braidotti's concept of the 'nomadic subject' as a subject who is both embodied (and interconnected) and in movement, seeks to embrace the Foucauldian emphasis on the fragmentary and constructed nature of identity, whilst retaining a politics, and an ethics, of sexual difference.

Cyborg Bodies

The most sustained attempt to articulate such ideas in the context of a feminist cultural studies can be found in the work of Donna Haraway. Haraway's work operates at the intersection of feminist cultural theory, cultural studies (the analysis of popular culture, film and advertising) and the cultural analysis of science, and returns us constantly to issues of the history, meanings and boundaries of female embodiment. Like Grosz and Braidotti, she reminds us that no return to a 'natural' body is either possible or desirable for feminism. Her account of the cultural moment of *Our Bodies, Ourselves*, as we have seen, is sympathetic but ultimately critical. The notion that women's liberation could be achieved through the reclaiming of the 'natural' body and its sexuality was, she writes, wrong on three counts. In 'seizing the masters' tools' (Lorde 1984) – the gynaecological speculum, the mirror and the flashlight – the women of the activist women's health movement of the 1970s acted in a spirit of self-help and self-empowerment, but, as we have seen, new visualizing technologies were already re-objectifying women's bodies as the territory of a masculinist medical science. The use of the masters' discourse – caricatured by Haraway as 'Land ho! We have discovered ourselves and claim the new territory for women' (1997: 41) – could only play into what Haraway calls the 'colonial narrative' of medical science which sees women's bodies as territories to be 'opened up' for exploration.

Secondly, such claims were based, as hooks (1990), Omolade (1983) and others have also pointed out, on a universalizing notion of women's bodies which ignores the very different meanings which the notion of the sexualized female body has had in black women's history. 'In the late twentieth century', writes Haraway, 'antiracist feminists cannot engage unproblematically in universalizing discourses about sexual pleasure as a sign of female agency without reinscribing feminism within one of the fundamental technologies for enforcing gendered racial inequality' (1990b: 146). To invoke the notion of an uncolonized *black* female body, as Hazel Carby has commented (1985), is to invoke a very different history and discourse. For white Western culture, blackness has represented corporeality: the black *is* the body, the biological. Ideologies of white femininity as passive and without desire have been erected upon the grounds of a racist discourse which assigns corporeality and the excesses of female desire to the black woman (Doane 1991, Gilman 1985). For white feminists to base claims for *women's* personhood upon the grounds of a reclaimed sexual body, therefore, is to ignore the coercive sexualization of non-white women which has characterized both slavery and more contemporary manifestations of colonialism. Black feminists, writes Carby, have understood that 'the struggle would have to take place on the terrain of the previously colonized' (1985: 276), with all the complexities of power and difference which that implies. To seek to reclaim a body 'unmarked' by those differences is to repeat the imperializing gesture.

Finally, as historian and cultural analyst of science, Haraway insists that we simply *cannot* return to a notion of the organic and natural body. Developments in biomedical sciences have translated the body into 'problems in genetic coding and read-out' (1990a: 206), and technologies of visualization and surgical intervention have disturbed our notion of what constitutes the 'inside' and the 'outside' of the body. Communications technologies and biotechnologies have converged, in other words, to render both organism and high-tech machine a matter of systems and networks, in which the boundaries of the human and the machine have become increasingly blurred. In a culture so saturated in science and technology, in which a powerful 'informatics of domination' is at work, argues Haraway, feminists *cannot* unite around a concept of the natural body.

Instead, she argues, feminism should welcome the conceptual blurring of boundaries that marks contemporary culture, and embrace a 'cyborg' identity. Western thought has been characterized, she writes, by conceptual dualisms which have served an imperialist project, marking boundaries which have opposed the 'self' (the 'unmarked' white male) against the 'other' (those marked as different by sex and/or race). The boundary between self/other, then, has been paralleled by the dualisms of mind/body, nature/culture, male/female, civilized/primitive, reality/appearance, whole/part, agent/resource, maker/made, active/passive, right/wrong, truth/illusion, total/partial, God/man (1990a: 219). The cyborg, embodied but not unitary, a figure of blurred boundaries and subject to regeneration rather than (re)birth, can neither be fixed within such dualisms nor explained by unitary myths of origin or psychoanalytic narratives of identity. It is historically and locally specific but globally connected. The metaphor of the cyborg offers, in short, a 'myth of political identity' which for Haraway expresses a feminist dream of 'situated knowledges' and partial identities which are nevertheless connected across difference and dispersion.

Haraway's 'Manifesto for Cyborgs', with its conclusion that 'I would rather be a cyborg than a goddess' (1990a: 223), has held powerful attractions for recent feminist writers, so that it is now possible to talk about a new kind of feminism: 'cyborg feminism'. Its central concept of an embodied female subjectivity which is not tied to the reclaiming of an 'original' or 'authentic' body – 'a kind of disassembled and reassembled, postmodern collective and personal self' (1990a: 205) – is attractive not only because it sidesteps traditional identifications of women with corporeality. It also links Haraway's 'postmodern' feminism with postcolonial theorists like Gayatri Chakravorty Spivak and Trinh T. Minh-ha. For Minh-ha, as for Foucault, colonial power is discursive power: it confers identity. It is thus impossible to look to a concept of 'authentic' experience on which to ground a politics of resistance, for one can never be outside the discourse which maps that experience. Our very denunciations of oppression are spoken within the terms of that oppression. The post-colonial subject can therefore never be unitary, must always have a 'hyphenated identity'. 'Differences', argues Minh-ha, 'do not only exist between outsider and insider – two entities – they are also at work within the outsider or insider' (1989: 147). Minh-ha's notion of the 'impure, both-in-one insider/outsider' or 'inappropriate/d other' is one upon which Haraway draws for her definition of the cyborg (her example of a contemporary cyborg identity is the 'fusion of outsider identities' called 'women of color'), but she extends it to include all women caught within the 'world system of production/reproduction and communication called the informatics of domination' (1990a: 205).

That Haraway's vision is particularly attractive to the white Western theorist – for whom it offers the dream of political connectedness whilst at the same time permitting a fantasy of embodiment unencumbered by any of the limitations of actual bodily existence – is a charge made by a number of writers within feminist cultural studies.[9] Haraway herself seeks always to tie her 'differential, diffracted feminist allegory' (1992: 300) to the specific analysis of both discursive histories and lived experience. Her insistence that *all* knowledge is situated knowledge, *all* categories 'discursively constituted and non-innocently deployed' (1997: 47), leads her both to the analysis of specific scientific discourses and histories, such as her studies of primatology, and to detailed accounts of the social and economic positioning of '*marked* groups – groups that do not fit the white, or middle-class, or other "unmarked" standard' (1997: 46) on issues like reproductive rights. Science studies, she insists, *are* cultural studies, articulating textual analysis with 'many kinds of sustained scholarly interaction among living people in living situations, historical and contemporary, documentary and *in vivo*' (1992: 234–5).

Nevertheless, the image of the cyborg remains curiously disconnected from such specificities in Haraway's work. Other writers have pointed to problems in the image itself. Jennifer Gonzalez, for example, has observed that the image of the cyborg, far from being a new one, dates back at least to the eighteenth century and has consistently functioned as a site for the representation of cultural fears and anxieties. Cyborg images, then, come already saturated in gender stereotypes, not 'float[ing] above the lingering, clinging past of differences, histories, stories, bodies, places' (1995: 272). Gonzalez cites as evidence a number of recent examples from popular culture, including a 1993 advertisement for Phoenix Technologies Ltd whose cyborg image, gendered female, presents 'not a cyborg of possibilities, [but] a cyborg of slavery' (1995: 273), and examples from comic books where the cyborg is marked not merely as female but also as racially 'other'. This latter image – of the ' "exotic" and vindictive cyborg who passes . . . as simply human' (1995: 277) – has been a common one in recent science-fiction films, such as the 1995 *Species*, and reminds us that the cyborg image – hybrid, fluid, able to 'pass' as one of 'us' – comes already laden with meanings about gendered and racial 'others'.

A glance at recent 'body cultures' such as the ones described earlier in this chapter also reminds us that the cyborg body is not so easily reclaimed for feminism. Cyborg bodies, Anne Balsamo points out, 'pump iron – physically fit, yet unnaturally crafted, they are hyperbuilt' (1988: 339). They may also be the silicone-filled bodies of the surgically reshaped woman, whose 'solidification', suggests Elizabeth Grosz, seeks to limit and control, in the service of a patriarchal ideal, the fluidity and indeterminacy associated with the female body (1994: 205). They may find their ultimate manifestation in the body and face of Michael Jackson, surgically altered to blur the boundaries of sex, race and age yet becoming in the process, as Susan Willis argues, 'the quintessential mass-cultural commodity', a 'simulacrum' who functions not to articulate but to deny cultural diversity (1991c: 120–30). As a final example, we might point to the discursive construction of the 'victims' of the AIDS virus – a virus which works precisely to blur the boundaries between self (healthy cells) and other (the virus) – as marginalized, contagious, and once again as 'the other' who seeks to 'pass' as one of 'us' (Balsamo 1988: 340).

The point made by these writers is that, however suggestive Haraway's image might be in reconceptualizing, in ways that are positive and Utopian, women's experience of their corporeal selves as non-unitary, fluid and fragmented, nevertheless the 'meaning of an image' in Anne Balsamo's words, 'is not easily won' (1988: 342). It is bound up in already existing discursive and cultural practices. The criticism they suggest of the universalizing tendency of some of Haraway's work is even more applicable to that of 'cyberfeminists' like Sadie Plant. Plant builds on Irigaray's argument that the traditions of Western thought are based on the 'imaginary' of the male body and its sexuality – unitary, penetrative, privileging the visual and the external. Women's bodies, in this 'dominant phallic economy', have served as the literal and metaphoric material of domination and exchange:

> The *one* of form, of the individual, of the (male) sexual organ, of the proper name, of the proper meaning . . . supplants, while separating and dividing, that contact of *at least two* (lips) which keeps woman in touch with herself, but without any possibility of distinguishing what is touching from what is touched. (Irigaray 1985: 26)

Woman, continues Irigaray, '*is neither one nor two*. Rigorously speaking, she cannot be identified either as one person, or as two' (1985: 26). It is time, she suggests, 'to return to that repressed entity, the female imaginary' (1985: 28). For Plant, cyberspace can realize this dream. The ones and zeros of machine code resist patriarchal binaries: like the woman or the cyborg, zero 'proliferates, replicates, and undermines the privilege of one' (1996: 179). Similarly, '[n]eural nets function in a way which has less to do with the rigours of orthodox logic than with the intuitive leaps and cross-connections which characterize what has been pathologized as hysteria', and it is touch, not vision, which is 'the sense of multi-media'. The forerunner of computing is not masculine technoscience but the feminine technology of weaving (1996: 177–9), and the future of cyberspace is not the phallic dream of 'total control and autonomy' but 'a dispersed, distributed emergence composed of links between women, women and computers, computers and communication links, connections and connectionist nets' (1996: 182).

The problem with this vision, as a number of writers point out, is that, whatever its claims to address the interrelationship between technology and the female body, there are in fact no bodies in it. What Virtual Reality technology offers is the illusion of escape from the body, reproducing traditional notions of transcendence ('I feel like God' claims one male researcher quoted by Alison Adam) or, even more worryingly, the illusion of control over 'unruly, gendered and raced bodies' (Adam 1998: 178). Ethnographic studies of the users of such technologies suggest, firstly that the dominant computer culture supports what Sherry Turkle calls a culture of 'hard mastery' (1984: 104). Whereas men feel comfortable with this discourse, women's attempts to appropriate the technology produce situations of discomfort or conflict (Turkle 1984, Honey 1994). Women, moreover, remain very much in the minority in Internet usage, and in both the culture of the Internet café and the discourses of the Internet itself, conventional gender values and behaviours, whilst they may be disrupted, are more often reinforced (Adam 1998, Wakeford 2000). Studies of cyberpornography have shown that computer-mediated communication, far from blurring gender boundaries, may actually magnify and accelerate inequalities and harassment (Adams 1996). To seek to invoke a 'female imaginary' through the use of metaphors of the female body (Plant's 'replicunts' and 'Amazones') is not the same, then, as to argue for the importance of embodied subjectivity or to trace its patterns in the lives of specific women. To mistake the two is to replace a politics of the body with a politics of the text – the metaphorical body, as Susan Bordo argues 'is no body at all' (1990: 145).

Embodied Knowledge

> I know that learning to be a feminist has grounded, or embodied, all of my learning and so en-gendered thinking and knowing itself. That engendered thinking and that embodied, situated knowledge (in Donna Haraway's phrase) are the stuff of feminist theory, whether by 'feminist theory' is meant one of a growing number of critical discourses – on culture, science, subjectivity, writing, visual representation, social institutions, etc. – or, more particularly, the critical elaboration of feminist thought itself . . . (de Lauretis 1990: 263)

What is interesting about de Lauretis' list of 'critical discourses' here is that the topics which she lists can all be included under the heading of cultural studies. For de Lauretis, however, feminist discussions of them, being the product of 'embodied, situated knowledge', must remain 'essentially' different from those of male theorists. If, looking back at the 1970s, we can argue, with Terry Lovell, that it was the space which cultural studies opened up for the study of 'women's lives as well as women's texts' (1990: 276) which made it so attractive to feminism, it is equally the case that, insofar as that study was both produced by and productive of a concern with female *embodiment*, the 'space' of cultural studies would always be an uncomfortable one for women to occupy. Insofar as feminism insists, too, that *all* knowledge is embodied, and investigates the gendered fantasies enacted in the discourses and practices of a 'neutral' science and medicine, its concerns lead it in directions which both challenge and disrupt those of (a masculine) cultural studies. The 'body politics' of feminism, always a disruptive force in the narratives of cultural studies, as Stuart Hall's (1992a) description of feminism's dramatic and 'unseemly' 'interruption' into cultural studies indicates, remains central to a *feminist* cultural studies.

Notes

1. The term comes from Julia Kristeva. In order for the child to gain access to the symbolic order, and become a speaking subject, Kristeva argues, it must first delimit its own 'clean and proper' body, separating its bounded, unified self from 'the improper, the unclean and the disorderly' (Grosz 1989: 71). Yet, argues Kristeva, what is excluded 'can never be fully obliterated but hovers at the borders of our existence, threatening the apparently settled unity of the subject with disruption and possible dissolution' (1989: 71). Abjection, then, disturbs identity, system and order, 'respecting no definite positions, rules, boundaries or limits. It is the body's acknowledgement that its boundaries and limits are the effects of desire not nature. It demonstrates the precariousness of the subject's grasp of its own identity'. It is 'the place where meaning collapses' (Grosz 1989: 74, Kristeva 1982: 2). Kristeva distinguishes three broad forms of abjection: abjection in relation to food, to (bodily) waste and to sexual difference. Abjection, then, is identified both with the feminine (menstrual blood as an index of sexual difference) and more specifically with the maternal. Placed on the side of the feminine and the maternal, in opposition to the masculine and paternal symbolic, it is the focus of both repulsion and desire.
2. Jacquelyn Dowd Hall quotes here from Rosalind Petchesky's 'Reproductive Freedom: Beyond "A Woman's Right to Choose"' (1980).
3. This is the title of the essay by Lee Comer in the 1974 anthology, *Conditions of Illusion*.
4. Hamblin draws substantially in her chapter on essays by Susan Lydon and Mary Jane Sherfey in Robin Morgan's 1970 anthology *Sisterhood is Powerful*, as well as on Ann Koedt's 1970 essay 'The Myth of the Vaginal Orgasm'. All of these essays in turn draw heavily on Masters and Johnson's *Human Sexual Response*, published in 1966.
5. Jane Campion's 1993 film, *The Piano*, deals with these issues particularly well, exploring the relationship between oppression and resistance, complicity and transgression, through the body and silence of its nineteenth-century protagonist, Ada.
6. Bordo links this with the patriarchal fantasy of the father as 'true parent' of the child – the mother supplying merely the 'housing' for its growth – which can be traced back at least as far as Aristotle. See Bordo (1993d: 88–90).
7. See Chapter 5, note 13.
8. Susan Willis, in 'Work(ing) Out' (1991d: 62–85) also focuses on Fonda's *Workout* book. For her, however, the book is a much less ambiguous text, exemplifying 'how far a feminist approach to exercise can go in a culture that continues to be defined by men and capitalism' (1991d: 67). Whilst the workout includes 'utopian dimensions' born of 'women's positive desires for strength, agility and the physical affirmation of self', she writes, such aspects are distorted and controlled through their transformation into a commodification of the body, a body which is produced with the aim of achieving 'the right look' (1991d: 70). Thus women are afforded 'the false gratification of seeing themselves in the self-made products they constitute'. Real power, however, remains elsewhere, 'in the

larger corporate structure', so that women merely enact 'the expropriation of ourselves as producers and the alienation of ourselves as consumers' (1991d: 84).

9. Susan Bordo, for example, argues that Haraway's use of the figure of the cyborg risks slipping into 'its own fantasy of escape from human locatedness. . . . To deny the unity and stability of identity is one thing. The epistemological fantasy of *becoming* multiplicity – the dream of endless multiple embodiments, allowing one to dance from place to place and self to self – is another. What sort of a body is it that is free to change its shape and location at will, that can become anyone and travel anywhere?' she asks, and concludes that 'the postmodern body is no body at all' (1990: 142–5).

|8|

Conclusion
Narratives of Displacement

Cultural studies . . . has no simple origins, though some of us were present at some point when it first named itself in that way. Much of the work out of which it grew, in my own experience, was already present in the work of other people. . . . Cultural studies has multiple discourses; it has a number of different histories. It is a whole set of formations; it has its own different conjunctures and moments in the past. It included many different kinds of work. I want to insist on that! It always was a set of unstable formations. . . . It had many trajectories; many people had and have different trajectories through it; it was constructed by a number of different methodologies and theoretical positions, all of them in contention. (Stuart Hall 1992a: 278)

'Identity', argues Stuart Hall elsewhere, 'is formed at the unstable point where the "unspeakable" stories of subjectivity meet the narratives of history, of a culture'. But, he continues, our acceptance of this 'fictional or narrative status of identity' must also necessitate – if we are to be able to act in the world – its opposite, 'the moment of arbitrary closure' (1987: 44–5). This moment of closure – the ending, however provisional, of the story – is what assures the narrative's structure and meaning. It is also the moment when it acquires the possibility of being *told*. The narrative of cultural studies, as Hall insists above, has 'multiple discourses' and 'different histories'; it is a matter of 'different conjunctures and moments in the past' and of contending methodologies and theoretical positions. Nevertheless, as told by Hall and by others, its outlines are clear. It has 'founding fathers', most commonly Raymond Williams, E.P. Thompson and Richard Hoggart. Its concerns centre initially on issues of class, but it is 'interrupted' or 'ruptured', first by feminism, then by the question of race. Finally, its theoretical path is dislocated by the 'necessary detour' in which questions of culture must be rethought in the light of theories of discourse.

Institutionally, it begins as marginal and displaced, but later acquires an uneasy 'disciplinary' status. These broad outlines can be found not only in masculine narratives of cultural studies (Brantlinger 1990, Storey 1993, Turner 1990) but also, though with a different emphasis, in those of feminists like Elizabeth Long who write of feminism's contribution to cultural studies as one of *extending* 'the Centre's substantive interests [and] methodological program' (1989: 429).

If we examine the terms of these narratives, however, they seem remarkably familiar. They look rather like Gillian Skirrow's account of the narrative structure of crime fiction, in which the 'most important relationships . . . are those between men, usually a father–son relationship' and 'the most important issue is male identity'. In these narratives, she writes, 'the characters from whose point of view we see events are on the side of the law and do not change from week to week', though the stories – the disturbances to equilibrium – do. In these stories women 'have very minor roles; even if they are the cause of the disturbance of equilibrium which sets off the narrative, the equilibrium which is restored in the end is a strictly male one' (1985: 175). Like these narratives of crime fiction, in fact, cultural studies narratives resemble the Oedipal narrative itself.[1] In it, as we have seen, feminism takes on the woman's role as disturber of the equilibrium by, as Hall recounts, 'breaking into' the house of cultural studies and 'crapp[ing] on the table' (Hall 1992a: 282).

In this, as Hall describes it, feminism's role is both *like* 'the question of race' and unlike it. The latter produced 'an internal struggle' which continued 'in what has since come to be known, but only in the rewritten history, as one of the great seminal books of the Centre for Cultural Studies, *The Empire Strikes Back*. In actuality,' Hall continues, 'Paul Gilroy and the group of people who produced the book found it extremely difficult to create the necessary theoretical and political space in the Centre in which to work on the project' (1992a: 283). In this account, 'the question of race' is thoroughly masculinized, a qualitatively *different* interruption to that of feminism whose actions, in 'crapp[ing] on the table of cultural studies', place it as cultural studies' aggressive and unclean 'other'. Moreover, the significance of feminism's 'interruption', unlike the 'actuality' which characterizes the account of the work on race, is seen to be – and this is emphasized twice – metaphorical: feminism's intervention is a 'metaphor for theory' (1992a: 283). Finally, feminism also serves another function: it opens up a 'new continent in cultural studies' for its disciplinary adventurers (1992a: 282).

That this is a masculine narrative is not surprising. Given its protagonists, it could not be otherwise, and in Stuart Hall's telling it is a self-aware and self-ironic narrative, one of interruptions, displacements and detours, always in process whatever 'arbitrary closures' might be temporarily drawn. But its masculinity, as this book has been concerned to show, has made it difficult for feminism to establish more than an uneasy relationship with cultural studies, despite the overlapping nature of their concerns.

Charlotte Brunsdon writes of 'the interstices, overlaps and contradictions of the relationships between attention to film and television in cultural studies and that in feminism' (1997: 2), and the editors of *Off Centre: Feminism and Cultural Studies* (Franklin *et al.* 1991) write of both 'overlaps' and 'contested territories' in the relationship. What I have been concerned to try to ask in this book is: what if, as we consider this narrative, we were to try reversing its terms? What if feminism's role were neither that of the protagonist's 'helper', as in Elizabeth Long's account of feminist 'contributions' to cultural studies, nor that of the 'ruptural' force which produces narrative disequilibrium – nor yet again that of the 'continent' (dark or not so dark) which is to be explored?[2] What if feminism, in short, were to be the subject, even the (autobiographical) hero, of this narrative? Such a reversal – and the further questions it provokes – is the issue to which I should now like to return, drawing together the ideas which have been traced in more narrative and historical terms throughout this book.

The Moving Subject

The first question we might ask concerns the precise identity of this new protagonist. Feminism, writes Rosalind Delmar, is 'a way of thinking created by, for, and on behalf of women ... Women are its subjects, its enunciators, the creators of its theory, of its practice and of its language' (1986: 27). But as Denise Riley has pointed out, the categories 'Woman', 'woman' and 'women' are all unstable ones, 'historically, discursively constructed, and always relatively to other categories which themselves change' (1988: 1–2). What it *means* to be a woman is not given at birth but constructed in culture and subject to historical change. Feminism, as the 'systematic fighting-out of that instability', is equally shifting. As 'the voicing of "women" from the side of "women", ... it cannot but act out the full ambiguities of that category' (1988: 5, 112). It, too, is historically and discursively constructed. It risks, then, becoming curiously disembodied, yet its embodiment as female is absolutely crucial to its identity. The category 'women's experience' may be an uncertain, multiple and potentially contradictory category, but it is central to any definition of feminism, and central in marking the difference from the narratives with which this chapter began. There is, in the end, as Teresa de Lauretis writes, 'an essential difference between a feminist and a non-feminist understanding of the subject and its relations to institutions; between feminist and non-feminist knowledges, discourses, and practices of cultural forms, social relations, and subjective processes; between a feminist and a non-feminist historical consciousness' (1990: 255). This recognition of 'a common ground of experience as women mutually engaged in a political task of resistance to *"Woman"* ', to the definitions of us imposed from elsewhere, is what marks, as Rosi Braidotti writes, the feminist subject (1994: 203).

Our protagonist acquires shape, then, as 'the female feminist subject', not defined once and for all, but rather shifting with historical and cultural change, but nonetheless embodied and *situated* within experience.[3] Our next question might concern how *active* this subject is. Is she merely – to use terms taken from narrative theory – the narrating subject, the one who is telling the story? Or is she also the subject of the action, 'the performative agency of action' (Cohan and Shires 1988: 69) – the narrative hero whose actions render her/him both visible and in control as s/he crosses space and time? Is she perhaps somewhat like that archetypal female protagonist, Jane Eyre, in the following passage, full of rebellious thoughts but never in control of the action?

> I was conscious that a moment's mutiny had already rendered me liable to strange penalties, and, like any other rebel slave, I felt resolved, in my desperation, to go all lengths.
> "Hold her arms, Miss Abbot: she's like a mad cat."
> "For shame! For shame!" cried the lady's-maid. "What shocking conduct, Miss Eyre, to strike a young gentleman, your benefactress's son! Your young master."
> "Master! How is he my master? Am I a servant?"
> "No; you are less than a servant, for you do nothing for your keep. There, sit down, and think over your wickedness." (Brontë, *Jane Eyre* 1971: 6)

Or does she, like the protagonist of the 'woman's film' of the 1940s, in Mary Ann Doane's (1984) account, repeatedly begin as active investigator, only to find herself persistently repositioned as object-victim, her identity uncertain, constantly slipping from narrative centrality? If, as Virginia Woolf writes, as women and as feminists 'we think back through our mothers' (1993: 69), can we be sure of finding them and understanding their significance in the same way as cultural studies can locate its 'founding fathers'?

Thirdly, we might want to understand the nature and the difficulties of the speaking voice which we encounter in this narrative. If writing as a feminist always also involves writing as a woman – however unstable the category 'woman' may be – the problem of writing position always arises. Nancy Miller has commented on the problems for feminism posed by Foucault's conclusion to his analysis of 'the author function' within discourse. In 'What is an Author?', Foucault analyses the different ways in which the category of 'the author' operates to control the circulation of discourse in society, attributing value and fixing meaning. Finally, he imagines a society 'without need for an author'.[4] What questions about the relations between discourse, power and subjectivity might we ask, he wonders, once we were no longer tied into issues of authenticity, originality and intentionality? The questions he offers are those with which we are familiar within cultural studies:

"What are the modes of existence of this discourse?"
"Where does it come from; how is it circulated; who controls it?"
"What placements are determined for possible subjects?"
"Who can fulfill these diverse functions of the subject?"

Behind all these questions, adds Foucault, 'we would hear little more than the murmur of indifference: "What matter who's speaking?" '. For women, Miller responds, it does matter; the signature *is* important. The female/feminist subject is always materially positioned; she has *not* always been able to lay claim to her own voice, or speak with it, either as author (think of 'Currer Bell' or 'George Eliot') or as legal signatory. 'Only those who have it can play with not having it', Miller writes. Foucault's own discourse, she adds, has itself an 'authorizing function'; it has 'authorized the "end of woman" without consulting her' (1990: 118). As 'woman', then, the feminist subject is caught always between the claim of equality – the 'right to speak', to 'author' her own work – and of difference – the claim to speak from somewhere else. She finds herself both within and outside the dominant discourse, the 'ultimate cultural dialectician'.[5] Luce Irigaray writes of the difficulties in seeking to answer – or ask – Foucault's questions concerning discourse, power and subjectivity, if one speaks as a woman:

> It is surely not a matter of interpreting the operation of discourse while remaining within the same type of utterance as the one that guarantees discursive coherence. . . . For to speak *of* or *about* woman may always boil down to, or be understood as, a recuperation of the feminine within a logic that maintains it in repression, censorship, nonrecognition. (1985: 78)

One cannot, she writes, analyse the gendered nature of culture by stepping out of the identity 'woman' into a gender-neutral discourse – by claiming an 'equal right' to speak – because there *is* no gender-neutral discourse; the public discourse of analysis is thoroughly masculine. To write from outside that discourse is, however, to be ignored. To do either is to remain within the terms of the dominant discourse. Her own proposed strategy is one of 'mimicry' – a deliberate assumption of 'the feminine role' as parody or masquerade. Others (Riley 1988, Kelly 1984, Snitow 1990) have preferred to write of the 'oscillations' or 'zigzagging' in the speaking voice of the female/feminist subject. We might look, then, for a narrative voice which, in Ann Snitow's words, 'keeps moving' (1990: 36).

Gender and Genre

A fourth question concerns the generic nature of our proposed narrative. Can it aspire to the status of a valued, public genre, or will it belong only to a 'trashy' sub-genre, the 'low culture' of the 'woman's genre'? There are two aspects to this question. The first concerns the gendered nature of culture itself. Celia Lury has written of the relationship between technologies of culture and the construction of the social category 'woman'. It is not enough, she argues, to point, as Foucault does, to the importance of 'the author function' in the emergence of modern societies. This concept of 'the individual' who is the source of value, judgement and authenticity, and whose supreme embodiment is the artist, is also a concept whose progressive *masculinization* (1993: 179) we can trace within the various categories of 'high culture' during the nineteenth century. In the field of art, for example, women, excluded from the academies, were confined to the 'lesser genres' of portraiture, still life and flowers, exhibiting as amateurs rather than as professional artists. Within print culture their involvement, whilst more developed, remained confined to the low-status activities of novel and periodical writing, areas where 'feminine values' prevailed. With the elevation of the novel to the status of high culture, as a public, realist form whose author could own the copyright to his work and hence lay claim to the status of a professional, it too became masculinized. Its author could now claim 'creative autonomy' in a struggle for 'self-expression', and literary criticism acquired its own authority (that of the 'man of letters'), and privileged status within the academy. The 'woman's novel' became 'women's fiction', a lower category lacking 'originality'. The high/low culture divide, then, is a thoroughly gendered one, corresponding to a division between mainstream cultural activity and public professionalism on the one hand, and a critically marginalized, privatized and less 'original' form of production on the other.

But it is not simply, argues Lury, that the constituting of culture as high/low, public/private corresponds to an already existing, socially structured sexual division. The category of the feminine, of 'Woman', is also constructed *through* these cultural distinctions. In the case of art, women's exclusion from the most highly regarded forms of painting because these genres included depictions of the naked human figure (1993: 179), also had the effect of constituting particular regimes of looking, with 'Woman' positioned always on the side of representation, the to-be-looked-at. Hence not only 'woman as image, as object to be looked at', but also a specifically gendered technique of objectification became naturalized, until finally this construction of the category 'Woman' is not recognized as representation at all (1993: 181). In the case of gendered divisions in modes of literary output, the 'feminization' of 'mass' cultural forms (the romance novel, the woman's magazine), in opposition to 'authored' writing, is not merely the *result* of gendered social divisions which identify the former with a privatized realm of content and consumption, and the latter with professionalism and public responsibility. It also helps *construct* notions of 'the feminine' which align it with commodification, standardization and passivity, and which maintain it within the sphere of the private, understood as subordinate, emotional and domestic. We might conclude, then, that any narrative which foregrounds the figure of woman in relation to culture will necessarily be a marginal(ized) one. If its focus is the exclusion of women from culture ('high', public or mainstream culture), it is telling a story of and from the margins. If it tells the story of female/feminine/feminist cultural production ('low' culture), it is no less a marginal story. Both, in omitting the (major) narrative of the public sphere, necessarily position themselves within a 'woman's genre'.

The second aspect of this question of genre concerns the gendered nature of cultural studies itself. In *'Am I That Name?'* (1988), Denise Riley offers a historical exploration of the shifting relationship between feminist thought and the category of 'women'. Writing of the emergence of 'women' as a modern social category in the nineteenth century, she argues that their position in relation to the newly constituted realm of 'the social' was quite different to that of 'man'. Whereas man, in the formulation 'man in society', was seen to *face* society, to be separate, individualized, his relationship to society in need of analysis, the categories 'women' and 'society' formed a continuum. Women, that is, were seen to be immersed in the social, so that 'society' (as opposed to politics, or the individual) was seen as always 'already permeated by the feminine' (1988: 15). 'Social issues' thus line up with 'women's issues', as distinct from 'political issues'. From this perspective we can think of 'low culture' as culture which is seen to be saturated with the (feminized) social, not, as with 'high culture' or 'high theory', critically separated from it. Feminists, who seek critical understanding of this divide and its implications *as women,* find themselves always similarly enmeshed, still 'saturated in the social' and hence doubly marginalized as theorists by the effort to speak at least partially from 'within'.

It is this problem which the CCCS Women's Studies Group describe in their 1978 account of the difficulties they encountered within the emerging field of cultural studies. Describing their project as an 'attempt to understand the material processes which constitute a social formation structured into division and conflict on the grounds of gender as well as class', they confess the following difficulty:

> To intervene effectively as feminists in other . . . areas of interest it seems we would have to conquer the whole of cultural studies, in itself multi-disciplinary, and *then* make a feminist critique of it. Or, the alternative we tended to adopt, we could concentrate on what we saw as the central issues of research *within* the WSG, and thus risk our concerns remaining gender-specific – our own concerns: the 'woman question' claimed by, and relegated to, the women. (1978a: 10)

Fifteen years later, Charlotte Brunsdon analyses the outcomes of this conflict. Since the 1970s, she argues, the relationship of the feminist critic to the category 'woman', the housewife or television viewer whose textual pleasures she studies, has had three phases. In the first, the two are thoroughly identified. The feminist speaks *as* woman, implicated in the gendered pleasures of the text – the soap opera or woman's magazine. There 'is no "otherness" between feminism and women'; the relationship is 'transparent' (1993: 312). The pronoun used is 'we'. The second, 'hegemonic' or 'recruitist' phase sees the feminist speaking as a *politicized* woman, her task to 'transform the feminine identifications of women to feminist ones' (1993: 313), to politicize their viewing or reading pleasures. This uneasy relationship is marked by both identification and disavowal, as the feminist intellectual, conscious of her distance from conventional femininity, strives to speak both *as* a woman and *about* women and their cultural pleasures. The final, 'fragmented' phase sees 'no necessary relationship' between the two, as the category 'woman' itself seems to dissolve into a host of differences – of class, ethnicity, age, language and so on. Both 'feminist' and 'woman' are now seen as fragmented identities, only partially, if at all, aligned; and in this exploration of identity and pleasure 'there are no pronouns beyond the "I"' (1993: 316). These three phases can be seen as different articulations of the problem identified by the Women's Studies Group. The field of feminist scholarship within cultural studies – what Charlotte Brunsdon calls the 'girlzone' – has been both constituted as a critique of, and yet defined by the terms and limits of the despised territory of the 'woman's genre'.

Elsewhere, Brunsdon cites Liesbet van Zoonen's use of John Corner's distinction between the two major emphases within media and cultural studies, that between a 'public knowledge project' and a 'popular culture project' (Corner 1991: 268), noting van Zoonen's comment (1994: 9) that this tends also to be a gendered distinction, with feminist work, as Brunsdon describes it, 'clustering in the "popular culture" domestic corner while citizenship, knowledge and the politics of information occupy the main square' (1997: 168). We might argue that not only does the latter align a masculine cultural studies with Riley's category of 'man in society' as man *facing* society; it also serves to rescue it from that immersion in the (feminized) social which might be seen to threaten a cultural studies that addresses issues of the popular and 'mass' culture. In this respect too, then, our narrative is a gendered one, slipping, like a secondary plotline, in and out of visibility in respect of the 'major' story, in this case that of the discipline of cultural studies itself. Charlotte Brunsdon ends her account of the difficulties in constructing 'feminist identities' within cultural studies with the vivid reminder of these difficulties provided by her favourite bookshop in London. On her visits there she finds she has to move constantly between the feminist section on the ground floor and the sections on philosophy, critical theory, film, media and cultural studies in the basement. The former includes most feminist books, but the latter gives an overview of 'what is being published in the field *generally*' (1997: 170). Her choices – though we can note that she is now free to oscillate between them – have not changed much, it seems, from those confronting the Women's Studies Group in 1978: 'the "woman question" claimed by, and relegated to, the women' on the one hand; 'the whole of cultural studies' on the other. Elsewhere even these choices have disappeared: in the academic bookshop in the town where I live, the 'public knowledge project' of cultural studies is subsumed within 'social policy'; whilst feminism has, in Nancy Miller's phrase, 'lost its signature', and its visibility, within the increasingly 'unmarked' field of 'gender studies', a place where, in Miller's words, the 'text's heroine [becomes] again no more than a fiction' (1990: 118).

Feminism's Exclusions

The final question we must ask if we are to reposition this hero(ine) at the centre of the narrative concerns feminism's own exclusions. Stuart Hall's 1992 narrative of cultural studies, as we have seen, cites two narrative 'interruptions'. The first is feminism; the second, 'the question of race'. Like other such accounts, this tends to make black *women* invisible in either category.[6] One of the key essays in that collection, however, is Hazel Carby's 'White Woman Listen! Black Feminism and the Boundaries of Sisterhood'. As its title indicates, the object of Carby's address here is not the discourse of cultural studies but that of (white) feminism; her concern is to rewrite the narrative of '*her*story' to include the experiences of black women. Writing at that 'transparent' moment in the relationship between feminist theory and 'woman' when the pronoun used by feminists is 'we', Carby demands of white feminists: 'what exactly do you mean when you say "WE"??' (1982: 233). It is not good enough, she insists, to write of *parallels* between race and gender oppression as white feminists have so persistently done. Black women 'are subject to the *simultaneous* oppression of patriarchy, class and "race"', so that to draw such parallels not only obscures the specificities of oppression within particular social formations (white women may oppress black women; black men may not have access to 'patriarchal' power), it also renders black women's 'position and experience not only marginal but also invisible' (1982: 213). As Mary Ann Doane points out, if 'race' is to do with black men and 'women' refers to white women, the position of the black woman – in cultural studies and feminist theory alike – becomes literally unthinkable: 'in terms of oppression, she is both black and a woman; in terms of theory, she is neither' (1991: 231).

A second exclusion is that of lesbian women. As Jane Gaines has argued, the opposition male/female, so central to feminist theory, 'is a powerful, but sometimes blinding construct'. It may 'lock us into modes of analysis which will continually misinterpret the position of many women' (1988: 15). 'The straight mind', to use Monique Wittig's term,[7] unable to conceive of desire or explain pleasure without reference to the binary opposition male/female, persistently conflates 'women's experience', 'women's pleasure', or 'women's desire' with that of white heterosexual (and middle-class) women. In thus operating its own exclusions, feminist theory risks remaining locked into the very conceptual structure which, as both Wittig and Irigaray argue, underlies existing structures of power/knowledge in Western society. If there are only *two* terms, one cannot but be privileged, acquiring its definition or shape through contrast with its less privileged 'other', and, as Simone de Beauvoir pointed out in 1949, woman in Western thought has consistently represented the Other that can confirm man's identity as Self, as rational thinking being (1988: 16).

Just as the narrative of cultural studies cannot simply be rewritten by *adding* 'women', however, so that of feminist theory cannot just add 'women of colour' or 'lesbian women' to remedy its exclusions. The 'imagined community' of 1970s British feminism, as Catherine Hall points out in terms which echo – though now more critically – those of the 1978 Women's Studies Group, was dependent on those exclusions. Writing specifically about issues of race, she comments:

> The political imperatives of the first phase of the women's movement were the imperatives of gender. The political identities we constructed, and which constructed us, were defined primarily in relation to the axes of gender and class. In the process of constructing identities, that is, 'the process of representing symbolically the sense of belonging which draws people together into an "imagined community" and at the same time defines who does *not* belong or is excluded from it',[8] we effectively excluded not only black women but those parts of ourselves which were identified in racial or ethnic terms. (1992: 21)

Our newly centred hero(ine), then, must now be decentred *from within*, and we might be pessimistic about the possibilities for a narrative with such an internally fragmented protagonist. Both the 'imagined community' of which Catherine Hall writes and the notion of 'woman' as an inclusive category, one that permits the feminist to speak as 'we', were, as Tania Modleski argues, always *utopian* concepts (1991b: 22). That is, they had a rhetorical, performative function essential to feminism if it were to be able to construct itself as an emancipatory narrative. When in 1851 the freed slave Sojourner Truth intervened in a women's rights gathering to demand rhetorically, 'Ain't I a Woman?',[9] her question shattered patriarchal definitions of femininity. The concept of 'woman' was forced open to include a black female corporeality and experience which had served as 'other' to a femininity conceptualized as delicate, spiritual, passive, white. But this shattering was done in the name of a greater inclusiveness, not an internal fracturing, and it was such a vision which drove 1970s feminist narratives of the future. Often 'written in the simple future tense, expressing a deep sense of determination, of certainty about the course of history and the irresistible emancipation of women', such writing seems to be, as Rosi Braidotti says, 'half prophecy and half utopia' (1994: 189). Yet the apparent certainty was polemical, its purpose political. As one feminist theorist has written, 'Suddenly a perspective on the world had unfolded that gave women a position to speak from, and things that had to be said not from choice but from political necessity' (Mulvey 1989d: viii).

If, then, we are to argue that this 'imagined community', with its fantasy of 'sisterly or woman-identified mutual support, anti-hierarchical and egalitarian relationships, an ethic of compassion and connection, an ease with intra-gender affectionate behavior and emotional sharing, and a propensity for mutual identification' (de Lauretis 1994: 185–6), in fact operates by means of crucial exclusions, we may conclude that it must therefore be resisted. Postmodern feminists have indeed argued this. Donna Haraway, for example, writes, 'We do not need a totality in order to work well. The feminist dream of a common language, like all dreams for a perfectly faithful naming of experience, is a totalizing and imperialist one' (1990a: 215). But if this re-envisaged feminist subject is now defined as 'the site of multiple, complex, and potentially contradictory sets of experiences, defined by overlapping variables such as class, race, age, lifestyle, sexual preference, and others' (Braidotti 1994: 4) – if, in Denise Riley's words, Sojourner Truth's question must be rephrased as 'Ain't I a fluctuating identity?' (1988: 1) – then the very possibility of a feminist narrative seems in doubt.

It is this problem which confronts feminist theory today: how, in Tania Modleski's words, to 'hold on to the category of woman while recognizing ourselves to be in the *process* (an unending one) of *defining and constructing the category*' (1991b: 20). If this delicate balance is not achieved, however, there is, as Modleski and others have pointed out, another narrative subject ready to assume the place of hero: postmodernism. Feminism and postmodernism have, at least at first glance, much in common. Both have argued that the 'grand' or 'master' narratives of Western culture have lost their legitimating power. Not only, they would both suggest, have claims put forward as universally applicable in fact proved to be valid only for men of a particular culture, class and race; the ideals which have underpinned these claims – of 'objectivity', 'reason' and the autonomous self – have been equally partial and contingent. Both also argue that Western *representations* – whether in art, literature or theory – are the product of access not to Truth but to power. Women, as both Celia Lury and Craig Owens point out, have been *represented* in countless images (and metaphors) throughout Western culture, often as symbol of something else – Nature, Truth, the Sublime, Sex – but have rarely seen their own representations accorded legitimacy. The representational systems of the West have, in Owens' words, admitted only 'one vision – that of the constitutive male subject' (1985: 58).

Yet for male postmodernist theorists like Owens, feminism is 'an *instance* of postmodern thought' (1985: 62, my emphasis); it is postmodernism which is the inclusive category. Feminism's place in this narrative – and it has recently been an influential narrative within cultural studies – is once more that of helper. The central protagonists are (as always) situated elsewhere. Feminists have been understandably suspicious of this move. 'Why is it,' asks Nancy Hartsock, 'that just at the moment when so many of us who have been silenced begin to demand the right to name ourselves, to act as subjects rather than objects of history, that just then the concept of subjecthood becomes problematic?' (1990: 163). It is no accident, she argues, that the category of woman disappears just when, as narrative subject, she begins to tell her own story. The narrative of the female feminist subject is already precarious, as we have seen throughout this book. Existing in tension with, and on the margins of, those other narratives, of culture and of cultural studies, its speaking voice is uncertain, its control of the action dubious. Subsumed within the multiple and fragmented identities of postmodernism, in which sexual difference is just one amongst many differences, it risks final disintegration.

Heroes and Heroines

Lastly, I should like to return to an autobiographical and theoretical narrative which does construct itself on the margins of, and in opposition to, the stories of those 'founding fathers' of cultural studies, Raymond Williams and Richard Hoggart: Carolyn Steedman's *Landscape for a Good Woman* (1986). It is about the lives of Steedman and her working-class mother, lives 'lived out on the borderlands, lives for which the central interpretative devices of the culture don't quite work' (1986: 5). Writing of Richard Hoggart's (1959) description of his own working-class childhood, *The Uses of Literacy*, she describes it as, like many other fictional and autobiographical narratives of the period, a 'narrative of escape'. Women, she continues, 'could not be heroines of the conventional narratives of escape. Women are, in the sense that Hoggart and Seabrook[10] present in their pictures of transition, without class, because the cut and fall of a skirt and good leather shoes can take you across the river and to the other side: the fairy-tales tell you that goose-girls may marry kings' (1986: 15–16). Steedman's reminder that women are outside the conventional structures of class because 'the working-class landscape has been made by men' (1986: 14), in drawing as it does on the narrative of fairy tale to make its point, also reminds us of another difference. Men may find transitions of class harder to make than women, but their narratives of escape always position them as subjects, and as subjects who, whilst still marked by their class origins, have nevertheless transcended them. The woman's narrative, as Teresa de Lauretis reminds us, is in an important sense never her own. She 'represent[s] and literally mark[s] out the place (to) which the hero will cross'. Her 'narrative is patterned on a journey, whether inward or outward, whose possible outcomes are those outlined by Freud's mythical story of femininity. In the best of cases, that is, in the "happy" ending, the protagonist will reach the place (the space) where a modern Oedipus will find her and fulfill the promise of his (off-screen) journey' (1984: 139–40). Ann Oakley offers a more contemporary version of this narrative image in her description of

the curiously impressive image of women as always waiting for someone or something, in shopping queues, in antenatal clinics, in bed, for
men to come home, at the school gates, by the playground swing, for
birth or the growing up of children, in hope of love or freedom or re-
employment, waiting for the future to liberate or burden them and the
past to catch up with them. (1981: 11)

The goose-girl, then, may marry the king, but she will never be the centre of
her own story and she can never transcend her gender – which is what defines
her – in the same way that the working-class hero can transcend class.

Steedman is of course aware of this. The stories she writes, she says,
'aren't stories in their own right: they exist in tension with other more
central ones'. But she also echoes Stuart Hall in arguing that 'The point of
a story is to present itself momentarily as complete, so that it can be said:
it does for now; it is an account that will last a while'. In constructing a
history, the writer has to first 'search backwards from the vantage point of
the present in order to appraise things in the past and attribute meaning to
them', then 'trace forward what we have already traced backwards, and
make a history' (1986: 21–2). If a common definition of feminist theory is
'a theory of gender oppression in culture', then the history (*her*story?) of
feminist theory, traced 'backwards from the vantage point of the present',
in the strictest sense already *is* a narrative of cultural studies. It is a narrative, however, which, like Steedman's, only exists 'in tension with other
more central ones', as I have tried to suggest, and it is one whose speaking
voice is, as we have seen, uncertain, struggling at times to break into, at
times to disrupt, at times to remain outside of those 'other more central'
discourses. For Teresa de Lauretis, however, who offers the definition
above, the narrative to be told is even more complex. If we define it as 'a
theory of *gender* oppression in culture', she writes, feminist theory can still
harbour its internal exclusions. What we need, she argues, is a definition
which will embrace the multiple and fragmented identities of 'women'
proposed by postmodern feminists whilst simultaneously insisting on the
centrality to them all of female *embodiment*. Feminist theory, she writes,
should be defined as

a developing theory of the female-sexed or female-embodied social
subject, whose constitution and whose modes of social and subjective existence include most obviously sex and gender, but also race,
class, and any other significant sociocultural divisions and representations; a developing theory of the female-embodied social subject
that is based on its specific, emergent, and conflictual history. (1990:
267)

It is this narrative, she argues, which must be both recounted and 'recon-
nect[ed] to the "external" discursive and social context from which it
finally cannot be severed' (1990: 266).

To return finally, then, to the question: what if feminism were to be the subject, even the (autobiographical) hero, of this narrative of 'feminism and cultural studies'? If, as Hall argues, identity 'is formed at the unstable point where the "unspeakable" stories of subjectivity meet the narratives of history, of a culture', then we must conclude that the identity of this hero is problematic indeed, for all three terms – subjectivity, history and culture – are not only split along lines of gender but also fractured across multiple differences. Still, it is a narrative whose telling is important, which, in dissolving feminism's 'false "we" ... into its real multiplicity and variety', seeks in Nancy Hartsock's words, 'out of this concrete multiplicity [to] build an account of the world as seen from the margins, an account which can expose the falseness of the view from the top and can transform the margins as well as the center'. The task, she suggests, is 'to develop an account of the world which treats our perspectives not as subjugated or disruptive knowledges, but instead as primary and constitutive' (1990: 171). In this recentred narrative it will be cultural studies rather than feminism which enters midway through, an ambiguous presence, not 'crapp[ing] on the table' as in Stuart Hall's account of feminism's illegitimate and ruptural/disruptive entry into the 'house' of cultural studies, but entering through the door, offering feminism a space in which to work but at the expense of ceding autonomy and perhaps also the 'signature' of feminist theory. As Charlotte Brunsdon notes, there is 'some doubt whether work by feminists ... that does not embrace the point of difference, in this case the feminine, is in fact *recognised* as feminist scholarship' (1997: 170). The metaphor which irresistibly suggests itself for this relationship is that of marriage – but then marriage, as we know, is an unstable, politically unsatisfactory and increasingly temporary institution.

Notes

1. See Teresa de Lauretis' discussion in *Alice Doesn't* (1984), where, particularly in the chapter 'Oedipus Interruptus' (134–56) she writes that narrative is 'governed by an Oedipal logic', its paradigmatic structure that of Freud's Oedipal journey. In the male-centred narrative this means the journey towards adult subjectivity and possession of the woman. In the female-centred narrative it means the relinquishing of desire, in favour of that state of passivity which for Freud characterized mature femininity, in which the woman accepts her role as object of desire for the man. In both, the female character represents the point of narrative closure. She is that portion of 'plot-space' which awaits the end of the *hero's* journey.

2. See Propp (1968) on the functions of characters in narrative, of which 'helper' is one, and Todorov (1977) on disequilibrium in narrative:

   An 'ideal' narrative begins with a stable situation which is disturbed by some power or force. There results a state of disequilibrium; by the action of a force directed in the opposite direction, the equilibrium is re-established; the second equilibrium is similar to the first, but the two are never identical. (1977: 111)

The reference to a 'dark continent' is of course to Freud's description of 'woman'. For a discussion of this, see Doane (1991) and Modleski (1991a).

3. See Braidotti's (1994) discussion of 'the female feminist subject'. The phrase 'situated knowledge' is from Donna Haraway (1988).

4. See 'What is an Author?' (Foucault 1986), in *The Foucault Reader* (ed. Rabinow 1986). The translation I give here, however, is that quoted by Miller, which differs slightly from that in *The Foucault Reader*.

5. The phrase is from B. Ruby Rich, who writes that 'a woman's experiencing of culture under patriarchy is dialectical in a way that a man's can never be: our experience is like that of the exile, whom Brecht once singled out as the ultimate dialectician for that daily working out of cultural oppositions within a single body' (1999: 45).

6. Paul Gilroy's own preface to the book is more open, confessing that 'We have not dealt satisfactorily with the struggles of black women' (1982: 7).

7. See Wittig, 'The Straight Mind' (1980: 107–11).

8. See note 10, Chapter 2.

9. See Schneir (1972) and Guy-Sheftall (1995) for transcripts of this now legendary speech. Guy-Sheftall points out, however (1995: 35), that the reliability of this transcript has been questioned.

10. Jeremy Seabrook, *Working Class Childhood* (1982).

Bibliography

ABEL, Elizabeth 1990: Race, class, and psychoanalysis? Opening questions. In Hirsch, M. & Fox Keller, E. (eds), *Conflicts in Feminism*. London: Routledge, 184–204.

ADAM, Alison 1998: Feminist AI projects and cyberfutures. In Adam, A., *Artificial Knowing: Gender and the Thinking Machine*. London: Routledge, 156–81.

ADAMS, Carol 1996: 'This is not our fathers' pornography': sex, lies and computers. In Ess, C. (ed.), *Philosophical Perspectives on Computer-Mediated Communication*. Albany, N.Y.: State University of New York Press, 147–70.

ALLEN, Sandra, SANDERS, Lee and WALLIS, Jan (eds) 1974: *Conditions of Illusion: Papers from the Women's Movement*. Leeds: Feminist Books.

ALTHUSSER, Louis 1977: *For Marx*. London: New Left Books.

ANDERSON, Benedict 1983: *Imagined Communities: Reflections on the Origin and Spread of Nationalism*. London: Verso.

ANG, Ien 1985: *Watching Dallas: Soap Opera and the Melodramatic Imagination*. London: Methuen.

ANG, Ien 1988: Feminist desire and female pleasure: on Janice Radway's *Reading the Romance*. *Camera Obscura* 16, 178–91.

ANG, Ien 1989: Wanted: audiences. On the politics of empirical audience studies. In Seiter, E., Borchers, H., Kreutzner, G. & Warth, E.-M. (eds), *Remote Control: Television, Audiences and Cultural Power*. London: Routledge, 96–115.

BAKHTIN, Mikhail 1965: *Rabelais and his World*, trans. Iswoy. Cambridge, Mass.: MIT Press.

BALLASTER, Ros, BEETHAM, Margaret, FRAZER, Elizabeth and HEBRON, Sandra 1991: *Women's Worlds: Ideology, Femininity and the Woman's Magazine*. London: Macmillan.

BALSAMO, Anne 1988: Reading cyborgs writing feminism. *Communication* 10, 331–44.

BANKS, Olive 1981: *Faces of Feminism: A Study of Feminism as a Social Movement*. New York: St Martin's Press.

BARRETT, Michele 1988: *Women's Oppression Today*. London: Verso.

BARRETT, Michele 1993: Introduction. In Woolf, V., *A Room of One's Own and Three Guineas*. Harmondsworth: Penguin, ix–liii.

BARTHES, Roland 1973 (1957): *Mythologies*. London: Granada Publishing.

BARTHES, Roland 1985 (1967): *The Fashion System*. London: Jonathan Cape.

BARTKY, Sandra Lee 1982: Narcissism, femininity and alienation. *Social Theory and Practice* 8(2), 127–43.

BAUDRILLARD, Jean 1990 (1979): *Seduction*, trans. Singer, B. London: Macmillan.

BEER, Gillian 1979: Beyond determinism: George Eliot and Virginia Woolf. In Jacobus, M. (ed.), *Women Writing and Writing about Women*. London: Croom Helm, 80–99.

BENJAMIN, Walter 1970: *Illuminations*. London: Fontana.

BENJAMIN, Walter 1973: *Charles Baudelaire: A Lyric Poet in the Era of High Capitalism,* trans. Harry Zohn. London: New Left Books.

BETTERTON, Rosemary 1987: Introduction: feminism, femininity and representation. In Betterton, R. (ed.), *Looking On: Images of Femininity in the Visual Arts and Media*. London: Pandora, 1–17.

BHABHA, Homi K. 1983: The other question – the stereotype and colonial discourse. *Screen* 24(6), 18–36.

BLAND, Lucy, BRUNSDON, Charlotte, HOBSON, Dorothy and WINSHIP, Janice 1978: Women 'inside and outside' the relations of production. In Women's Studies Group, CCCS, *Women Take Issue: Aspects of Women's Subordination*. London: Hutchinson, 35–78.

BOBO, Jacqueline and SEITER, Ellen 1991: Black feminism and media criticism. *Screen* 32(3), 286–302.

BORDO, Susan 1989: The body and the reproduction of femininity. In Bordo, S. & Jaggar, A. M. (eds), *Gender/Body/Knowledge: Feminist Reconstructions of Being and Knowing*. London: Rutgers University Press, 13–33.

BORDO, Susan 1990: Feminism, postmodernism, and gender-scepticism. In Nicholson, L. (ed.), *Feminism/Postmodernism*. London: Routledge, 133–56.

BORDO, Susan 1993a: Introduction: feminism, western culture, and the body. In Bordo, S., *Unbearable Weight: Feminism, Western Culture, and the Body*. London: University of California Press, 1–42.

BORDO, Susan 1993b: Whose body is this? Feminism, medicine, and the conceptualization of eating disorders. In Bordo, S., *Unbearable Weight: Feminism, Western Culture, and the Body*. London: University of California Press, 45–69.

BORDO, Susan 1993c (1985): Anorexia nervosa: psychopathology as the crystallization of culture. In Bordo, S., *Unbearable Weight: Feminism, Western Culture, and the Body.* London: University of California Press, 139–64.

BORDO, Susan 1993d: Are mothers persons? Reproductive rights and the politics of subjectivity. In Bordo, S., *Unbearable Weight: Feminism, Western Culture, and the Body.* London: University of California Press, 71–97.

BORDO, Susan 1993e (1990): 'Material girl': the effacements of postmodern culture. In Bordo, S., *Unbearable Weight: Feminism, Western Culture, and the Body.* London: University of California Press, 245–75.

BOSTON WOMEN'S HEALTH CLUB COLLECTIVE 1976: *Our Bodies, Ourselves: A Book by and For Women,* second edition. New York: Simon and Schuster.

BOURDIEU, Pierre 1984 (1979): *Distinction: A Social Critique of the Judgement of Taste.* London: Routledge and Kegan Paul.

BOURDIEU, Pierre 1986: The aristocracy of culture. In Collins, R., Curran, J., Garnham, N., Scannell, P., Schlesinger, P. & Sparks, C. (eds), *Media, Culture and Society: A Critical Reader.* London: Sage, 164–93.

BOWLBY, Rachel 1985: *Just Looking: Consumer Culture in Dreisen, Gissing and Zola.* London: Methuen.

BOWLBY, Rachel 1987: Modes of modern shopping: Mallarmé at the *Bon Marché.* In Armstrong, N. & Tennenhouse, L. (eds), *The Ideology of Conduct: Essays in Literature and the History of Sexuality.* London: Methuen, 185–205.

BOWLBY, Rachel 1992: *Still Crazy after all these Years: Women, Writing and Psychoanalysis.* London: Routledge.

BOWLBY, Rachel 1993: *Shopping with Freud.* London: Routledge.

BRAIDOTTI, Rosi 1994: *Nomadic Subjects: Embodiment and Sexual Difference in Contemporary Feminist Theory.* New York: Columbia University Press.

BRANTLINGER, Patrick 1990: *Crusoe's Footprints: Cultural Studies in Britain and America.* London: Routledge.

BRODY, Miriam 1992: Introduction. In Mary Wollstonecraft, *A Vindication of the Rights of Woman,* Brody, M. (ed.). London: Penguin, 1–70.

BRONTE, Charlotte 1971 (1847): *Jane Eyre.* New York: Norton.

BROWN, Mary Ellen 1994: *Soap Opera and Women's Talk.* London: Sage.

BRUNSDON, Charlotte 1978: 'It is well known that by nature women are inclined to be rather personal'. In Women's Studies Group, CCCS, *Women Take Issue: Aspects of Women's Subordination.* London: Hutchinson, 18–34.

BRUNSDON, Charlotte 1981: *Crossroad*s: notes on soap opera. *Screen* 22(4), 32–7.

BRUNSDON, Charlotte 1989: Text and audience. In Seiter, E., Borchers, H., Kreutzner, G. & Warth, E.-M. (eds), *Remote Control: Television, Audiences and Cultural Power.* London: Routledge, 116–29.

BRUNSDON, Charlotte 1993: Identity in feminist television criticism. *Media, Culture and Society* 15(2), 309–20.

BRUNSDON, Charlotte 1996: A thief in the night: stories of feminism in the 1970s at CCCS. In Morley, D. & Kuan-Hsing Chen (eds), *Stuart Hall: Critical Dialogues in Cultural Studies*. London: Routledge, 276–86.

BRUNSDON, Charlotte 1997: *Screen Tastes: Soap Opera to Satellite Dishes*. London: Routledge.

BURNISTON, Steve, MORT, Frank and WEEDON, Christine 1978: Psychoanalysis and the cultural acquisition of sexuality and subjectivity. In Women's Studies Group, CCCS, *Women Take Issue: Aspects of Women's Subordination*. London: Hutchinson, 109–31.

BUSBY, Linda J. (1975) Sex-role research on the mass media. *Journal of Communication* Autumn, 107–31.

BUTLER, Judith 1990: *Gender Trouble: Feminism and the Subversion of Identity*. London: Routledge.

BUTLER, Judith 1999: Performativity's social magic. In Shusterman, R. (ed.), *Bourdieu: A Critical Reader*. Oxford: Blackwell, 113–28.

CARBY, Hazel 1982: White woman listen! Black feminism and the boundaries of sisterhood. In Centre for Contemporary Cultural Studies, *The Empire Strikes Back: Race and Racism in 70s Britain*. London: Hutchinson, 212–35.

CARBY, Hazel 1985: 'On the threshold of a woman's era': lynching, empire, and sexuality in Black feminist theory. *Critical Enquiry* 12, 262–77.

CARTER, Erica 1984: Alice in the consumer wonderland. In McRobbie, A. & Nava, M. (eds), *Gender and Generation*. London: Macmillan, 185–214.

CHODOROW, Nancy 1978: *The Reproduction of Mothering: Psychoanalysis and the Sociology of Gender*. Los Angeles: University of California Press.

CITRON, Michelle, LE SAGE, Julia, MAYNE, Judith, RICH, B. Ruby, TAYLOR, Anna Marie and the editors of *New German Critique* 1978: Women and film: a discussion of feminist aesthetics. *New German Critique* 13, 83–107.

CLARKE, John 1976: Style. In Hall, S. & Jefferson, T. (eds), *Resistance Through Rituals: Youth Subcultures in Post-War Britain*. London: HarperCollins, 175–91.

CLARKE, John, HALL, Stuart, JEFFERSON, Tony and ROBERTS, Brian 1976: Subcultures, cultures and class: a theoretical overview. In Hall, S. & Jefferson, T. (eds), *Resistance Through Rituals: Youth Subcultures in Post-War Britain*. London: HarperCollins, 9–74.

COHAN, Steven and SHIRES, Linda M. 1988: *Telling Stories: A Theoretical Analysis of Narrative Fiction*. London: Routledge.

COLLINS, Patricia Hill 1990: *Black Feminist Thought*. London: Routledge.

COMER, Lee 1974: Medical mystifications. In Allen, S., Sanders, L. & Wallis, J. (eds), *Conditions of Illusion: Papers from the Women's Movement*. Leeds: Feminist Books, 45–50.

CORNER, John 1991: Meaning, genre and context: the problematics of 'public knowledge' in the new audience studies. In Curran, J. & Gurevitch, M. (eds), *Mass Media and Society*. London: Arnold, 267–84.

COWARD, Rosalind 1984: *Female Desire: Women's Sexuality Today*. London: Paladin.

COWIE, Elizabeth 1984: Fantasia. *m/f* 9, 71–104.

DE BEAUVOIR, Simone 1988 (1949): *The Second Sex*. London: Pan Books.

DE LAURETIS, Teresa 1984: *Alice Doesn't: Feminism, Semiotics, Cinema*. London: Macmillan.

DE LAURETIS, Teresa 1986: Feminist studies/critical studies: issues, terms and contexts. In de Lauretis, T. (ed.), *Feminist Studies/Critical Studies*. Indianapolis: Indiana University Press, 1–19.

DE LAURETIS, Teresa 1987: *Technologies of Gender: Essays on Theory, Film, and Fiction*. London: Macmillan.

DE LAURETIS, Teresa 1990: Upping the anti (sic) in feminist theory. In Hirsch, M. & Fox Keller, E. (eds), *Conflicts in Feminism*. London: Routledge, 255–70.

DE LAURETIS, Teresa 1994: *The Practice of Love: Lesbian Sexuality and Perverse Desire*. Indianapolis: Indiana University Press.

DELMAR, Rosalind 1986: What is feminism? In Mitchell, J. & Oakley, A. (eds), *What Is Feminism?* Oxford: Blackwell.

DOANE, Mary Ann 1982: Film and the masquerade: theorising the female spectator. *Screen* 23(3–4), 74–87.

DOANE, Mary Ann 1984: The 'woman's film': possession and address. In Doane, M. A., Mellencamp, P. & Williams, L. (eds), *Re-Vision: Essays in Feminist Film Criticism*. Los Angeles: American Film Institute, 67–82.

DOANE, Mary Ann 1987: *The Desire to Desire: The Woman's Film of the 1940s*. London: Macmillan.

DOANE, Mary Ann 1991: Dark continents: epistemologies of racial and sexual difference in psychoanalysis and the cinema. In *Femmes Fatales: Feminism, Film Theory, Psychoanalysis*. London: Routledge, 209–48.

DONALD, James (ed.) 1991: On the threshold: psychoanalysis and cultural studies. In Donald, J. (ed.), *Psychoanalysis and Cultural Theory*. Basingstoke: Macmillan, 1–10.

DREIFUS, Claudia 1973 (1971): The selling of a feminist. In Koedt, A., Levine, E. & Rapone, A. (eds), *Radical Feminism*. New York: Quadrangle Books, 358–61.

EAGLETON, Terry 1978: *Criticism and Ideology: A Study in Marxist Literary Theory*. London: Verso.

EAGLETON, Terry 1989: Base and superstructure in Raymond Williams. In Eagleton, T. (ed.), *Raymond Williams: Critical Perspectives*. Cambridge: Polity.

EHRENREICH, Barbara, HESS, Elizabeth and JACOBS, Gloria 1992: Beatlemania: girls just want to have fun. In Lewis, L. A. (ed.), *The Adoring Audience: Fan Culture and Popular Media*. London: Routledge, 84–106.

EVANS, Caroline and THORNTON, Minna 1989: *Women and Fashion: A New Look*. New York: Quartet Books.

FALK, Pasi and CAMPBELL, Colin (eds) 1997: *The Shopping Experience*. London: Sage.

FANON, Frantz 1986 (1952): *Black Skin, White Masks*. London: Pluto.

FIGES, Eva 1978 (1970): *Patriarchal Attitudes*. London: Virago.

FIRESTONE, Shulamith 1979 (1970): *The Dialectic of Sex: The Case for Feminist Revolution*. London: The Women's Press.

FISKE, John 1987: *Television Culture*. London: Methuen.

FOUCAULT, Michel 1979a: *Discipline and Punish: The Birth of the Prison*, trans. Alan Sheridan. Harmondsworth: Penguin.

FOUCAULT, Michel 1979b: *Power, Truth, Strategy*, Morris, M. & Patton, P. (eds). Sydney: Feral Publications.

FOUCAULT, Michel 1981: *The History of Sexuality*, Vol. 1. Harmondsworth: Penguin.

FOUCAULT, Michel 1986: What is an author? In Rabinow, P. (ed.), *The Foucault Reader*. Harmondsworth: Penguin, 101–20.

FRANKLIN, Sarah 1991: Fetal fascinations: new dimensions to the medical-scientific construction of fetal personhood. In Franklin, S., Lury, C. & Stacey, J. (eds), *Off Centre: Feminism and Cultural Studies*. London: HarperCollins, 190–205.

FRANKLIN, Sarah, LURY, Celia and STACEY, Jackie 1991: Feminism and cultural studies: pasts, presents, futures. In Franklin, S., Lury, C. & Stacey, J. (eds), *Off Centre: Feminism and Cultural Studies*. London: HarperCollins, 1–19.

FREEMAN, Jo 1975: *The Politics of Women's Liberation*. New York: David McKay Co.

FREUD, Sigmund 1955 (1913–14): *Totem and Taboo*, trans. James Strachey. Standard Edition Vol. XIII. London: The Hogarth Press, ix–164.

FREUD, Sigmund 1977 (1931): Female sexuality. In Freud, S., *On Sexuality*. Pelican Freud Library Vol. 7. London: Penguin, 367–92.

FRIEDAN, Betty 1965 (1963): *The Feminine Mystique*. London: Penguin.

GAINES, Jane 1988: White privilege and looking relations: race and gender in feminist film theory. *Screen* 29(4), 12–27.

GAINES, Jane 1990: Introduction: fabricating the female body. In Gaines, J. & Herzog, C. (eds), *Fabrications: Costume and the Female Body*. London: Routledge, 1–27.

GAINES, Jane and HERZOG, Charlotte (eds) 1990: *Fabrications: Costume and the Female Body*. London: Routledge.

GALLOP, Jane 1982: *Feminism and Psychoanalysis: The Daughter's Seduction*. London: Macmillan.

GALLOP, Jane 1989: Moving backwards or forwards. In Brennan, T. (ed.), *Between Feminism and Psychoanalysis*. London: Routledge, 27–39.

GELDER, Ken and THORNTON, Sarah (eds) 1997: *The Subcultures Reader*. London: Routledge.

GILMAN, Charlotte Perkins 1973 (1912): Are women human beings? In Hogeland, R. W. (ed.), *Women and Womanhood in America*. Lexington: D.C. Heath and Company, 133–5.

GILMAN, Charlotte Perkins 1979 (1915): *Herland*. London: The Women's Press.

GILMAN, Charlotte Perkins 1981a (1892): The yellow wallpaper. In Lane, A. J. (ed.), *The Charlotte Perkins Gilman Reader*. London: The Women's Press, 3–20.

GILMAN, Charlotte Perkins 1981b (1914): If I were a man. In Lane, A. J. (ed.), *The Charlotte Perkins Gilman Reader*. London: The Women's Press, 32–8.

GILMAN, Charlotte Perkins 1981c: *The Charlotte Perkins Gilman Reader*, Lane, A. J. (ed.). London: The Women's Press.

GILMAN, Charlotte Perkins 1998 (1898): *Women and Economics*. Mineola, N.Y.: Dover Publications Inc.

GILMAN, Sander L. 1985: *Difference and Pathology: Stereotypes of Sexuality, Race and Madness*. Ithaca: Cornell University Press.

GILROY, Paul 1982: Preface. In CCCS, *The Empire Strikes Back: Race and Racism in Contemporary Britain*. London: Hutchinson, 7–8.

GONZALEZ, Jennifer 1995: Envisioning cyborg bodies: notes from current research. In Gray, C. H. (ed.), *The Cyborg Handbook*. London: Routledge, 267–79.

GRAY, Ann 1992: *Video Playtime: The Gendering of a Leisure Technology*. London: Routledge.

GRAY, Chris Hables (ed.) 1995: *The Cyborg Handbook*. London: Routledge.

GREER, Germaine 1971 (1970): *The Female Eunuch*. St Albans: Granada Publishing.

GRIMSHAW, Jean 1986: *Philosophy and Feminist Thinking*. Minneapolis: University of Minnesota Press.

GRIMSHAW, Roger, HOBSON, Dorothy and WILLIS, Paul 1980: Introduction to ethnography at the Centre. In Hall, S., Hobson, D., Lowe, A. & Willis, P. (eds), *Culture, Media, Language*. London: Hutchinson, 73–7.

GROSSBERG, Lawrence, NELSON, Cary and TREICHLER, Paula (eds) 1992: *Cultural Studies*. London: Routledge.

GROSZ, Elizabeth 1989: *Sexual Subversions: Three French Feminists*. London: Allen & Unwin.

GROSZ, Elizabeth 1994: *Volatile Bodies: Towards a Corporeal Feminism*. Indianapolis: Indiana University Press.

GROSZ, Elizabeth 1995: *Space, Time and Perversion*. London: Routledge.

GUY-SHEFTALL, Beverly (ed.) 1995: *Words of Fire*. New York: The New Press.

HALL, Catherine 1992: *White, Male and Middle Class: Explorations in Feminism and History*. Cambridge: Polity.

HALL, Jacquelyn Dowd 1983: 'The mind that burns in each body': women, rape, and racial violence. In Snitow, A., Stansell, C. & Thompson, S. (eds), *Powers of Desire: The Politics of Sexuality*. New York: Monthly Review Press, 328–49.

HALL, Stuart 1980a: Cultural studies and the Centre: some problematics and problems. In Hall, S., Hobson, D., Lowe, A. & Willis, P. (eds), *Culture, Media, Language*. London: Hutchinson, 15–47.

HALL, Stuart 1980b: Encoding/decoding. In Hall, S., Hobson, D., Lowe, A. & Willis, P. (eds), *Culture, Media, Language*. London: Hutchinson, 128–38.

HALL, Stuart 1986: Cultural studies: two paradigms. In Collins, R., Curran, J., Garnham, N., Scannell, P., Schlesinger, P. & Sparks, C. (eds), *Media, Culture and Society: A Critical Reader*. London: Sage, 33–48.

HALL, Stuart 1987: Minimal selves. In ICA Documents 6, *Identity, The Real Me: Postmodernism and the Question of Identity*. London: ICA, 44–6.

HALL, Stuart 1992a: Cultural studies and its theoretical legacies. In Grossberg, L., Nelson, C. & Treichler, P. (eds), *Cultural Studies*. London: Routledge, 277–94.

HALL, Stuart 1992b: Introduction. In Hall, S. & Gieben, B. (eds), *Formations of Modernity*. Oxford: Polity, 1–16.

HALL, Stuart 1994: Reflections upon the encoding/decoding model: an interview with Stuart Hall. In Cruz, J. & Lewis, J. (eds), *Viewing, Reading, Listening: Audiences and Cultural Studies*. Boulder, Col.: Westview Press, 253–74.

HALL, Stuart and JEFFERSON, Tony (eds) 1976: *Resistance Through Rituals: Youth Subcultures in Post-War Britain*. London: HarperCollins.

HALL, Stuart, HOBSON, Dorothy, LOWE, Andrew and WILLIS, Paul (eds) 1980: *Culture, Media, Language*. London: Hutchinson.

HAMBLIN, Angela 1974: The suppressed power of female sexuality. In Allen, S., Sanders, L. & Wallis, J. (eds), *Conditions of Illusion: Papers from the Women's Movement*. Leeds: Feminist Books, 86–98.

HARAWAY, Donna 1988: Situated knowledges: the science question in feminism and the privilege of partial perspective. *Feminist Studies*, Vol. 14, No. 3, 575–600.

HARAWAY, Donna 1990a (1985): A manifesto for cyborgs: science, technology, and socialist feminism in the 1980s. In Nicholson, L. J. (ed.), *Feminism/Postmodernism*. London: Routledge, 190–233.

HARAWAY, Donna 1990b: Investment strategies for the evolving portfolio of primate females. In Jacobus, M., Keller, E. F. & Shuttleworth, S. (eds),

Body/Politics: Women and the Discourses of Science. London: Routledge, 139–62.

HARAWAY, Donna 1991: *Simians, Cyborgs, and Women.* London: Free Association Books.

HARAWAY, Donna 1992: The promises of monsters: a regenerative politics for inappropriate/d others. In Grossberg, L., Nelson, C. & Treichler, P. (eds), *Cultural Studies.* London: Routledge, 295–337.

HARAWAY, Donna 1997: The virtual speculum in the new world order. *Feminist Review* 55, 22–72.

HARRISON, Rachel 1978: *Shirley:* relations of reproduction and the ideology of romance. In Women's Studies Group, CCCS, *Women Take Issue: Aspects of Women's Subordination.* London: Hutchinson, 176–95.

HARTSOCK, Nancy 1990 (1987): Foucault on power: a theory for women? In Nicholson, L. J. (ed.), *Feminism/Postmodernism.* London: Routledge, 157–75.

HEATH, Stephen 1982: *The Sexual Fix.* Basingstoke: Macmillan.

HEBDIGE, Dick 1979: *Subculture: The Meaning of Style.* London: Routledge.

HOBSON, Dorothy 1978: Housewives: isolation as oppression. In Women's Studies Group, CCCS, *Women Take Issue: Aspects of Women's Subordination.* London: Hutchinson, 79–95.

HOBSON, Dorothy 1980: Housewives and the mass media. In Hall, S., Hobson, D., Lowe, A. & Willis, P. (eds), *Culture, Media, Language.* London: Hutchinson, 105–14.

HOBSON, Dorothy 1982: *'Crossroads': The Drama of a Soap Opera.* London: Methuen.

HOGGART, Richard 1958: *The Uses of Literacy.* Harmondsworth: Penguin.

HONEY, Margaret 1994: The maternal voice in the technological universe. In Bassin, D., Honey, M. & Kaplan, M. M. (eds), *Representations of Motherhood.* New Haven: Yale University Press, 220–39.

HOOKS, bell 1984: *Feminist Theory: From Margin to Centre.* Boston, MA: South End Press.

HOOKS, bell 1990: *Yearning: Race, Gender and Cultural Politics.* Boston, MA: South End Press.

HOOKS, bell 1992: *Black Looks: Race and Representation.* London: Turnaround.

HUYSSEN, Andreas 1988: Mass culture as woman: modernism's other. In Huyssen, A., *After the Great Divide: Modernism, Mass Culture and Postmodernism.* London: Macmillan, 44–62.

IRIGARAY, Luce 1985 (1977): *This Sex Which is not One,* trans. Catherine Porter. Ithaca: Cornell University Press.

JACOBUS, Mary 1979a: The difference of view. In Jacobus, M. (ed.), *Women Writing and Writing about Women.* London: Croom Helm, 10–21.

JACOBUS, Mary 1979b: The buried letter: feminism and romanticism in *Villette*. In Jacobus, M. (ed.), *Women Writing and Writing about Women*. London: Croom Helm, 42–60.

JACOBUS, Mary (ed.) 1979c: *Women Writing and Writing about Women*. London: Croom Helm.

JACOBUS, Mary, KELLER, Evelyn Fox and SHUTTLEWORTH, Sally 1990: Introduction. In Jacobus, M., Keller, E. F. & Shuttleworth, S. (eds), *Body/Politics: Women and the Discourses of Science*. London: Routledge, 1–10.

JAMESON, Fredric 1983: Pleasure: a political issue. In Formations Editorial Board (eds), *Formations of Pleasure*. London: Routledge & Kegan Paul, 1–13.

JANUS, Noreene 1977: Research on sex roles in the mass media. *Insurgent Sociologist* 7, 19–31.

JOHNSTON, Claire 1973: Women's cinema as counter-cinema. In Johnston, C. (ed.), *Notes on Women's Cinema*. London: SEFT, 24–31.

KAPLAN, Cora 1986a (1979): Radical feminism and literature: rethinking Millett's *Sexual Politics*. In Kaplan, C., *Sea Changes: Essays on Culture and Feminism*. London: Verso, 15–30.

KAPLAN, Cora 1986b: Introduction. In Kaplan, C., *Sea Changes: Essays on Culture and Feminism*. London: Verso, 1–12.

KAPLAN, Cora 1986c: Speaking/writing/feminism. In Kaplan, C., *Sea Changes: Essays on Culture and Feminism*. London: Verso, 219–28.

KELLY, Joan 1984: The doubled vision of feminist theory. In *Women, History and Theory*. Chicago: University of Chicago Press.

KOEDT, Anne 1973 (1970): The myth of the vaginal orgasm. In Koedt, A., Levine, E. & Rapone, A. (eds), *Radical Feminism*. New York: Quadrangle Books, 198–207.

KOEDT, Anne, LEVINE, Ellen and RAPONE, Anita (eds) 1973: *Radical Feminism*. New York: Quadrangle Books.

KRISTEVA, Julia 1982: *Powers of Horror: An Essay on Abjection*. New York: Columbia University Press.

KUHN, Annette 1988: The body and cinema: some problems for feminism. In Sheridan, S. (ed.), *Grafts: Feminist Cultural Criticism*. London: Verso, 11–23.

KUHN, Annette 1995a: *Family Secrets: Acts of Memory and Imagination*. London: Verso.

KUHN, Annette 1995b: Introduction. *The Power of the Image: Essays on Representation and Sexuality*. London: Routledge and Kegan Paul, 1–8.

KUHN, Annette and WOLPE, AnnMarie (eds) 1978: *Feminism and Materialism: Women and Modes of Production*. London: Routledge and Kegan Paul.

LANE, Ann J. 1979: Introduction. In Charlotte Perkins Gilman, *Herland*. London: The Women's Press, v–xxiii.

LAPLACE, Maria 1987: Producing and consuming the woman's film:

discursive struggle in *Now, Voyager*. In Gledhill, C. (ed.), *Home is Where the Heart Is: Studies in Melodrama and the Woman's Film*. London: BFI, 138–66.

LAPLANCHE, Jean and PONTALIS, Jean-Bertrand 1986 (1964): Fantasy and the origins of sexuality. In Burgin, V., Donald, J. & Kaplan, C. (eds), *Formations of Fantasy*. London: Routledge, 5–34.

LÉVI-STRAUSS, Claude 1949: *Les Structures Elementaires de la Parente*. Paris: PUF.

LÉVI-STRAUSS, Claude 1972: *Structural Anthropology*. Harmondsworth, Penguin.

LONG, Elizabeth 1989: Feminism and cultural studies. *Critical Studies in Mass Communication* 6, 427–35.

LOPATE, Carol 1978: Jackie! In Tuchman, G. (ed.), *Hearth and Home*. New York: Oxford University Press, 130–40.

LORDE, Audre 1984: *Sister Outsider*. Freedom, Calif.: The Crossing Press.

LOVELL, Terry 1990: Introduction: feminist criticism and cultural studies. In Lovell, T. (ed.), British Feminist Thought: A Reader. Oxford: Blackwell, 271–80.

LUNDBERG, Ferdinand and FARNHAM, Marynia F. 1947: *Modern Woman: The Lost Sex*. New York: Harper & Bros.

LURY, Celia 1993: *Cultural Rights: Technology, Legality and Personality*. London: Routledge.

LURY, Celia 1996: *Consumer Culture*. Oxford: Polity.

LYDON, Susan 1970: The politics of orgasm. In Morgan, R. (ed.), *Sisterhood is Powerful*. New York: Random House, 197–205.

LYON, Elizabeth 1988 (1980): The cinema of Lol V. Stein. In Penley, C. (ed.), *Feminism and Film Theory*. London: BFI, 244–71.

McNAY, Lois 1992: *Foucault and Feminism*. Oxford: Polity.

McNEIL, Maureen and FRANKLIN, Sarah 1991: Science and technology: questions for cultural studies and feminism. In Franklin, S., Lury, C. & Stacey, J. (eds), *Off Centre: Feminism and Cultural Studies*. London: HarperCollins, 129–46.

McROBBIE, Angela 1978: Working class girls and the culture of femininity. In Women's Studies Group, CCCS, *Women Take Issue: Aspects of Women's Subordination*. London: Hutchinson, 96–108.

McROBBIE, Angela 1989: Second-hand dresses and the role of the rag-market. In McRobbie, A. (ed.), *Zoot Suits and Second-Hand Dresses: An Anthology of Fashion and Music*. London: Macmillan, 23–49.

McROBBIE, Angela 1991a (1980): Settling accounts with subcultures: a feminist critique. In McRobbie, A., *Feminism and Youth Culture: From Jackie to Just Seventeen*. London: Macmillan Education, 16–34.

McROBBIE, Angela 1991b: *Feminism and Youth Culture: From Jackie to Just Seventeen*. London: Macmillan Education.

McROBBIE, Angela 1991c (1982): The politics of feminist research: between talk, text and action. In McRobbie, A., *Feminism and Youth*

Culture: From Jackie *to* Just Seventeen. London: Macmillan Education, 61–80.

McROBBIE, Angela 1999: Bridging the gap: feminism, fashion and consumption. In McRobbie, A., *In the Culture Society: Art, Fashion and Popular Music*. London and New York: Routledge, 31–45.

McROBBIE, Angela and GARBER, Jenny 1976: Girls and subcultures: an exploration. In Hall, S. & Jefferson, T. (eds), *Resistance Through Rituals: Youth Subcultures in Post-War Britain*. London: HarperCollins, 209–22.

McROBBIE, Angela and NAVA, Mica (eds) 1984: *Gender and Generation*. London: Macmillan.

MANSFIELD, Alan and McGINN, Barbara 1993: Pumping irony: the muscular and the feminine. In Scott, S. & Morgan, D. (eds), *Body Matters*. London: The Falmer Press, 49–68.

MARCUS, G. E. 1992: Past, present and emergent identities: requirements for ethnographies of late twentieth-century modernity world-wide. In Lash, S. & Friedman, J. (eds), *Modernity and Identity*. Oxford: Blackwell, 309–31.

MARCUS, G. E. and FISCHER, M. 1986: *Anthropology as Cultural Critique: An Experimental Moment in the Human Sciences*. Chicago: University of Chicago Press.

MARX, Karl 1977 (1869): *The Eighteenth Brumaire of Louis Bonaparte*. Moscow: Progress Publishers.

MASTERS, W. H. and JOHNSON, V. E. 1966: *Human Sexual Response*. Boston: Little, Brown and Co.

MAYHEW, Henry 1851: *London Labour and the London Poor*, Vol. 1. London: George Woodfall.

MILLER, Nancy 1990: The text's heroine: a feminist critic and her fictions. In Hirsch, M. & Fox Keller, E. (eds), *Conflicts in Feminism*. London: Routledge, 112–20.

MILLETT, Kate 1977 (1970): *Sexual Politics*. London: Virago.

MINH-HA, Trinh T. 1989: Outside in inside out. In Pines, J. & Willemen, P. (eds), *Questions of Third Cinema*. London: BFI, 133–49.

MITCHELL, Juliet 1971: *Woman's Estate*. Harmondsworth: Penguin.

MITCHELL, Juliet 1975 (1974): *Psychoanalysis and Feminism*. Harmondsworth: Penguin.

MITCHELL, Juliet 1984: *Women: The Longest Revolution*. London: Virago, 1984.

MITCHELL, Juliet and OAKLEY, Ann (eds) 1976: *The Rights and Wrongs of Women*. Harmondsworth: Penguin.

MODLESKI, Tania 1979: The search for tomorrow in today's soap operas. In *Film Quarterly* 33(1), 12–21.

MODLESKI, Tania 1984: *Loving with a Vengeance: Mass Produced Fantasies for Women*. London: Methuen, 85–109.

MODLESKI, Tania 1986: Femininity as mas(s)querade: a feminist approach to mass culture. In MacCabe, C. (ed.), *High Theory/Low Culture*. Manchester: Manchester University Press, 37–52.

MODLESKI, Tania 1991a: Cinema and the dark continent: race and gender in popular film. In Modleski, T., *Feminism without Women: Culture and Criticism in a 'Postfeminist' Age*. London: Routledge, 115–34.

MODLESKI, Tania 1991b: Postmortem on postfeminism. In Modleski, T., *Feminism without Women: Culture and Criticism in a 'Postfeminist' Age*. London: Routledge, 3–22.

MOI, Toril 1991: Appropriating Bourdieu: feminist theory and Pierre Bourdieu's sociology of culture. *New Literary History* 22, 1017–49.

MOI, Toril 1994: *Simone de Beauvoir: The Making of an Intellectual Woman*. Oxford: Blackwell.

MOORE, Jane 1989: Promises, promises: the fictional philosophy in Mary Wollstonecraft's *Vindication of the Rights of Woman*. In Belsey, C. & Moore, J. (eds), *The Feminist Reader: Essays in Gender and the Politics of Literary Criticism*. Basingstoke: Macmillan, 155–74.

MOORES, Shaun 1993: *Interpreting Audiences: The Ethnography of Media Consumption*. London: Sage.

MORGAN, Robin (ed.) 1970: *Sisterhood is Powerful*. New York: Random House.

MORGAN, Robin 1993a (1968): Women *vs.* the Miss America pageant. In Morgan, R., *The Word of a Woman: Selected Prose 1968–92*. London: Virago, 1993, 21–9.

MORGAN, Robin 1993b (1974): Theory and practice: pornography and rape. In Morgan, R., *The Word of a Woman: Selected Prose 1968–92*. London: Virago, 1993, 78–89.

MORGAN, Robin 1993c (1974): On women as a colonized people. In Morgan, R., *The Word of a Woman: Selected Prose 1968–92*. London: Virago, 1993, 74–7.

MORLEY, David 1980a: *The 'Nationwide' Audience*. London: BFI.

MORLEY, David 1980b: Texts, readers, subjects. In Hall, S., Hobson, D., Lowe, A. & Willis, P. (eds), *Culture, Media, Language*. London: Hutchinson, 163–73.

MORLEY, David 1986: *Family Television: Cultural Power and Domestic Leisure*. London: Comedia.

MORLEY, David 1989: Changing paradigms in audience studies. In Seiter, E., Borchers, H., Kreutzner, G. & Warth, E.-M. (eds), *Remote Control: Television, Audiences and Cultural Power*. London: Routledge, 16–43.

MORRIS, Meaghan 1988: *The Pirate's Fiancée: Feminism, Reading, Postmodernism*. London: Verso.

MULVEY, Laura 1989a (1973): Fears, fantasies and the male unconscious *or* 'You don't know what is happening, do you, Mr Jones?' In Mulvey, L., *Visual and Other Pleasures*. London: Macmillan, 6–13.

MULVEY, Laura 1989b (1975): Visual pleasure and narrative cinema. In Mulvey, L., *Visual and Other Pleasures*. London: Macmillan, 14–26.

MULVEY, Laura 1989c (1977): Notes on Sirk and melodrama. In Mulvey. L., *Visual and Other Pleasures*. London: Macmillan, 39–44.

MULVEY, Laura 1989d: Introduction. *Visual and Other Pleasures*. London: Macmillan, vii–xv.

NAVA, Mica 1992: Consumerism and its contradictions. In Nava, M., *Changing Cultures: Feminism, Youth and Consumerism*. London: Sage, 162–8.

NAVA, Mica 1997: Modernity's disavowal: women, the city and the department store. In Falk, P. & Campbell, C. (eds), *The Shopping Experience*. London: Sage, 56–91.

NIGHTINGALE, Virginia 1996: *Studying Audiences: The Shock of the Real*. London: Routledge.

OAKLEY, Ann 1981: *From Here to Maternity: Becoming a Mother*. Harmondsworth: Penguin.

OKELY, Judith 1986: *Simone de Beauvoir*. London: Virago.

OMOLADE, Barbara 1983: Hearts of darkness. In Snitow, A., Stansell, C. & Thompson, S. (eds), *Powers of Desire: The Politics of Sexuality*. New York: Monthly Review Press, 350–70.

OWENS, Craig 1985: The discourse of others: feminists and postmodernism. In Foster, H. (ed.), *Postmodern Culture*. London: Pluto, 57–82.

PARTINGTON, Angela 1992: Popular fashion and working-class affluence. In Ash, J. & Wilson, E. (eds), *Chic Thrills: A Fashion Reader*. London: Pandora, 145–61.

PENLEY, Constance 1989: Untitled entry. *Camera Obscura* 20/21, 256–60.

PENLEY, Constance 1992: Feminism, psychoanalysis, and the study of popular culture. In Grossberg, L., Nelson, C. & Treichler, P. (eds), *Cultural Studies*. London: Routledge, 479–500.

PETCHESKY, Rosalind Pollack 1980: Reproductive freedom: beyond "a woman's right to choose". *Signs* 5, 661–85.

PETCHESKY, Rosalind Pollack 1987: Foetal images: the power of visual culture in the politics of reproduction. In Stanworth, M. (ed.), *Reproductive Technologies: Gender, Motherhood and Medicine*. Oxford: Polity, 57–80.

PLANT, Sadie 1996: On the matrix: cyberfeminist simulations. In Shields, R. (ed.), *Cultures of Internet: Virtual Spaces, Real Histories, Living Bodies*. London: Sage, 170–83.

PLANT, Sadie 1998: *Zeros and Ones: Digital Women and the New Technoculture*. London: Fourth Estate.

POLLOCK, Griselda 1987 (1977): What's wrong with images of women? In Betterton, R. (ed.), *Looking On: Images of Femininity in the Visual Arts and Media*. London: Pandora, 40–8.

PRATT, Mary Louise 1986: Interpretive strategies/strategic interpretations. In Arac, J. (ed.), *Postmodernism and Politics*. Minneapolis: University of Minnesota Press.

PROBYN, Elspeth 1993: *Sexing the Self: Gendered Positions in Cultural Studies*. London: Routledge.

PROPP, Vladimir 1968 (1928): *The Morphology of the Folk Tale*, Wagner, L. A. (ed.), trans. Laurence Scott. Austin: University of Texas Press.

RABINOW, Paul (ed.) 1986: *The Foucault Reader*. Harmondsworth: Penguin.

RADNER, Hilary 1995: *Shopping Around: Feminine Culture and the Pursuit of Pleasure*. London: Routledge.

RADWAY, Janice 1986: Identifying ideological seams: mass culture, analytical method, and political practice. *Communication* 9, 93–123.

RADWAY, Janice 1987 (1984): *Reading the Romance*. London: Verso.

RICH, Adrienne 1977: *Of Woman Born: Womanhood as Experience and Institution*. London: Virago.

RICH, Adrienne 1986 (1980): Compulsory heterosexuality and lesbian existence. In Rich, A., *Blood, Bread, and Poetry: Selected Prose*. London: W.W. Norton & Co., 23–75.

RICH, B. Ruby 1999 (1978): The crisis of naming in feminist film criticism. In Thornham, S. (ed.), *Feminist Film Theory*. Edinburgh: Edinburgh University Press, 41–7.

RILEY, Denise 1988: *'Am I that Name?': Feminism and the Category of 'Women' in History*. Basingstoke: Macmillan.

ROONEY, Ellen 1990: Discipline and vanish: feminism, the resistance to theory, and the politics of cultural studies. *Differences: A Journal of Feminist Cultural Studies* 2(3), 14–28.

ROSE, Jacqueline 1986: *Sexuality in the Field of Vision*. London: Verso.

ROSEN, Marjorie 1974 (1973): *Popcorn Venus*. New York: Avon Books.

ROSSI, Alice S. 1988: *The Feminist Papers: From Adams to de Beauvoir*. Boston: Northeastern University Press.

ROTHMAN, Barbara Katz 1986: *The Tentative Pregnancy*. New York: Viking.

ROWBOTHAM, Sheila 1973: *Woman's Consciousness, Man's World*. Harmondsworth: Penguin.

SARUP, Madan 1992: *Jacques Lacan*. Hemel Hempstead: Harvester Wheatsheaf.

SCHNEIR, Miriam (ed.) 1972: *Feminism: The Essential Historical Writings*. New York: Vintage Books.

SCHULZE, Laurie 1990: On the muscle. In Gaines, J. & Herzog, C. (eds), *Fabrications: Costume and the Female Body*. London: Routledge, 59–78.

SEABROOK, Jeremy 1982: *Working Class Childhood*. London: Gollancz.

SEITER, Ellen, BORCHERS, Hans, KREUTZNER, Gabriele and WARTH, Eva-Maria (eds) 1989: Introduction. *Remote Control: Television, Audiences and Cultural Power*. London: Routledge, 1–15.

SHERFEY, Mary Jane 1970: A theory on female sexuality. In Morgan, R. (ed.), *Sisterhood is Powerful*. New York: Random House, 220–30.

SHOHAT, Ella and STAM, Robert 1994: *Unthinking Eurocentrism: Multiculturalism and the Media*. London: Routledge.

SHOWALTER, Elaine 1977: *A Literature of their Own: British Women Novelists from Bronte to Lessing*. Princeton: Princeton University Press.

SHOWALTER, Elaine 1986: Introduction: the feminist critical revolution. In Showalter, E. (ed.), *The New Feminist Criticism: Essays on Women, Literature and Theory*. London: Virago.

SILVERMAN, Kaja 1986: Fragments of a fashionable discourse. In Modleski, T. (ed.), *Studies in Entertainment: Critical Approaches to Mass Culture*. Indianapolis: Indiana University Press, 139–52.

SKEGGS, Beverley 1995a: Introduction. In Skeggs, B. (ed.), *Feminist Cultural Theory: Process and Production*. Manchester: Manchester University Press, 1–29.

SKEGGS, Beverley 1995b: Theorising, ethics and representation in feminist ethnography. In Skeggs, B. (ed.), *Feminist Cultural Theory: Process and Production*. Manchester: Manchester University Press, 190–206.

SKEGGS, Beverley 1997: *Formations of Class and Gender*. London: Sage.

SKIRROW, Gillian 1985: *Widows*. In Alvarado, M. & Stewart, J. (eds), *Made for Television: Euston Films Limited*. London: BFI, 174–84.

SMITH, Barbara 1986 (1977): Toward a black feminist criticism. In Showalter, E. (ed.), *The New Feminist Criticism: Essays on Women, Literature, and Theory*. London: Virago, 168–85.

SNITOW, Ann 1990: A gender diary. In Hirsch, M. & Fox Keller, E. (eds), *Conflicts in Feminism*. London: Routledge, 9–43.

SNITOW, Ann, STANSELL, Christine and THOMPSON, Sharon (eds) 1983: *Powers of Desire: The Politics of Sexuality*. New York: Monthly Review Press.

SPENDER, Dale 1985: *For the Record: The Making and Meaning of Feminist Knowledge*. London: The Women's Press.

SPIVAK, Gayatri Chakravorty 1990: *The Post-Colonial Critic: Interviews, Strategies, Dialogues*, ed. Sarah Harasym. London: Routledge.

SPRAFKIN, Joyce N. and LIEBERT, Robert M. 1978: Sex-typing and children's television preferences. In Tuchman, G. (ed.), *Hearth and Home*. New York: Oxford University Press, 228–39.

STACEY, Jackie 1994: *Star Gazing: Hollywood Cinema and Female Spectatorship*. London: Routledge.

STANWORTH, Michelle (ed.) 1987: *Reproductive Technologies: Gender, Motherhood and Medicine*. Oxford: Polity.

STEEDMAN, Carolyn 1986: *Landscape for a Good Woman*. London: Virago.

STOREY, John 1993: *An Introductory Guide to Cultural Theory and Popular Culture*. London: Harvester Wheatsheaf.

SULEIMAN, Susan R. 1986: (Re)Writing the body: the politics and poetics of female eroticism. In Suleiman, S. R. (ed.), *The Female Body in Western Culture*. Cambridge, Mass.: Harvard University Press, 7–29.

THOMPSON, E. P. 1980 (1968): *The Making of the English Working Class*. Harmondsworth: Penguin.

THORNHAM, Sue 1997: *Passionate Detachments: An Introduction to Feminist Film Theory*. London: Arnold.

TODD, Janet (ed.) 1989: *A Wollstonecraft Anthology*. Cambridge: Polity.

TODOROV, Tzvetan 1977: *The Poetics of Prose*, trans. Richard Howard. Ithaca: Cornell University Press.

TREICHLER, Paula 1990: Feminism, medicine, and the meaning of childbirth. In Jacobus, M., Keller, E. F. & Shuttleworth, S. (eds), *Body/Politics: Women and the Discourses of Science*. London: Routledge, 113–38.

TRUTH, Sojourner 1972 (1851): Ain't I a woman? In Schneir, M. (ed.), *Feminism: The Essential Historical Writings*. New York: Vintage Books, 93–5.

TUCHMAN, Gaye 1978a: Introduction: the symbolic annihilation of women by the mass media. In Tuchman, G. (ed.), *Hearth and Home*. New York: Oxford University Press, 3–38.

TUCHMAN, Gaye (ed.) 1978b: *Hearth and Home*. New York: Oxford University Press.

TUCHMAN, Gaye 1979: Women's depiction by the mass media. *Signs: Journal of Women in Culture and Society* 4(3), 528–42.

TURKLE, Sherry 1984: *The Second Self: Computers and the Human Spirit*. New York: Simon and Shuster.

TURKLE, Sherry 1996: *Life on the Screen: Identity in the Age of the Internet*. London: Weidenfeld & Nicolson.

TURNER, Graeme 1990: *British Cultural Studies: An Introduction*. Boston: Unwin Hyman.

WAKEFORD, Nina 2000 (1998): Gender and the landscapes of computing in an internet café. In Kirkup, G., Janes, L., Woodward, K. & Hovenden, F. (eds), *The Gendered Cyborg*. London: Routledge, 291–304.

WALKERDINE, Valerie 1984: Some day my prince will come. In McRobbie, A. & Nava, M. (eds), *Gender and Generation*. London: Macmillan, 162–84.

WALKERDINE, Valerie 1989 (1986): Video replay: families, films and fantasy. In Burgin, V., Donald, J. & Kaplan, C. (eds) *Formations of Fantasy*. London: Routledge, 167–99.

WALKERDINE, Valerie 1997: *Daddy's Girl: Young Girls and Popular Culture*. London: Macmillan.

WANDOR, Michelene (ed.) 1990: *Once a Feminist: Stories of a Generation*. London: Virago, 1990.

WARE, Cellestine 1970: *Woman Power: The Movement for Women's Liberation*. New York: Tower Publications.

WILLIAMS, Linda 1990: *Hard Core*. London: Pandora.

WILLIAMS, Linda 1991: Film bodies: gender, genre and excess. *Film Quarterly* 44(4), 2–13.

WILLIAMS, Raymond 1961 (1958): *Culture and Society 1780–1950*. Harmondsworth: Penguin.

WILLIAMS, Raymond 1965 (1961): *The Long Revolution*. Harmondsworth: Penguin.

WILLIAMS, Raymond 1977: *Marxism and Literature*. Oxford: Oxford University Press.

WILLIAMS, Raymond 1979: *Politics and Letters: Interviews with New Left Review*. London: New Left Books.

WILLIAMS, Raymond 1980: *Problems in Materialism and Culture*. London: Verso.

WILLIAMS, Raymond 1983: *Keywords*. London: Fontana.

WILLIAMSON, Judith 1978: *Decoding Advertisements*. London: Marion Boyars.

WILLIS, Susan 1991a: Learning from the Banana. In Willis, S., *A Primer for Daily Life*. London: Routledge, 41–61.

WILLIS, Susan 1991b: *A Primer for Daily Life*. London: Routledge.

WILLIS, Susan 1991c: I want the black one: is there a place for Afro-American culture in commodity culture? In Willis, S., *A Primer for Daily Life*. London: Routledge, 108–32.

WILLIS, Susan 1991d: Work(ing) out. In Willis, S., *A Primer for Daily Life*. London: Routledge, 62–85.

WILSON, Elizabeth 1985: *Adorned in Dreams: Fashion and Modernity*. London: Virago.

WILSON, Elizabeth (with Angela Weir) 1986a: The British women's movement. In Wilson, E., *Hidden Agendas: Theory, Politics and Experience in the Women's Movement*. London: Tavistock Publications, 93–133.

WILSON, Elizabeth 1986b: Psychoanalysis: psychic law and order. In Wilson, E., *Hidden Agendas: Theory, Politics and Experience in the Women's Movement*. London: Tavistock Publications, 148–68.

WILSON, Elizabeth 1990: All the rage. In Gaines, J. & Herzog, C. (eds), *Fabrications: Costume and the Female Body*. London: Routledge, 28–38.

WILSON, Elizabeth 1992: The invisible *flâneur*. *New Left Review* 191, 90–110.

WINSHIP, Janice 1978: A woman's world: *Woman* – an ideology of femininity. In Women's Studies Group, CCCS, *Women Take Issue: Aspects of Women's Subordination*. London: Hutchinson, 133–54.

WINSHIP, Janice 1980: Sexuality for sale. In Hall, S., Hobson, D., Lowe, A. & Willis, P. (eds), *Culture, Media, Language*. London: Hutchinson, 217–23.

WITTIG, Monique 1980: The straight mind. *Feminist Issues* Summer, 107–11.

WOLFF, Janet 1985: The invisible *flâneuse*: women in the literature of modernity. *Theory, Culture & Society* 2(3), 37–46.

WOLFF, Janet 1995: The artist and the *flâneur*: Rodin, Rilke and Gwen John in Paris. In Wolff, J., *Resident Alien: Feminist Cultural Criticism.* Oxford: Polity, 88–114.

WOLLSTONECRAFT, Mary 1976 (1788): *Mary: A Fiction.* In Wollstonecraft, M., *Mary* and *The Wrongs of Woman*, ed. and introd. Gary Kelly. Oxford: Oxford University Press, 1–68.

WOLLSTONECRAFT, Mary 1976 (1798): *The Wrongs of Woman: or Maria. A Fragment.* In Wollstonecraft, M., *Mary* and *The Wrongs of Woman*, ed. and introd. Gary Kelly. Oxford: Oxford University Press, 69–231.

WOLLSTONECRAFT, Mary 1960 (1790): *A Vindication of the Rights of Men.* Facsimile by Scholars Facsimiles & Reprints.

WOLLSTONECRAFT, Mary 1992 (1792): *A Vindication of the Rights of Woman*, Brody, M. (ed.). London: Penguin.

WOMEN'S STUDIES GROUP, CCCS 1978a: Trying to do feminist intellectual work. In Women's Studies Group, *Women Take Issue: Aspects of Women's Subordination.* London: Hutchinson, 7–17.

WOMEN'S STUDIES GROUP, CCCS 1978b: *Women Take Issue: Aspects of Women's Subordination.* London: Hutchinson.

WOOLF, Virginia 1992: *A Woman's Essays: Selected Essays Vol. 1*, ed. Rachel Bowlby. Harmondsworth: Penguin.

WOOLF, Virginia 1993 (1929): *A Room of One's Own.* In Barrett, M. (ed.), *A Room of One's Own and Three Guineas.* Harmondsworth: Penguin, 1–114.

WOOLF, Virginia 1993 (1931): Professions for women. In Barrett, M. (ed.), *A Room of One's Own and Three Guineas.* Harmondsworth: Penguin, 356–61.

WOOLF, Virginia 1993 (1938): *Three Guineas.* In Barrett, M. (ed.), *A Room of One's Own and Three Guineas.* Harmondsworth: Penguin, 115–323.

YOUNG, Robert 1991: Psychoanalysis and political literary theories. In Donald, J. (ed.), *Psychoanalysis and Cultural Theory.* Basingstoke: Macmillan, 139–57.

ZOONEN, Liesbet van 1994: *Feminist Media Studies.* London: Sage.

Subject index

Name index